# Gardening for
# Butterflies

A variegated fritillary (*Euptoieta claudia*) rests on coreopsis, a plant commonly used in gardens.

# Gardening for Butterflies

## How you can attract and protect beautiful, beneficial insects

**THE XERCES SOCIETY**

Scott Hoffman Black | Brianna Borders | Candace Fallon | Eric Lee-Mäder | Matthew Shepherd

**FOREWORD BY ROBERT MICHAEL PYLE**

**Timber Press**
**PORTLAND, OREGON**

Published in 2016 by Timber Press, Inc.

The Haseltine Building
133 S.W. Second Avenue, Suite 450
Portland, Oregon 97204-3527
timberpress.com

Printed in China
Text design by Jen Wick Studio
Cover design by Anna Eshelman

Library of Congress Cataloging-in-Publication Data

Black, Scott Hoffman, author.
    Gardening for butterflies: how you can attract and protect beautiful, beneficial insects/
the Xerces Society (Scott Hoffman Black, Brianna Borders, Candace Fallon, Eric Lee-Mader,
Matthew Shepherd); foreword by Robert Michael Pyle.—First edition.
        pages cm
    Includes index.
    ISBN 978-1-60469-598-4
    1. Butterfly gardening. 2. Butterflies.  I. Title.
    QL544.6.B56 2015
    638'.5789—dc23                                    2015029810

# Contents

**I AM OFTEN ASKED** why a butterfly guy such as I resides in what is arguably one of the worst locations to be found for butterflies. Well, it's true, I do: the rain forest of the Maritime Northwest is among the least conducive places for both diversity and abundance of butterflies. There are good reasons for that, and also for why I live here—among them, the chance to do original fieldwork in a region largely ignored by naturalists on account of its very subtlety. Another thing that keeps me here is how much one comes to appreciate each and every butterfly, a sense more difficult to maintain in the teeming tropics. Most salient to the present book is this: through judicious gardening, almost any precinct can be made more friendly for butterflies—even this one.

Somehow the question with which I began loses its barb when I am entranced by a gorgeous big female *Clodius parnassian*, smoky white with jet and ruby spots, cruising my garden in search of nectar and the wild bleeding hearts of my woods on which to deposit her eggs. I don't feel bad about where I live as I watch woodland skippers by the score and half a dozen mylitta crescents queueing together like so many animated gold nuggets around the Douglas asters of late summer; nor wish to move elsewhere when the several species of swallowtails sail about the old farmyard lilacs and rhododendrons. And, as with almost anywhere, certain kinds of butterflies are well adapted even here, such as linen-like margined whites and ice-blue echo azures. By the plants I choose to grow, I can help make sure these butterflies and others proliferate.

The authors of *Gardening for Butterflies*, all consummate professionals in the field of pollinator conservation, have taken this beloved practice into new territory. First introducing butterflies and moths as the animals they are, then placing them into an ecological context, they set the stage for successful backyard (or back forty) management on behalf of the bright wings of summer. In delightfully readable yet authoritative prose, they take the gardener and the butterfly lover each by the hand and lead them into territory they may profitably share. Discussing the best plants for each region and garden type, they help the reader make suitable decisions and designs well before the seed catalogues arrive for spring. It can be even more fun planning the butterfly garden than actually planting it . . . at least until the invited guests show up! Then all the effort becomes worthwhile, and you can sit back, enjoy the added color and life in your own home habitat, and thank these authors.

The habitat of home: that's what all wildlife gardens are about, and butterfly gardens are one of the most responsive kinds—the nectar and larval host plants responsive to your care and good choices for where you live, and the butterflies responsive, in turn, to them. By nurturing, enriching, and diversifying your own habitat of home, you are taking part in real butterfly conservation—a very needful activity these days. You might not influence many endangered species directly, but you can surely help keep the more common and widespread kinds from getting that way. If this claim seems overblown, consider the fact that the monarch, our tri-national icon as North American butterflies go, is as of this writing in early 2015 under consideration for federal listing under the Endangered Species Act. Its future depends in no small part on landscape decisions, small and large, to be taken across southern Canada and the United States. Butterfly gardeners will play a distinct role in bringing back the monarch, just as they may in keeping great spangled fritillaries abundant for the children to chase and marvel at in days and years to come.

When Xerces appeared on the scene in 1971, I was much inspired by L. Hugh Newman's British book *Create a Butterfly Garden*. Now that the Society is thriving, it is very exciting to see it produce with Timber Press that pioneering book's state-of-the-art successor. It will prove excellent company for aspiring butterfly gardeners, whether advanced or beginner.

Perhaps you're beginning with a cottage garden stocked with traditional ornamentals. You'd like to keep your zinnias (great for painted ladies!) but augment them with native plants coevolved with local insects. Or let's say you have a vegetable plot free of weeds and pests but equally innocent of butterflies, which you miss. Or maybe you share your yard with bluegrass turf and know you could do better. No matter your starting point, this essential and welcome book will help you bring about the garden you desire—for the butterflies, for yourself, and for the earth. If I can do it here in the temperate rain forest, you surely can too, wherever you live!

Robert Michael Pyle
*Gray's River, Washington*

# Butterfly gardeners can change the world

**A COUPLE OF US** writing this book grew up during the last gasp of the American muscle car. We have teenage memories of rocketing in Plymouth Barracudas and Chevy Novas down old country roads in the Midwest and the Great Plains. Even a short drive back then resulted in hundreds of dead bugs splattered across the grille, so we were always washing those cars. Returning to our teenage haunts today with a few gray hairs, vastly more fuel-efficient cars, and the lens of professional conservationists, we are awestruck by the lack of bugs. Drive across the entire state of North Dakota, Nebraska, or Iowa now, and your car will be practically spotless when you get to the other side. Animals, including insects, are disappearing.

A global assessment of wildlife populations in 2014 released by the World Wide Fund for Nature and the Zoological Society of London (ZSL) found that the sheer number of vertebrates on earth had declined by more than 50 percent since 1970. While the ZSL report did not assess insect populations, irrefutable evidence of their decline and clear examples of insect extinctions can be found. Many of the rare insects have always been rare, but now once-common insects are becoming rare as well. The most striking example of this is the iconic monarch butterfly, whose population has declined by 80 percent across North America since monitoring efforts began in the mid-1990s.

Loss and degradation of habitat is driving this disappearing act. Urban landscapes divide up, pave over, and fragment formerly green spaces. Agriculture favors fewer types of crops, leaves fewer edges unplowed and untrampled, and tolerates ever fewer "pests." The wild places that remain bear the indignities of invasive species, climate uncertainties, and hardscrabble resource extraction such as mining and logging. The net result is that 7 billion humans have finally created a fully human-dominated world.

Despite the biodiversity crisis unfolding in real time all around us, we believe that butterflies and other animals can have a secure future. However, such a future will require reconciliation between the human environment and a more natural one. Policies

An Eastern tiger swallowtail (*Papilio glaucus*) drinks nectar from redbud flowers, demonstrating the importance of flowering shrubs and trees in providing nourishment.

In not much more than one human generation, the number of wild animals on earth has declined by more than 50 percent. Butterfly gardening is one way to help reverse this trend.

you can play a critical role right now in saving the earth's butterflies. You don't need a large space. A small yard with just a few native plants can attract and sustain dozens of butterfly species. And beyond aiding butterflies, your yard can become a wildlife refuge for all of the creatures that pollinate crops and wildflowers in your region. Your efforts will support countless other creatures as well, from lady beetles to songbirds. The insect populations that grow and thrive in native grasses and forbs around your patio will increase in number and disperse, and their descendants will ultimately go on to feed fish and bears and bats. If you manage larger landscapes, the gardening concepts described in this book can easily be scaled up to provide habitat on roadsides or in parks and natural areas.

Finally, when you share what you do, your garden can become a platform for science education, connecting kids to the amazing life cycle of butterflies, from caterpillars and their host plants to the incredible process of metamorphosis, to the colorful adults drinking nectar from equally colorful flowers; this exposure can build a new generation of conservationists. Similarly, by sharing your efforts with neighbors, other gardeners, community groups, and local conservation agencies, you are giving those people a living template to inspire their own efforts. You are changing expectations about what our human-dominated landscapes should look like; you are exposing gigantic manicured lawns and insecticides as embarrassingly uncool; you are

that could accelerate such a reconciliation are desperately needed. At the same time, as individuals we cannot simply stand by and do nothing while we wait for those policies. At least in the case of butterflies, every one of us who gardens has the potential to change the world.

This book is designed to be a blueprint for that change. Whether you live in California's Central Valley, upstate New York, or the panhandle of Texas,

How you tend your garden directly affects the butterflies and other wildlife that visit or live in it. A few flowers can go a long way toward supporting once-abundant butterfly populations.

creating a world where it is no longer weird to be the person with the overgrown, wildflower-filled yard and instead making it weird to *not* be that person.

When you create this world, you will bring back the butterflies, the other bugs, and ultimately all of the animals that have become so absent from our lives. Who would have thought that some simple landscaping could do all of that?

The monarch (*Danaus plexippus*) may be the best-loved butterfly in North America.

# Why butterflies matter—and why they are in trouble

**B**UTTERFLIES MAY WELL BE the best loved of all insects. For millennia, they have attracted the attention and admiration of people around the world. This is not surprising as they are large and showy for insects, and they do not bite or sting. Their metamorphosis from caterpillar to winged adult has captured the imagination of many writers and artists, and this process has come to symbolize beauty, freedom, and transformation. What many people do not realize is just how important butterflies are as pollinators of plants and food sources for other animals, not to mention their role in important scientific discoveries.

At the same time, butterflies are in trouble. Butterfly populations undergo normal fluctuations from year to year, and there can be large differences in both abundance (number of butterflies) and diversity (number of different kinds of butterflies) in any given landscape. Although these fluctuations often account for year-to-year differences, evidence is mounting that many butterflies are now declining at unprecedented rates.

The good news is that as a gardener or land manager, you can help by providing habitat and limiting the use of insecticides. When you understand why butterflies are an important part of the ecosystem and why they are currently in trouble, you can make choices in your own garden that will make a real difference in conserving these amazing creatures.

## THE IMPORTANCE OF BUTTERFLIES AND MOTHS

Butterflies and moths make up the second largest order of insects, the Lepidoptera, with some 160,000 recognized species worldwide. Moth species make up

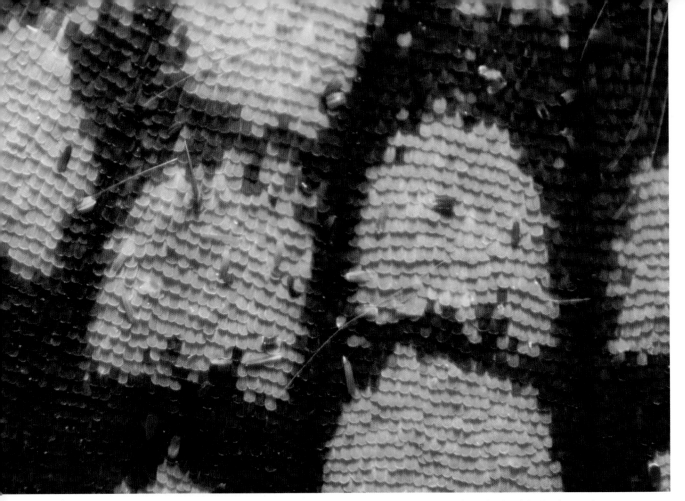

A butterfly's wing is covered with tiny overlapping scales. These gave rise to the name Lepidoptera, from the Greek for "scaly wing."

the vast majority of this total. Butterfly species number approximately 20,000 globally, with 800 of those in North America. Moth species number 11,000 or so in North America.

The name Lepidoptera comes from the Greek words *lepidōtos* (scaly) and *pteron* (wing), in recognition of the thousands of tiny overlapping scales that cover the wings much like shingles on a roof. Each scale is a single color, and collectively these scales create the complex color patterns seen on a butterfly's wing. These scales also distinguish butterflies and moths from other insects.

Found in many different habitats, butterflies successfully live in environments from the rain forests of the equator to the northern tundra and from deserts to the highest peaks in the American West. It is no wonder that they play a role in ecosystems and have captured the imaginations of children, scientists, artists, and gardeners.

## BUTTERFLIES AS POLLINATORS

While moths have always been known to pollinate plants, the role of butterflies as pollinators has been debated. But now a growing body of evidence suggests

Why butterflies matter—and why they are in trouble

# Butterfly or moth?

**BUTTERFLIES AND MOTHS** are closely related and can sometimes be difficult to tell apart. Butterflies are often thought of as brightly colored and flying by day while moths are perceived to be more muted in their appearance and fly by night. While this may hold as a broad-brush division, it is not entirely true and exceptions abound. Moths such as burnets, foresters, tigers, and ctenuchas are day flying and colorful, as are some hawk moths. On the other hand, the butterflies known as grass skippers may appear mothlike with small and fuzzy brown, tan, or dark gray bodies.

It is easier to separate moths from butterflies when they are at rest. Butterflies tend to hold their wings either partially open in a V shape or pressed together, upright over their bodies. With wings together, they can look like tiny sailboats. Most moths, on the other hand, hold their wings flat, like paper airplanes, or slightly pitched, with the forewings over the hind wings, covering their body like a tent. Moths also tend to be stouter and hairier than butterflies. And butterfly antennae are a single filament with a clubbed, bulblike tip, while antennae of moths can be either feathery (for males) or a single filament that tapers to a point (for females).

**TOP:** This regal fritillary (*Speyeria idalia*) illustrates the basic features of a butterfly: wings held upright like a sailboat and antennae with clubbed, bulblike tips. **MIDDLE:** Male moths—such as this male luna moth (*Actias luna*)—have feathery antennae that help them detect female sex pheromones. **BOTTOM:** At first sight, this may appear to be a butterfly, but wings held flat give it away as a moth—a mournful thyris (*Thyris sepulchralis*)—and the single-filament antennae as a female.

Butterflies are known to pollinate some types of flowers. Pollen is clearly visible on the legs of this obscure skipper (*Panoquina panoquinoides*).

that counter to what many researchers have long believed, butterflies are significant pollinators of at least some plants.

For plants, pollination—the sharing of pollen among their own flowers or with those of other plants—is an essential step in producing seed and reproducing. Plants, however, cannot move about in order to accomplish this transfer. Approximately 20 percent of flowering plants release and receive their pollen on the wind; grasses are a primary example of wind-pollinated plants. But the vast majority of flowering plants (the

other roughly 80 percent) rely on animals, mostly insects, to move their pollen from flower to flower.

For some animals, particularly bees, the pollen is a source of food, which is reason enough in itself to visit a flower. But for many other insects, as well as birds and other animals, the nourishment that draws them is nectar. Nectar is the primary food source for most adult butterflies and moths. Brightly colored flowers or heady fragrances advertise the presence of nectar, and special color patterns and markings help direct the pollinators quickly to their reward. While moving

Why butterflies matter—and why they are in trouble

around and feeding, the animals inadvertently pick up pollen grains, which they transfer to other flowers of the same plant species. Plants can help ensure that just the right pollinator visits their flowers by hiding nectar deep within the flower; in this way they also ensure that the visitor seeking that nectar contacts the pollen in just the right way.

Numerous birds pollinate: hummingbirds in the Americas, sunbirds in Africa, honeyeaters in Australia and the Pacific islands. Mammals are also known to pollinate plants. Several species of bats pollinate trees in the tropics, and others pollinate saguaro cacti in the deserts of the southwestern United States. Non-flying mammals that pollinate include sugar gliders in Australia and lemurs on Madagascar; those lemurs, at more than five pounds, may be the heaviest pollinators in the world.

The most significant pollinators, however, are tiny: bees (order Hymenoptera), beetles (Coleoptera), flies (Diptera), and butterflies and moths (Lepidoptera). Bees are by far the dominant pollinators of crops, and it is generally agreed that in temperate areas of the world bees are the most important pollinators for plants of all kinds. Flies are more important for pollination in high-elevation and high-latitude regions, while beetles are more important as pollinators in tropical and equatorial areas, and are major pollinators of rain forest trees.

Which brings us to butterflies. Although not as centrally critical for pollination as bees are, moths and butterflies do play a significant role in the pollination of flowering plants. Plenty of established evidence indicates that moths can be important pollinators, but some have questioned whether butterflies are pollinators at all. Butterflies certainly pick up pollen when visiting flowers for their nectar; grass skippers have been observed carrying pollen, and in photographs pollen can clearly be seen on the legs and bodies of skippers. Skippers may well be important pollinators

The six-spot burnet (*Zygaena filipendulae*) rests on a fragrant orchid (*Gymnadenia conopsea*), one of several European orchids that are adapted for pollination by moths.

of prairie areas, since their short legs and stout hairy bodies lend themselves to moving pollen from flower to flower. Similarly, monarch butterflies (*Danaus plexippus*) may be seen with pollinia—small bundles of pollen—hanging from their legs, picked up from the milkweed flowers they visit.

For any animals to be successful pollinators, they must carry pollen from the flower of a particular kind of plant to another flower of the same kind. Bees are efficient pollinators in part because they demonstrate considerable flower constancy, moving consistently among flowers of the same species and even returning again and again to a single species in separate foraging flights to gather more pollen. Although butterflies show less constancy to flower species, they are consistently drawn to flowers from which they can efficiently get nectar. Butterflies and moths may not be as effective as bees at moving pollen and thereby pollinating plants, but even so, it has been documented that many plants benefit from the pollen transfer they accomplish.

In North America, the western prairie fringed orchid (*Platanthera praeclara*) is pollinated by several species of hawk moths in Midwest prairies; the mountain parnassian butterfly (*Parnassius smintheus*) pollinates *Senecio* and other yellow flowers in the daisy family in montane areas of the western states and northward through Canada into Alaska; and in the meadows and forests of the Pacific Northwest, swallowtail butterflies (*Papilio* species) are pollinators of

# Butterflies' protective tactics

**PREDATION ON BUTTERFLIES** is actually not a completely one-sided situation. Butterflies often depend on toxic compounds and other protective tactics to avoid being eaten. Monarchs, pipevine swallowtails (*Battus philenor*), and atalas (*Eumaeus atala*) concentrate poisons from their host plants within their own bodies, making them distasteful to other animals. Birds and other predators that do attempt to eat them find them unpalatable and quickly learn to avoid them. A study famous among butterfly enthusiasts found that blue jays need to eat a monarch only once to know not to eat one again; the cover of the journal with this study showed a blue jay retching after eating its first monarch. It must be admitted, though, that some predators have adapted to unpalatable butterflies; black-backed orioles (*Icterus abeillei*), black-headed grosbeaks (*Pheucticus melanocephalus*), and black-eared mice (*Peromyscus melanotis*) eat several million monarchs every year at the butterflies' Mexican overwintering sites.

Many species have evolved additional defenses such as irritating hairs or elaborate horns and spikes to further thwart predators. Larvae may use protective behaviors such as twitching violently when approached closely to discourage parasitoids. Some butterflies have taken protection a step further and enlisted bodyguards. Several species of blues and hairstreaks have evolved a relationship with ants; the caterpillars exude sugary honeydew that the ants consume and in exchange the ants protect the caterpillars from other predators.

Butterflies and caterpillars also use camouflage to hide in plain sight. The caterpillars of some moths attach plant debris to themselves. Caterpillars of other species resemble dead leaves or bark or some other part of a tree or plant, and the young larvae of most swallowtail butterflies (*Papilio* species) look like bird droppings—distinctly unpalatable! Adult butterflies and moths with wings closed often blend well with vegetation and if disturbed may use startling colors or large eye spots to surprise a bird or other would-be predator, causing the predator to set its sights elsewhere or giving them just long enough to escape. And adult butterflies may roost or puddle in groups, proving that old adage of safety in numbers. If a bird attacks, the massed fluttering of wings may confuse the bird, allowing most butterflies to escape.

the Columbia tiger lily (*Lilium columbianum*). In Central America, the firecracker plant (*Russelia* species), a shrub with vibrantly colored flowers, is pollinated by the orange-barred sulphur butterfly (*Phoebis philea*); the shrub's weeping branches cause its flowers to hang in a way that makes the flowers difficult for other insects to pollinate.

Europe also has a number of plants, in particular orchids, that are pollinated by Lepidoptera. The fragrant orchid (*Gymnadenia conopsea*) and the closely related short-spurred fragrant orchid (*G. odoratissima*) are both pollinated by owlet and forester moths. The greater and lesser butterfly orchids (*Platanthera chlorantha* and *P. bifolia*) may be misnamed, as owlet and hawk moths are their most frequent visitors. Each of these orchids produces copious amounts of nectar, unlike the pyramidal orchid (*Anacamptis pyramidalis*)—which doesn't produce any, and which still somehow attracts enough butterflies and moths to achieve adequate pollination.

Another example of butterfly-pollinated flowers comes from the fynbos shrublands of South Africa's Cape Province. What makes this instance most notable is that one butterfly, the Table Mountain beauty (*Aeropetes tulbaghia*), is the pollinator of a group of about fifteen unrelated but visually similar flowers; such dependence on a single species of pollinator is rarely found in plants, let alone in a group of different species. These flowers all bloom in late summer and have large red flowers with straight, narrow nectar tubes; the butterfly appears to be attracted primarily to the red color of the flowers, while the nectar tubes discourage birds that would otherwise visit red flowers. At least one of these species, the rust red orchid (*Disa ferruginea*), does not offer nectar but instead, in order to attract the butterfly, mimics species that do.

Butterfly-pollinated plants often display a similar set of features. They tend to bloom during the day and to provide nectar at the bottom of a long, narrow

The Table Mountain beauty (*Aeropetes tulbaghia*) is the pollinator of a group of about fifteen unrelated but visually similar red flowers.

tube or spur. The flowers, growing singly or clustered together in a group, often have a sweet odor and typically provide a large enough surface for a butterfly to land on. The flowers are also in colors that butterflies can see, usually red through violet and often ultraviolet. To make it even easier for butterflies to find the nectar (and thus further aid the plant's reproductive success), some plant species have evolved nectar

Butterflies and their caterpillars are a very important food source for many types of birds. This willow warbler (*Phylloscopus trochilus*) has a beak full of caterpillars, likely to feed its young.

guides—colorful lines or markings on the flower that help direct the pollinator to the nectar. In some cases, these nectar guides contain ultraviolet patterns that only particular flower visitors can see. Flower species with nectar guides are more frequently visited by pollinators than those without guides.

## BUTTERFLIES AS FOOD FOR OTHER ANIMALS

One thing to remember as you plant and nurture your butterfly garden is that some of the animals you are providing for will be eaten by other larger animals.

While we have yet to measure the full importance of butterfly populations as a food source, they undoubtedly play an integral role in providing sustenance to a variety of life on the planet. Many birds and lizards, as well as spiders, dragonflies, and other invertebrates in your garden, eat butterflies and moths. Try not to be too concerned, as this is part of nature. The fact is that if the population of butterflies is healthy, they can withstand this predation. If you see predation, it means you are providing for a robust population of butterflies and moths and that they in turn are feeding other necessary creatures. You are not just gardening for

Why butterflies matter—and why they are in trouble

butterflies; you are providing for a wider ecosystem.

Birds are an important predator of butterflies, particularly in the caterpillar stage. Warblers and other songbirds seek out caterpillars to sustain the high energy levels required to complete their spring migration. Songbirds would not survive without invertebrates—including butterfly and moth caterpillars—to feed their young. Parasites also feed on caterpillars. Some wasps and flies lay their eggs on top of or within a caterpillar; after hatching, the parasitic larvae burrow into the host and slowly eat it from the inside, eventually killing the caterpillar and emerging as adults. Stink bugs search for caterpillars in foliage, stabbing their prey with strawlike mouthparts and dissolving the tissues so they can suck up a nutrient-rich soup, and wasps and hornets sting and immobilize caterpillars to be brought back to the nest. Ground beetles and tiger beetles prey on both caterpillars and adult butterflies, using speed and enormous mandibles to capture their prey. Small mammals such as mice, chipmunks, and ground squirrels also dine on caterpillars. Beyond caterpillars, pupae undoubtedly serve as food to many of the same predators, but observations of pupal predation are not as common.

Adult butterflies are important food for many animals including bats, lizards, birds, and frogs, as well as spiders. Dragonflies and robber flies snatch butterflies midflight, while praying mantids, ambush bugs, and flower spiders lurk among blooms to seize butterflies when they land. Sometimes a predator catches only wing fragments; in fact, you may find a butterfly with a noticeable triangular, beak-shaped wedge missing from its hind wing.

Even humans can be considered butterfly predators. People in many countries eat pupae and larvae of moths, although here in North America we may be most familiar with caterpillars as "food" in the form of the agave worm in a tequila bottle.

Caterpillars are voracious eaters. Some are large and obvious, such as this tetrio sphinx (*Pseudosphinx tetrio*) caterpillar, while others are noticeable only by the chewed leaves.

## BUTTERFLIES AS HERBIVORES

When growing a butterfly garden, you need to be prepared to have some plants chewed and eaten since more than 99 percent of all moths and butterflies feed on plants. The goal is to put plants in the landscape that butterflies will lay their eggs on and that will in turn be consumed by caterpillars. Caterpillars are voracious eaters, and as herbivores they are critically important to the transfer of energy through the food chain. Not only do they make energy harnessed by plants available to higher organisms by becoming food for other animals, they also return nutrients to the soil through their abundant excretions (known as frass).

Because of their voracious appetites, caterpillars are helpful in controlling plant populations. Some species are even being used as biocontrol agents for controlling noxious invasive weeds; for example, in the western United States tansy ragwort (*Senecio jacobaea*),

a threat to farmers due to its livestock toxicity, is being controlled with the cinnabar moth (*Tyria jacobaeae*).

## AESTHETIC VALUE OF BUTTERFLIES

The beauty and brilliance of butterflies have captured the imaginations of countless people throughout the ages. Artistic depictions of butterflies appear in 3500-year-old Egyptian hieroglyphs, and ancient Hopi, Mayan, and Aztec cultures often represented butterflies in their drawings and figures. Ritual butterfly dances and ceremonies were performed by several ancient cultures. Aristotle gave the Greek name *psyche* (soul) to butterflies, and the butterfly has come to represent the human spirit.

Many different cultures have come to view butterflies as the souls of the dead. This is true in Mexico, where monarch butterflies return just before the Day of the Dead celebrations, and was true in seventeenth-century Ireland, where white butterflies were thought to be the souls of deceased children and where the killing of these butterflies was prohibited. Literature from the Bible to Shakespeare and from poetry to music lyrics makes many references to butterflies and moths. The renowned lepidopterist and novelist Vladimir Nabokov exquisitely shared his experiences with these animals in his autobiography, *Speak, Memory*. Numerous artists, including Salvador Dali, have depicted butterflies.

Europe during the Victorian era saw intense interest in collecting butterflies. Old World explorers would travel across the globe searching for new and unknown butterflies, while close to home young children and men and women alike would go on daytime collecting trips in the fields outside town. These vast collections contributed not only to the interests of the day but also to a scientific legacy.

Today, butterflies are widely used in art and jewelry. They are mounted in frames, embedded in resin, displayed in bottles, laminated in paper, and used in mixed media artworks and furnishings. British artist Damien Hirst uses butterflies in hugely controversial pieces of modern art, from collaging hundreds of individuals in kaleidoscopic paintings to releasing thousands of pupae and adults into stark white rooms to live out their short lives among museum visitors. Images of butterflies are commonly used in advertising and labeling, often to represent something natural or environmentally friendly; small monarch icons now grace U.S. foods that are certified GMO-free.

Butterflies mean business and an income source in some developing countries. Butterfly farms earn income from visiting tourists as well as from selling chrysalises to butterfly houses.

A recent study suggests that people in the United States value monarch butterflies (*Danaus plexippus*) as much as they do endangered whooping cranes.

## BUTTERFLIES AS BUSINESS

Beyond the ecosystem and aesthetic value of butterflies, they are important economically. Butterfly watching generates millions a year for local communities. In places like the monarch overwintering grounds of Mexico, tourists are drawn by the thousands to a handful of towns, adding to the local economy through purchases of food, lodging, tours, transportation, gifts, and other memorabilia. Other Lepidoptera hot spots include Valley of the Butterflies on the Greek island of Rhodes, where the Jersey tiger moth (*Euplagia quadripunctaria*) aggregates every summer, and the Maolin Ecological Park in Taiwan, which hosts up to a million overwintering purple crow butterflies (*Euploea* species) each year. In tropical regions around the world, eco-resorts are now being developed that offer tourists chances to see spectacular equatorial species. Costa Rica alone has more than 2500 species of butterflies, and Peru boasts 3500 or more. In the past, butterfly tours were tailored to collectors, but as interest grows in watching butterflies rather than collecting them, more tours are being offered simply to watch butterflies in their natural habitats.

Public butterfly houses and gardens at museums, arboretums, and botanic gardens also attract visitors from around the world. Butterfly World opened in Florida in 1988, and since then additional sites have opened in Georgia, California, Colorado, and elsewhere. Natural history museums often include some sort of butterfly house or butterfly garden for visitors to experience butterflies from faraway lands. The Smithsonian National Museum of Natural History in Washington DC has a year-round butterfly garden and exhibit, and the California Academy of Sciences in San Francisco boasts a three-story living rain forest complete with free-flying birds and butterflies.

A niche market in the home gardening world has opened up to provide plants labeled to inform gardeners that these species are best for attracting butterflies. These same plants are often attractive to hummingbirds and bees as well.

In developing countries, sustainable butterfly farming, in which small farms provide specimens of adults to collectors and larvae to butterfly houses, is a source of income for some people. Papua New Guinea took this to new levels when the national government designated insects a national resource and included butterfly farming in the country's village economic development plans. In rural villages where people have few opportunities to make a living, butterfly farming offers a chance to generate an income from using the land in a sustainable way.

Assigning a value to butterfly species and the services they provide is inherently difficult but may improve conservation of certain species. For example, a 2014 study suggested U.S. citizens are willing to support monarch butterfly conservation at high levels, up to about $6.5 billion if extrapolated to all U.S.

Butterflies like this common buckeye (*Junonia coenia*) are highly recognizable visitors to gardens.

households—a number in line with the public's valuation of many higher-profile endangered species such as whooping cranes and one that suggests donations to conservation groups and monarch-friendly plant purchases could generate much-needed action to protect this species.

## BUTTERFLIES IN SCIENCE AND EDUCATION

Butterflies are among the most studied insects; in England, naturalists have studied them for almost three hundred years. Butterflies (and moths to a lesser extent) are an extremely important group of model organisms used in biological research, including biodiversity and conservation biology studies, habitat assessments, animal population monitoring, and

Butterfly collections have helped scientists and conservationists understand and protect butterflies and their habitat.

Monarch butterflies (*Danaus plexippus*) like these seen overwintering along the California coast are threatened by habitat loss and climate change.

# The monarch butterfly: A common species at risk

**MONARCH BUTTERFLIES** are ubiquitous in North America and common garden visitors in many areas of the United States. These well-known butterflies make annual trips of hundreds or thousands of miles from summer breeding grounds to overwintering groves in California and Mexico. But despite populations still numbering in the millions, the monarch butterfly is quickly becoming a prime example of a once-common species now undergoing drastic population declines.

When monitoring efforts first began in the 1990s, an estimated half a billion monarchs made the epic flight each fall from the northern plains of the United States and Canada to sites in the oyamel fir forests north of Mexico City. An additional one million monarchs overwintered in forested groves along the California coast. Now, researchers and citizen scientists estimate that only about 50 million monarchs remain, representing a more-than-80-percent drop across North America. In the face of these declines and mounting threats from habitat loss and degradation, pesticide use, and climate change, the annual migration was declared an endangered biological phenomenon by the International Union for Conservation of Nature, and the North American population is being considered as of this writing in late 2015 for threatened species protection under the U.S. Endangered Species Act.

The fate of the monarch is uncertain, but the good news is that the governments of the United States, Canada, and Mexico are taking unprecedented collaborative conservation actions for both the summer breeding grounds (offering stands of the monarchs' host plant, milkweed) and overwintering groves in Mexico. More than two dozen conservation, education, and research partners from across the United States have joined together to form the Monarch Joint Venture (monarchjointventure.org) to conserve the monarch migration and teach gardeners how to help. Gardeners can actively promote monarch and pollinator conservation simply by planting locally appropriate milkweed species, providing a variety of nectar sources from spring through fall, and avoiding the use of insecticides.

genetic studies. Their sheer abundance, diversity, and relatively well-documented taxonomy and biology, in addition to the ease of observing them in the field, make them ideal indicators of a healthy environment and ecosystem. Because of the generally positive public view of butterflies, they can act as flagships for the protection of a suite of other organisms that share the same habitat and are thus an important focus of conservation projects.

With their fascinating life cycles, butterflies and moths are used in many countries to teach children about the natural world. Their transformation from egg to caterpillar to chrysalis and finally winged adult is a wonder of nature, and butterflies can be used in the classroom to teach a plethora of other scientific lessons, including ones on migration, mimicry, and the use of intricate wing patterns and iridescence.

The study of butterflies has led to some incredible scientific theories and innovations. Research on the wing structure of butterflies led to new aircraft designs. Studies on the reflection and scattering of light by the scales on wings of swallowtail butterflies led to the innovation of more efficient light-emitting diodes (electric components that allow an electrical current to move in one direction but not the other). Monarchs, queens (*Danaus gilippus*), and viceroys (*Limenitis archippus*) sparked the study of mimicry.

## THREATS TO THE WORLD'S BUTTERFLIES

Our lives would be greatly impoverished without butterflies and moths. As you have seen, they are of vital importance to ecosystems, inspire poetry and art, provide livelihoods, offer a window into the natural world, and bring beauty into our cities and neighborhoods. But unfortunately, the world's butterflies are in peril. Although we know relatively little about the status of each species, the information we do have

The growth of San Francisco has smothered much habitat and led to the extinction of three butterflies: the sthenele wood nymph (*Cercyonis sthenele sthenele*), the Xerces blue (*Glaucopsyche xerces*), and the pheres blue (*Plebejus icarioides pheres*).

is not encouraging. Recent reports from practically every continent are now documenting unprecedented declines in a broad suite of butterflies.

Studies in Europe have revealed that grassland butterfly species have declined by almost 50 percent since the early 1990s and three-quarters of the butterflies in the United Kingdom are in decline. In the United States alone, at least five butterflies have gone extinct since 1950; an additional twenty-five butterflies are listed as endangered nationwide, and four are listed as threatened. NatureServe, one of the leading sources of information about rare and endangered species, has assessed all 800 butterfly species in the United States and has found that 17 percent are currently at risk of extinction.

Most of the butterflies at risk of extinction are rare endemics—those species that have a narrow geographic range or very specific habitat requirements. However, lepidopterists across the United States are reporting that broadly distributed butterflies are also in decline. These downward trends are troubling and are being mirrored by many other groups of animals and plants. What is happening in our global landscapes

Why butterflies matter—and why they are in trouble

to cause such alarming losses? Butterflies face a wide range of threats including habitat loss, climate change, disease, pesticides, and invasive plants. More localized threats, such as overcollecting and roadside mowing, can also have negative consequences. Chief among these threats is loss and fragmentation of habitat.

## HABITAT LOSS AND FRAGMENTATION

Habitat loss is the most significant factor leading to declines in butterflies. It includes both the outright destruction of habitat and the fragmentation of habitat into small, isolated patches. In urban areas the loss of wild habitat is apparent, but the fragmentation of habitat in rural areas is no less a problem. Farming and ranching practices can leave the landscape green but covered in fields that provide little for butterflies. Loss of both larval host plants and nectar sites can have a profound impact on butterfly populations and is the leading factor in the decline of most imperiled butterflies. This includes species like grass skippers that do not fly far in the landscape as well as the migratory monarch butterfly.

Habitat loss takes many forms, including conversion of grasslands and wetlands to agriculture, urban growth and sprawl, clear cutting of forests and replanting with single-species stands, and tree and shrub encroachment into meadows, which impacts meadow- and grassland-dependent species. One of the major problems with human-caused habitat loss and fragmentation is that it happens very quickly, so local species don't have time to adapt. Natural changes, on the other hand, often occur over a much longer span of time, giving local species the chance to adjust.

Perhaps the best-known case of habitat loss leading to a butterfly's extinction is that of San Francisco, California, a city that now almost entirely covers what was once one of the major coastal dune ecosystems in western North America. Three dune butterflies that

Habitat loss is not restricted to farmland or development sites. Many landscapes provide little or no habitat for butterflies because they lack flowers and host plants.

lived only in this region are now extinct: the sthenele wood nymph (*Cercyonis sthenele sthenele*), the Xerces blue (*Glaucopsyche xerces*), and the pheres blue (*Plebejus icarioides pheres*). Three other butterflies, the Calippe silverspot (*Speyeria callippe callippe*), the San Bruno elfin (*Callophrys mossii bayensis*), and the mission blue (*Icaricia icarioides missionensis*), are now limited to San Bruno Mountain and just a few other locations south of San Francisco, the final remnant of the once-extensive San Francisco hills ecosystem.

Beyond urbanization, agriculture is the single largest component of global land use, and with 36 percent of the earth's surface devoted to agriculture it is vital that we protect butterflies and other animals within this landscape. Unfortunately, the advent of large-scale monoculture agriculture in recent decades has led to huge declines in available habitat for our butterflies. Until recently, plants that butterflies could use for host plants or nectar sources grew within and adjacent to agricultural fields, but that has now changed. To eradicate weeds, genetically modified corn and soy in the

Climate change may negatively impact a variety of butterflies and moths that live in alpine areas such as the mountains of Colorado.

American Midwest are sprayed with glyphosate herbicides, which unfortunately also target many beneficial plants including milkweed, the monarch butterfly's host plant. As monarch numbers plummet, this loss of milkweed (and subsequent loss of available breeding ground) is thought to be one of the primary culprits.

## CLIMATE CHANGE

We have all heard about the issue of climate change and how it may impact our environment. The terms *climate change* and *global warming* do not really articulate how greenhouse gases are impacting our world, and in fact these terms can be somewhat confusing.

It's true that some places are getting hotter and drier, but some are actually getting wetter or colder. In many places, the climate is just a lot more variable—cold one year, hot and dry the next, late snows or no snows at all. All of these changes impact a butterfly's ability to survive in the environment.

We are already seeing the impact of climate change on butterflies. The Uncompahgre fritillary (*Boloria acrocnema*) is one of the first butterflies known to be impacted by climate change. This imperiled butterfly was protected under the Endangered Species Act in 1991, and it was the first time climate change was listed as a threat to an animal in an Endangered Species Act

Why butterflies matter—and why they are in trouble

listing. The Uncompahgre fritillary is remarkable in that it is found only above 13,000 feet in the mountains of southern Colorado, some of the tallest peaks in the United States. Because of the harsh climate at this elevation (the summer often lasts only four to six weeks), it takes two to three years for a butterfly to complete its life cycle. Snowfields persist year-round on the north slopes, and the snowmelt provides a plentiful water supply for snow willow, the butterfly's host plant. Unfortunately, those snowfields will likely be gone before the middle of this century, which may lead to extinction of this butterfly.

It is not just butterflies living in high mountains that may suffer. Many butterflies that reside along coastlines are already seeing habitat loss due to rising oceans and larger storm events. Even meadow butterflies may suffer as climate change alters moisture availability and dries up wet areas where these species' host plants grow. Ongoing severe drought conditions in California that may be linked to climate change are likely causing declines in monarch overwintering populations on the California coast. Drought in Texas also impacts monarch butterflies looking for breeding sites as they fly north from overwintering sites in Mexico. Studies on the California drought found that some populations of checkerspots went locally extinct because adults could not find host plants on which to lay eggs.

Some butterflies are moving as a result of climate change. Scientists have already documented that some species are shifting their entire distribution northward or to higher elevations in order to find the habitats and resources they need to survive. What we don't know is how many species are capable of this type of movement. Many species can survive only in certain types of habitats and are not able to fly far enough to find suitable new areas. Loss of habitat makes matters worse as butterflies often need to go farther through agricultural fields or urban or suburban developments to find new homes.

One additional problem is that some plant species are emerging earlier or later than they have in the past—and this can put them out of sync with the butterflies that use them. As some species of butterflies emerge earlier, they also run the risk of encountering frost or missing their host plants entirely.

Despite the challenges inherent in these changes, there are some success stories. The Quino checkerspot (*Euphydryas editha quino*), a once-abundant California butterfly that declined due to urban sprawl in San Diego and Los Angeles, has now moved to higher altitudes and even adopted a new host plant. This is the first butterfly known to science to change both its location and its host plant so rapidly, and it serves as a reminder that some species may be more resilient to climate change than we initially expected. Still, in order to make shifts like this possible, human-managed nature reserves, wild lands, and appropriate habitat corridors are becoming even more important. Without these links available, many species may have no place to go.

## PESTICIDES

The use of pesticides, including insecticides and herbicides, is detrimental to a healthy community of butterflies. Insecticides, as the term implies, kill insects and can kill butterflies and moths if used where they feed. Herbicides can kill plants that butterflies depend on and reduce the amount of food available to them.

**INSECTICIDES** Insecticide use is now ubiquitous around the globe; more than one billion pounds of insecticides are used annually in just the United States. Insecticides are widely used in agriculture, on rangelands, in woodlands and other natural areas, in waterways, on golf courses, on residential lawns and gardens, on sports fields, along roadsides, and on street trees. Interestingly, several studies show that more insecticides are used in urban and suburban areas than in agricultural areas.

According to the U.S. Geological Survey, more pesticides are often used per acre in urban and suburban areas than in agriculture.

Many insecticides were designed to control moth pests of commercial crops, which means they can be especially toxic to butterflies. Studies have shown that butterflies in and around agricultural fields are impacted when the fields are sprayed. Even butterflies that use habitat on the edges of fields are at risk because these chemicals can drift away from the areas that have been treated. Other uses also affect butterflies. In Florida, aerial spraying of malathion and other pesticides for adult mosquito control has devastated some local butterfly populations. The Schaus swallowtail (*Heraclides aristodemus ponceanus*) was listed under the Endangered Species Act in part because of mosquito spraying.

A new class of insecticides called neonicotinoids is especially concerning. These synthetic chemicals are similar in structure and action to nicotine and work by blocking nerve impulses in insects and other invertebrates. Currently the most widely used group of insecticides in the world, neonicotinoids are employed broadly in the nursery industry and beyond; the U.S. Geological Survey routinely finds these chemicals in stream samples across the United States. Neonic-

otinoids are currently under scientific scrutiny for the potentially substantial threats that they pose to pollinators (including butterflies and moths), aquatic invertebrates, soil-dwelling invertebrates, and birds. The use of these insecticides has led to the loss of millions of honey bees in recent years, and in a single event more than fifty thousand bumble bees were killed when trees near a shopping center were treated.

What makes neonicotinoids different from other insecticides is that they have a systemic mode of action; this means they are taken up into every part of the plant including the nectar and the pollen. Neonicotinoids can also be persistent for long periods in plants and soil. They can remain in soil for months or even years after a single application, and untreated plants may absorb chemical residues in the soil from the previous year. Measurable amounts of residues have been found in woody plants up to six years after a single application.

Many products containing neonicotinoids are sold for use in gardens; some of the most common include the active chemical ingredients imidacloprid, dinotefuran, clothianidin, and thiamethoxam. What makes this especially troubling is that products approved for home and garden use may be applied to ornamental and landscape plants, as well as turf, at significantly higher rates (up to thirty-two times higher) than those approved for agricultural crops. Many scientists from all over the world have come together to call for bans on these chemicals, especially in garden situations. These insecticides should not be used in the garden if your goal is to help provide for butterflies or other pollinators.

**HERBICIDES** Herbicides kill plants and can impact the butterflies that depend on them. Herbicide use has eliminated milkweed from much of the Midwest farm landscape and is likely a major factor in the decline of the monarch butterfly. The key issue with herbicides is how they are applied. The broadcast application of a nonselective herbicide can kill all of

# The mardon skipper:
# A conservation success

**MANY OF OUR MOST** imperiled butterflies are found in highly restricted habitats with only a handful of known populations. While these localized endemics probably won't be found in your garden, it's important to realize how actions at both local and regional levels can contribute to the conservation or decline of these species.

The mardon skipper (*Polites mardon*) is a rare butterfly found only in the Pacific Northwest. In 2000 the mardon skipper was listed as a candidate species under the U.S. Endangered Species Act. In an unprecedented cooperative effort to conserve this butterfly, the Xerces Society for Invertebrate Conservation, the Forest Service / Bureau of Land Management Interagency Special Status / Sensitive Species Program, the Washington Department of Fish and Wildlife, Washington State University,

the Oregon Zoo, the Six Rivers National Forest, and the Center for Natural Lands Management quickly joined together on a number of research and monitoring projects. These projects include developing and implementing surveys across the species' range, studying host plant preference and the impacts of management activities, and implementing restoration activities and management actions at specific mardon sites.

This ongoing process has led to the discovery of many new populations and an improved outlook for the butterfly. Although continued work is needed to recover the butterfly, the U.S. Fish and Wildlife Service did not ultimately list the species under the Endangered Species Act. This process serves as a model for protecting additional U.S. butterfly species.

the plants in an area, effectively eliminating or reducing floral resources and host plants for butterflies. If you find you must use an herbicide, it is very important to target treatments to ensure host plants and nectar sources are not impacted.

## INVASIVE SPECIES

Invasive plants are a large and growing threat in our natural landscapes. These are plants that are not native to a region that have a tendency to spread out over large areas, quickly crowding out native plants. For many butterflies that have specific host plant requirements, the encroachment of invasive plants may lead to a decline in their host plant and subsequently a decline in the butterfly. Grass skippers such as the federally threatened Dakota skipper (*Hesperia dacotae*), which rely on specific grasses in their larval stage, are negatively impacted by invasive grasses that crowd out native species.

Invasive animals can also pose a threat. For example, the introduced green iguana in South Florida can be a major herbivore of the nickerbean, the host plant for the endangered Miami blue butterfly (*Cyclargus thomasi bethunbakeri*). This butterfly has a tiny population limited to only one or two sites in the Florida Keys and a nearby island. By eating the leaves of these plants, iguanas not only remove the food source for larval Miami blues, they also likely destroy eggs and larvae already on the plant.

The introduced green iguana in South Florida eats the host plant of the endangered Miami blue butterfly (*Cyclargus thomasi bethunbakeri*).

Over the past century, nonnative insects have been released in order to control—as predators, parasites, or herbivores—pest insects and nonnative invasive plants. This biological control is often touted as a safe alternative to chemicals and is now frequently applied. However, increasing evidence suggests that the negative impacts of such releases on nontarget, native species can be significant.

Studies in Illinois have demonstrated that lady beetles introduced to control aphids on crops also feed upon young caterpillars of monarch butterflies. Similarly, a study in Hawaii found that 83 percent of parasitoids found in native moths were species that had originally been introduced for biological control and that now parasitize a wide range of native host species. An introduced parasitic fly is also thought to be a factor in the decline of large silkmoths in the eastern United States.

Indirectly, insects released for the purpose of controlling nonnative invasive plants can affect native pollinators by reducing food availability. For example, two European weevil species released in North America to control nonnative thistles now adversely impact native thistles, limiting an important nectar source for a range of butterflies.

## MASS RELEASES OF BUTTERFLIES

For many years butterflies have been released at weddings, funerals, and other events. People are thrilled by the majesty of dozens or hundreds of butterflies fluttering over these events. Although we do not know how many butterflies are sold and released each year

Why butterflies matter—and why they are in trouble

because the butterfly-rearing industry does not give out its records, we believe that hundreds of thousands are sold, shipped across the United States, and released away from where they were raised. Unfortunately, the transfer and release of butterflies for weddings and other events may cause several problems for native butterflies.

Mass butterfly releases may spread diseases and parasites to wild populations. Mass production of butterflies makes it easy to transmit disease. Butterflies did not evolve under conditions in which they developed in large groups, and they are very susceptible to diseases that can be transmitted among larvae. Breeders are not required to follow specific disease-preventing protocols, nor do outside agencies routinely test captive stock for diseases.

Another threat of butterfly releases involves introducing unhelpful genes into local populations, which could negatively influence the survivorship potential of native butterflies. Genetic transfer can occur when released butterflies mate with wild butterflies and they produce offspring; the genetic makeup of the offspring will include traits from both the wild and reared butterfly parents. Though this threat is difficult to quantify and demonstrate, it should certainly be approached through the precautionary principle, with the burden of proof on potential releasers to prove the harmlessness of their proposed activity.

These releases also confuse studies of butterfly distribution and make it hard to prioritize habitat conservation. In order to prioritize conservation, we need to know where butterflies live, breed, and move within the environment. When butterflies are released into the environment, they muddle our ability to understand these important issues. As one example, monarch butterflies have shown up in the San Juan Islands in northern Washington State in recent years—a place where they have never been seen before. We do not know whether these monarchs made it to the islands naturally and may be expanding their range due to climate change or whether they arrived because of releases.

Another problem is that many of the animals we release die from exposure or starvation because it is the wrong time of year or the wrong locality for them to survive. If they do succeed in reproducing in the new territory, the other problems are only magnified. Treating butterflies as commercial ornaments to be grown, shipped, and released at will is not an appropriate way to increase respect and care for wild butterflies. Birds have been protected from such treatment for decades, and it is time to extend the same kind of concern to butterflies. It doesn't harm butterflies to collect them locally and raise them for release, but captive rearing of butterflies must be done carefully. The practice of mass releases is opposed by many organizations including the Xerces Society and the North American Butterfly Association.

## OTHER THREATS

Other activities such as overcollecting may threaten butterflies, although this is likely only a threat to butterflies whose populations are already imperiled. Light pollution is also a concern; the lights that brighten our streets and highways at night are apparently responsible for losses of nocturnal insects, particularly large moths. Many of the threats we've discussed are human caused in some way, but natural threats in the form of predators, parasites, disease, and natural disasters also take their toll on butterfly populations.

Despite the many threats to butterflies and their habitats, the situation is far from hopeless. By providing pesticide-free habitat in your garden, you can be part of the solution. If enough people take action to plant flowers, provide host plants, and offer overwintering areas, butterflies will have a better future and we will have beautiful landscapes to enjoy.

As a butterfly gardener, you should be prepared to have your plants chewed on and eaten by caterpillars. This black swallowtail (*Papilio polyxenes*) caterpillar is feeding on dill.

# Knowing butterflies and what they need

IN AN INCREASINGLY ALTERED and fragmented global landscape, butterflies are suffering from lack of flowers. Yards, gardens, and parks are often filled with turfgrass or cultivars that are beautiful to look at but provide no food for these insects. Habitat on farms has decreased as farmers seek to maximize production, and areas like roadsides are often mowed right when the flowers start blooming. Large quantities of pesticides are also used in all of these landscapes.

A well-designed garden can offer all a butterfly or moth needs to complete its life cycle. Providing host plants and nectar sources will go a long way toward attracting and keeping butterflies and is a very good place to start your butterfly gardening efforts. Adding sites where butterflies and moths can overwinter will round out your garden and make it truly a butterfly paradise. Knowing about the variety of butterflies that exist and the life stages of these animals will allow you to tailor your garden to their needs.

## THE BUTTERFLY FAMILIES

To help you know the butterflies you see in your garden, we introduce you here to the broad groupings of butterflies known as families, some of which are broken down further into subfamilies. Although representatives of most of these groups can be found in all areas across North America, the species you see will vary depending on where you live. To identify specific butterflies, we encourage you to check out one of the many good national and regional guides to butterflies that can be found in bookstores and libraries (some of which are listed at the back of this book).

At 6 inches, the wingspan of North America's largest butterfly, the giant swallowtail (*Papilio cresphontes*, right), is nearly twelve times that of the continent's smallest, the western pygmy-blue (*Brephidium exilis*, below).

## SKIPPERS (FAMILY HESPERIIDAE)

The rapid, skipping flight of these butterflies gives the family its common name. Skippers are small to medium size and are distinct from other butterflies in having larger bodies in proportion to the wings. They can also be distinguished from other butterflies by the hooked bulb at the end of each antenna. On skippers, this bulb is bent almost 90 degrees to the side, rather than straight as in other butterflies.

Most North American species are grouped in one of two subfamilies: the monocot (grass) skippers and the dicot (flowering plant) skippers. There are approx-

Grass skippers often hold their wings partially open with the forewing separated from the hind wing, making two Vs.

imately 200 species of skippers in the United States. You can encourage them to visit your garden if you provide their grass host plants.

**GRASS SKIPPERS (SUBFAMILY HESPERI-INAE)** Grass skippers resemble moths, being hairier and more robust than most other butterflies, but unlike most moths they fly during the day. These skippers tend to have short wings and must flap them rapidly ("skip") to fly. Most North American species are orange-brown and lack the brighter colors and complex wing patterns of the other butterflies, although this is not true of tropical species. When at rest, they often hold their wings partially open with the forewing separated from the hind wing, making two Vs, one inside the other, when observed from the front or back. Males of many species have dark patches or streaks on the upper side of the forewing containing special scales that produce pheromones for attracting a mate. Skipper caterpillars frequently curl the blades of grasses

# What's in a name?

**THE TWO-PART** Latin name given after the common name for each butterfly mentioned here is known as scientific nomenclature. This naming system groups every living thing into a hierarchy of categories that begins with the broadest category of kingdom and proceeds down through phylum, class, order, and family to genus and species. The genus-species name is the unique identifier for each species.

As an example of this classification system, the full classification of a monarch butterfly looks like this:

KINGDOM **Animalia** (animals)
PHYLUM **Arthropoda** (arthropods)
CLASS **Insecta** (insects)
ORDER **Lepidoptera** (butterflies and moths)
FAMILY **Nymphalidae** (brush-footed butterflies)
GENUS *Danaus* (tiger, milkweed, soldier, and queen butterflies)
SPECIES *plexippus* (monarch butterfly)

or sedges with silk to form nests in which they feed, overwinter, and pupate.

**DICOT OR SPREAD-WINGED SKIPPERS (SUBFAMILY PYRGINAE)** Perhaps three dozen dicot skippers such as duskywings and cloudywings are native in North America. Dicot skippers are usually darker than grass skippers, either black or dark brown and often with white spots or checkers. They have broad wings that are commonly opened flat—not in the double-V pattern—when the butterflies are perched, hence "spread-winged" skippers.

Dicot skippers are often dark and mothlike, as exemplified by this common sootywing (*Pholisora catullus*), but still have the clubbed antennae characteristic of butterflies.

# SWALLOWTAILS (FAMILY PAPILIONIDAE)

The swallowtail family includes the largest and most easily recognized butterflies in the world, which are also among the most common butterflies seen in gardens. There are about 550 species worldwide. The aptly named giant swallowtail (*Papilio cresphontes*), with a wingspan up to 6 inches, is the largest butterfly in North America.

Swallowtails are well loved because of their size and beauty, and several species are formally recognized as state symbols. The eastern tiger swallowtail (*Papilio glaucus*) is the state insect of Virginia and the state butterfly of Georgia, Delaware, and South Carolina. The black swallowtail (*Papilio polyxenes*) is the state butterfly of Oklahoma, and the Oregon swallowtail (*Papilio oregonius*) is the state insect of Oregon.

The wings of swallowtails are often black and yellow or black and white. Most species have tails on their hind wings reminiscent of the elegant forked tails of barn swallows and other similar birds. These tails may serve as a way to escape predators such as birds. When a bird strikes, it often takes off just the end of the tail on the wing of the butterfly, which does no real harm. Next time you see a swallowtail in your garden, look to see if it has escaped a bird.

The related parnassians (subfamily Parnassiinae) do not have tails and are often mostly white with red spots and only small, fine black stripes. The wings are often off-white or ashen because parnassians have a thinner covering of scales on the outer half of their wings, making them translucent and the colors less intense. Five species of parnassians are found in North America.

Adult swallowtails are strong fliers and may pass over your garden as often as they stop in it. In open areas and parks, they often patrol back and forth along the edges of wooded areas or streams. Some species gather in large groups at mud puddles and damp stretches of sand. These are mostly males who sip at the moisture to glean salts and other nutrients not available from flowers.

Swallowtail larvae are excellent mimics, and young caterpillars of some species mimic bird droppings with extraordinary accuracy as a means of camouflage. When disturbed or handled, older caterpillars of some species have an impressive defensive display: a bright orange, forked, foul-smelling organ called an osmeterium is pushed out just behind the head. The osmeterium likely startles predators, and the smell may deter them.

Caterpillars of some species of swallowtail display a bright orange, forked, foul-smelling organ called an osmeterium to ward off predators.

Swallowtails get their name from the tails on their hind wings, reminiscent of the elegant forked tails of barn swallows.

41

Whites like this Sara's orangetip (*Anthocharis sara*) often have bright orange wingtips and black marginal wing patterns.

Male sulphurs are often a bright, clear lemon yellow like this orange sulphur (*Colias eurytheme*), while females are more likely to be off-white.

## WHITES, MARBLES, AND SULPHURS (FAMILY PIERIDAE)

Butterflies in this family vary in size from small to swallowtail size and are most often white, marbled, yellow, or orange. Bright orange wingtips and black marginal patterns are common. In some species, the males and females have visibly different wing patterns or coloration. Males can be a bright, clear lemon yellow, while females are off-white with small dark markings. Some say that the word *butterfly* originated from a European member of this family, the brimstone (*Gonepteryx rhamni*), which centuries ago was called the butter fly in Britain for its pale yellow color.

In many areas of North America these are among the earliest butterflies to emerge, so they are the first ones to look for in early spring. They fly in a continuous fluttering pattern and are common along roadsides, in meadows, and in gardens. Sulphurs can be particularly quick moving, spending only a moment at a flower before flying on. Dozens of individuals, usually male, often group together on a patch of damp mud to drink and take in minerals and salts.

Larvae of most whites feed on the plants in the mustard family such as cabbage, and most sulphurs feed on plants in the pea family. Although very few butterfly caterpillars are pests, this family includes two: the orange sulphur (*Colias eurytheme*), which can be a pest of alfalfa, and the cabbage white (*Pieris rapae*), introduced from Europe and now one of the most common butterflies in gardens and a likely pest if you grow cabbage or broccoli. The widespread abundance and distribution of the cabbage white is not typical of this family, as many whites and sulphurs have restricted ranges and their caterpillars occur only on specific host plants.

## GOSSAMER-WINGED BUTTERFLIES (FAMILY LYCAENIDAE)

The family Lycaenidae is a highly diverse group of small butterflies. The group includes the blues,

As illustrated by this Melissa blue (*Plebejus melissa*), blues are small, usually less than 1½ inches across, but stunningly beautiful, with shimmering wings that are often dotted with bold spots or zigzag lines.

Damage to the wings of butterflies from bird strikes is relatively common. This gray hairstreak (*Strymon melinus*) survived thanks to wing markings that fooled the bird into striking the wrong end.

coppers, hairstreaks, and metalmarks. It is the second largest group of butterflies, with approximately 5000 species worldwide and about 150 species in North America. Despite their small size, they are often strikingly beautiful, with wings shimmering in blue, green, or copper. Rather than being pigmented, the wing scales on male lycaenids have a structure that refracts light, leading to iridescent colors that change with the angle of viewing. The females are less brightly colored. On the underside, the wings of both males and females may be dotted with bold spots or zigzag lines.

Many of these butterflies have hairlike tails and bright eyespots at the rear of their hind wings. Together, these mimic the head and antennae, an adaptation intended to fool predators such as birds; they strike the wing instead of the head, getting nothing but a mouthful of dry, scaly wing and allowing the butterfly to escape, torn but essentially unharmed.

This group includes the smallest butterfly in the United States (and one of the smallest in the world), the western pygmy-blue (*Brephidium exilis*), which measures little more than ½ inch from wingtip to wingtip. Blues are common residents of gardens in many areas of the country. Plants in the buckwheat family and the heath and heather family as well as shrubs such as dogwood, elderberry, and huckleberry can help attract them.

Many butterflies in this family, including blues and coppers, have an unusual relationship with ants. In some species, caterpillars feeding on the host plant are attended to and protected by ants, and the ants receive sugar-rich honeydew produced by the caterpillars in return. With particular species of ants, only the first part of the caterpillar's life is spent on the plant, and the remainder of the caterpillar life span is spent in the ant nest. Once the ants bring the caterpillar into the nest, they may feed it ant regurgitations, or in some cases the caterpillar eats the ant larvae. Some ants bring the chrysalis up out of the nest; others let the butterfly emerge from the chrysalis inside the nest, in which case the butterfly must crawl out of the nest before it can expand its wings.

## BRUSH-FOOTED BUTTERFLIES (FAMILY NYMPHALIDAE)

Nymphalidae is the largest and most diverse butterfly family, encompassing many of the best-known butterflies, such as monarchs and painted ladies. The family also includes fritillaries, crescents, checkerspots, anglewings, admirals, and longwings. They are called brush-foots because the forelegs of these butterflies are greatly reduced in size and covered in hair—brushlike. They are held close to the head and are used primarily for tasting potential food. Because the forelegs are so small and tucked away, these butterflies appear to have only four legs.

The great diversity of butterflies in this family means no single characteristic—other than the appearance of having only four legs—unites them or makes

Many caterpillars in the family Nymphalidae have large spines, as illustrated by this variegated fritillary (*Euptoieta claudia*).

them easy to identify as a group. The nymphalids are often colored in shades of orange, brown, and black, sometimes checkered or dotted, sometimes having eyespots or spots of silver. Some are even shaped and patterned like dead leaves. Nymphalid caterpillars feed on a wide variety of plant families. Most caterpillars in this family have large spines, and their chrysalises are usually sharply angled and adorned with silver or gold colors.

**LONGWINGS AND FRITILLARIES** Longwings are tropical butterflies that breed on and are closely co-evolved with passionflowers. They are among the few butterflies to feed on pollen. Most species have long, narrow wings with stripes of color. The zebra heliconian (*Heliconius charithonia*) is the most widespread in the United States. It is commonly seen in Florida but may be found as far west as California and as far north as North Carolina. In contrast, fritillaries are widespread throughout North America and can be found in many different environments. The wings of fritillaries are orange or warm brown with black markings and often have glistening silver spots below.

The zebra heliconian (*Heliconius charithonia*) is a longwing that can be seen throughout much of the southern United States from Florida to California.

The appearance of having only four legs is a defining characteristic of the brush-footed butterflies. The "missing" legs of this Baltimore checkerspot (*Euphydryas phaeton*) are the same orange color as the others and can be seen held close to the head.

**CHECKERSPOTS AND CRESCENTS** As the name suggests, checkerspots often bear a checkerboard-like pattern in black, white, and orange. They are usually medium size (wingspan less than 2½ inches) and are relatively strong flyers. The crescents are generally smaller and typically have dark, crescent-shaped bands along the edges of their wings. This group includes some of our most endangered butterflies. On the West Coast, three closely related subspecies, the Taylor's checkerspot (*Euphydryas editha taylori*), the bay checkerspot (*Euphydryas editha bayensis*), and the

Crescents like this pearl crescent (*Phyciodes tharos*) typically have dark, crescent-shaped bands along the edges of their wings.

Knowing butterflies and what they need

Quino checkerspot (*Euphydryas editha quino*), are all protected under the U.S. Endangered Species Act. Two other members of this family, the Baltimore checkerspot (*Euphydryas phaeton*) in the east and the Sacramento Mountains checkerspot (*Euphydryas anicia cloudcrofti*) in New Mexico, also need conservation attention.

**TRUE NYMPHS (ANGLEWINGS, COMMAS, TORTOISESHELLS, LADIES, BUCKEYES, AND ADMIRALS)** As strong fliers that travel broadly across the landscape, true nymphs include many butterflies that frequent gardens. They are almost all medium size but are highly variable in shape and color (as the long list of names here might suggest). The anglewings, commas, and tortoiseshells are remarkable mimics of bark or leaves, with the camouflaged underside of the wings completely masking the brightly colored upper side when closed together. Anglewings enhance this camouflage by having uneven edges to their wings; tortoiseshells have broader wings with less-ragged edges. The commas often have a silvery white, comma-shaped mark on the ventral hind wing. The ladies—including the painted lady (*Vanessa cardui*)—are strong fliers with orange or pink-tinted wings tipped with black and white. The underside is predominantly covered in intricate patterns in brown and cream with a line of obvious spots. The

The American lady (*Vanessa virginiensis*) is a frequent visitor to gardens.

The admirals, exemplified by this red admiral (*Vanessa atalanta*), are relatively large butterflies with bold bands of white or orange said to resemble the stripes of military uniforms.

buckeyes, as you might expect, have large eyespots on their wings. The admirals are larger than the other true nymphs, with bold bands of white or orange that resemble the stripes of military uniforms.

**SATYRS, BROWNS, AND RINGLETS** Members of this group are medium size and often drab. They are usually various shades of brown and often have darker eyespots on their wings. They have a weak, bobbing flight and can be seen near woods, prairies, or alpine areas among grasses, which are their larval host plants. They also feed on bamboo and palms.

The satyrs, browns, and ringlets are not the most colorful butterflies but have a subtle beauty, as shown by this common wood-nymph (*Cercyonis pegala*).

Knowing butterflies and what they need

The queen (*Danaus gilippus*, top) is often mistaken for a monarch (*Danaus plexippus*, bottom). They are closely related and both feed on milkweed as caterpillars.

**MILKWEED BUTTERFLIES** The milkweed butterflies include our best-known and best-studied butterfly, the monarch (*Danaus plexippus*). This familiar species is a remarkably strong flier, migrating great distances every year to overwintering roosts in California and central Mexico. Monarchs have a very interesting life cycle (more on this later when we discuss migration), and gardeners can take advantage of the fact that they spread out across the United States every year to draw them to gardens. This group also includes numerous other, mainly tropical, equally large species. In the southern United States, the queen butterfly (*Danaus gilippus*) can easily be mistaken for a monarch. This butterfly also feeds on milkweed and is only slightly smaller, with similar orange and black markings. Looking at how the markings are arranged and oriented allows for positive identification.

## THE BUTTERFLY LIFE CYCLE

The life cycle of a butterfly is a miraculous phenomenon. Whereas the young of mammals and birds look like small versions of the adults, butterflies and moths go through a major transformation that restructures their entire bodies. Who would dream that a slow-moving, fat, crawling, leaf-chewing caterpillar could transform into a flying, nectar-drinking, colorful adult butterfly?

To achieve this transformation, a butterfly or moth passes through four distinct stages: egg, caterpillar (or larva), chrysalis (or pupa), and adult. An entomologist, or insect scientist, would describe this as complete metamorphosis because the form the butterfly takes is different at each stage. Compare this with simple or incomplete metamorphosis, in which the animal does not have a pupal stage and once hatched from an egg looks very much like it did at every prior life stage as it grows. Grasshoppers and shield bugs are examples of creatures that go through incomplete metamorphosis.

Some butterfly species (known as univoltine species) produce only one generation or brood per year, while many complete two or more generations per year. In each generation, an adult butterfly lays its eggs and the caterpillar grows and pupates and emerges as an adult. With two generations, this happens twice over the growing season. Generations from eggs laid during the spring or summer will complete their life

The butterfly and moth life cycle has four distinct stages—egg, caterpillar (or larva), chrysalis (or pupa), and adult—as illustrated by the Taylor's checkerspot (*Euphydryas editha taylori*) butterfly. A well-designed butterfly garden provides for all of these life stages.

cycle within three to eight weeks; those generations from eggs, larvae, or pupae that overwinter may take six to eight months. Regardless of the season in which breeding occurs, univoltine species take twelve months to complete their life cycle.

## EGGS

Butterfly eggs are singularly beautiful objects. Without a hand lens, you may see them as colored specks on a plant. Up close, they may be smooth and shiny or intricately structured with ridges or bumps, and may be spherical, flattened, or elongated. They may be white or yellow, green or red, and may have colored bands or

The Gulf fritillary (*Agraulis vanillae*) lays its eggs directly on tendrils of the passionflower vine.

Tucked underneath leaves or on plant stems, butterfly eggs can be hard to find, but you'll be rewarded with the sight of intricate jewels. Eggs of different species often differ in shape, size, and color.

spots. Some resemble tiny sea urchins, others currants and gooseberries. The eggs can vary quite a bit in size, shape, and color from family to family and even species to species.

Depending on the species, a female butterfly may lay a few dozen to many hundreds of eggs in her lifetime. She carefully selects particular plants, called host plants, on which to lay her eggs, singly or in clusters. She will most often deposit her eggs on the undersides of leaves, alighting on the leaf and curling her body to lay eggs from the tip of her abdomen. Eggs may also be laid on flower buds, stems, or, in the case of the Gulf fritillary (*Agraulis vanillae*), on the tendrils of their host plant (the passionflower vine).

How long the eggs remain unhatched varies with the species. Some butterflies, such as many blues and hairstreaks, overwinter as eggs. For these species, the eggs last many months. For butterflies that lay eggs in spring or summer, development begins immediately and the eggs usually hatch after a few days.

## CATERPILLARS (OR LARVAE)

The first thing newly hatched caterpillars do is eat, starting with their own egg shells—a good source of

Butterfly and moth caterpillars need to shed their skin to be able to grow. This Gulf fritillary (*Agraulis vanillae*) caterpillar has just molted; its freshly shed skin is behind it.

protein to jump-start their rapid growth—and then the plant on which the egg was laid. Caterpillars spend most of their time eating, and because they are particular about what they eat, it is critical for the adult female to lay her eggs on or very near an appropriate food source lest her offspring starve. Caterpillars can consume a tremendous amount of biomass relative to their size and ultimately grow to many times their original proportions.

Like most insects, butterflies have an exoskeleton, even as caterpillars. This exoskeleton is basically their bone structure, a hard shell on the outside of their bodies with corresponding organs and muscles underneath. Because the exoskeleton does not expand to accommodate growth, a caterpillar must shed it several times in a process known as molting. The caterpillar is the only life stage that molts. Once a butterfly emerges as an adult, it no longer grows. Depending on

All butterflies form a chrysalis in which they transform from a caterpillar into an adult. The chrysalises of many butterflies hang from silk buttons called cremasters, as with the monarch chrysalises on the left, or are held upright by silken girdles, like the black swallowtail chrysalis on the right.

the species, molting generally occurs four to six times. Each stage between molts is called an instar, and the caterpillar at each instar is larger than the previous one. In the final molt the caterpillar transforms into a pupa, or chrysalis, the mummylike quiescent stage between larva and adult.

Molting is regarded as one of the most vulnerable processes a caterpillar goes through. In the period immediately before and after shedding its old skin, the caterpillar is immobile and can easily fall prey to a predator.

As with eggs, the length of time a butterfly spends as a caterpillar depends largely on whether it passes the winter in this stage (as many skippers do). If the

caterpillar doesn't overwinter, it will spend a few days to a week in each instar between molts, with development typically completed within three to eight weeks.

## CHRYSALISES (OR PUPAE)

After a caterpillar has gone through four to six instars, it stops eating and searches for a safe place to pupate. During pupation, the caterpillar's entire physiology undergoes drastic changes as its body restructures itself to eventually emerge as a winged adult. *Chrysalis* is the term for both this stage in development and the encasing at this stage, during which the structure of the insect is being completely reorganized. The term is derived from *chrysós*, Greek for "gold," referring to the

This sequence of photos of a black swallowtail (*Papilio polyxenes*) shows how the chrysalis changes color just before the butterfly's emergence and then splits open so the butterfly can crawl out. Once free from its chrysalis, the butterfly pumps fluid from its body into its still-crumpled wings.

metallic-gold coloration of many chrysalises.

*Pupa* and *chrysalis* have the same meaning: the transformative stage between the larva and the adult. While *pupa* can refer to this naked stage in a butterfly or moth, *chrysalis* is used strictly for the butterfly pupa. A cocoon is the silk casing that a moth caterpillar spins around itself before it turns into a pupa.

The chrysalises of many butterflies hang from silk buttons called cremasters or are held upright by silken girdles. Some are disguised to blend into their surroundings, being generally green or brown and resembling leaves, stems, or wood. Others are covered in thornlike bumps. Some butterflies, such as swallowtails, overwinter as chrysalises. For butterflies completing development in a single season, the chrysalis stage lasts a couple of weeks.

Just before the butterfly's emergence, the chrysalis usually changes color. You may also begin to see the markings of the wings through the now-translucent casing. It breaks open across the back and the butterfly crawls out from it. Once free of the chrysalis, the butterfly pumps fluid from its swollen body to its still-crumpled wings. The freshly emerged butterfly clings to the plant or structure next to its chrysalis to

Knowing butterflies and what they need

It might appear counter to their beauty, but many butterflies feed at seemingly noxious sources such as mud puddles or animal scat. Here eight species of butterflies—eastern tailed-blue, northern pearly-eye, red admiral, silvery checkerspot, spicebush swallowtail, spring azure, cloudywing, and hoary edge—are feeding on one coyote scat.

complete the process of metamorphosis, letting its wings dry and harden before taking flight in search of food and a mate.

## ADULTS (OR IMAGOES)

The primary activities of adult butterflies are feeding, mating, and egg laying. Nearly all butterflies need to feed as adults. Nectar from flowers and sugar from tree sap, overripe fruit, or aphid honeydew provide most, but not all, of the nutrition that most butterfly and moth species need. To acquire additional nutrients, minerals, and salts, sometimes butterflies (males in particular) imbibe liquid from carcasses, animal waste, mud puddles, and moist soil. A few species of butterflies—such as tropical longwings, which can be found in the southern United States—eat pollen as well as nectar. Longwings collect pollen around their mouthparts and then combine it with their own saliva to break down the amino acids before ingesting it. This protein-rich meal enables them to live longer

A male butterfly like this fiery skipper (*Hylephila phyleus*) may "court" the female by flying around her and rapidly beating his wings.

air together. This courtship is sometimes confused with a male warding off another male from its territory because both involve two butterflies flying around each other. If the female accepts the male, they couple end to end, with the tips of their abdomens joined. They may remain coupled for an hour or more, sometimes even overnight.

During mating, the male passes a packet of sperm and nutrients called a spermatophore to the female. The sperm then fertilizes each egg as it passes down the female's egg-laying tube. After mating, female butterflies locate appropriate host plants by sight or scent and usually land on or near the plant to oviposit (lay eggs) singly or in clusters on or under the leaves. Some grass skippers do not land at all; they fly over their chosen host plant and drop the eggs one by one.

than most other butterflies and may even give them a reproductive advantage.

Male butterflies find females by sight or sometimes using chemicals called pheromones—natural perfume—at close range. The male may "court" the female by flying around her, and they may spiral up into the

## HOW BUTTERFLIES USE YOUR GARDEN

As humans, we need safe places to live, healthy food to eat, and protection from poisons. Butterflies are no different. To survive and complete their life cycle, but-

# Carnivorous butterflies

**WHILE THE VAST** majority of butterfly species feed on plant matter as larvae, there are a few exceptions. Caterpillars of the large blue (*Maculinea arion*), a European butterfly, start life eating thyme but finish their development in ant nests, eating the grubs. Caterpillars of the North American harvester butterfly (*Feniseca tarquinius*) take this one step further. They are strictly carnivorous, growing on a diet of woolly aphids and sometimes scale insects or treehoppers. Females lay eggs in or near woolly aphid

colonies so their young have immediate access to food. This protein-rich food source enables them to grow quickly, often reaching pupation in just two to three weeks. Some harvester caterpillars have been observed feeding on aphid carcasses under silken threads that may give them protection from ants that tend aphids. As adults, harvesters remain closely linked to their woolly hosts, sipping aphid-produced honeydew rather than floral nectar.

The best butterfly gardens provide both nectar and host plants and secure places for butterflies to pupate and overwinter.

terflies need food plants for their caterpillars (which ecologists refer to as host plants or larval host plants), nectar to fuel their activities, safe places to take shelter, and protection from pesticides. Your garden can provide all a butterfly needs in a single space. Providing plants for caterpillars to eat, food for adults, and a secure place to pupate or overwinter can all be accomplished even in a relatively small yard. Later in the book you will find a directory of some of the best plants for supporting butterflies in garden settings; here we describe butterflies' plant needs in general.

## HOST PLANTS

Many species of wildflowers, grasses, shrubs, and trees are butterfly hosts. Caterpillars of some species will eat only a single species of plant or several very closely related plants, while other species will eat a wide range of plants from multiple families. Often, butterflies and moths have specialized relationships with native larval host plants. For example, research by Douglas Tallamy and his colleagues at the University of Delaware revealed that in the eastern United States, native plants support four times as many native butterfly and

Most butterflies lay their eggs directly on a host plant. This female silver-banded hairstreak (*Chlorostrymon simaethis*) is placing the egg carefully from the tip of her abdomen.

moth species as do introduced plants. This relationship between plants and butterflies is the result of a long history of coevolution.

For the many butterflies that are host-plant specific, such as monarchs with their milkweed, the availability of these host plants is critical to their survival. These butterflies are limited to areas where their host plants thrive. For example, the federally endangered Fender's blue butterfly (*Icaricia icarioides fenderi*) feeds almost exclusively on Kincaid's lupine (*Lupinus sulphureus* subsp. *kincaidii*), which is itself threatened. Both species are found mainly in a narrow region of northwest Oregon, although the lupine enjoys a slightly larger range north into southern Washington and south into parts of central Oregon. As with all species that are highly selective with their food plants, the Fender's blue will not survive without its host plant. At the opposite end of the spectrum is the gray hairstreak

(*Strymon melinus*), a butterfly found from coast to coast in the United States. Its caterpillars feed on a huge variety of plants; more than eighty different plant species from at least two dozen plant families have been documented.

Most butterflies lay their eggs directly on host plants so that caterpillars after hatching do not have to travel far to begin feeding. When flying through a landscape—over gardens, across a meadow, around the edge of a woodlot—butterflies locate and identify host plants through a combination of sight and scent. From a distance, the females use both visual and chemical cues to guide them, picking up scent using their antennae. When a female butterfly lands on a potential larval host plant, she "tastes" it with chemoreceptors located at the tips of her legs to determine its suitability. (She can be choosy; a female seldom lays eggs on the first plant she visits.) A butterfly's ability to find specific

Knowing butterflies and what they need

Tropical milkweed (*Asclepias curassavica*) in the landscape can encourage monarchs to lay eggs outside of their regular breeding season, possibly disrupting their migratory cycle. Planting native species is the better option.

# Tropical milkweed: Bad for butterflies?

**MILKWEEDS** (*Asclepias* species) are the key host plants for the monarch butterfly (*Danaus plexippus*), and more than seventy milkweed species are native to the United States and Canada. Tropical milkweed (*Asclepias curassavica*) is a related species that has been introduced to the United States and is often available from nurseries. The native range of the species is not well documented but includes South America and Mexico. While tropical milkweed is a popular garden plant due to its showy flowers and its attractiveness to monarchs, some monarch scientists have expressed concerns about the species' potential impacts on monarch health, particularly when it is grown in the southern United States.

These concerns stem from tropical milkweed's potential to have foliage year-round when it grows in areas with mild winter temperatures and adequate moisture. In contrast, the majority of native U.S. and Canadian milkweeds are deciduous and do not have any foliage during late fall and winter. Tropical milkweed can flower and produce new leaves well into the fall months, and some scientists are concerned that the plants' presence in the landscape can encourage some monarchs to lay eggs outside of their regular breeding season, possibly disrupting their migratory cycle. Additionally, research from the University of Georgia indicates that the evergreen nature of tropical milkweed may result in an increase in the rate at which monarchs are infected by the parasite *Ophryocystis elektroscirrha*.

Given the concerns around the introduction of tropical milkweed to areas of the southern and southwestern United States and the fact that many native milkweed species are aesthetically pleasing and available from nurseries, planting only natives is the ecologically appropriate choice.

# Butterfly feeders and houses

**AS YOU PREPARE** your garden to attract butterflies, keep in mind that some species are also attracted to rotting fruit, mud puddles, and tree sap rather than or in addition to nectar. You can easily create a simple homemade butterfly feeder by filling a plate with overripe fruits and hanging it from a tree with a plant hanger. Suspending the plate helps keep it safe from ants and other animals. Use the ripest fruits you can find, particularly bananas, peaches, pears, and watermelon. You can add a little water or orange juice to keep things juicy and appealing to butterflies for several days. At night, it may attract moths as well. You can also attract puddling males by providing a moist area, such as a birdbath filled with sand and placed on the ground. Open areas of soil work well for this too; just moisten the ground with some water and see who comes to visit.

Commercial butterfly feeders are also available. These feeders, similar to hummingbird feeders, are composed of a bottom compartment that is filled with a sugar water solution and a top area where butterflies can perch and slip their proboscises into the liquid. However, in most areas these commercial feeders do not seem to work very well, and a home-made feeder with fruit will likely be much more enticing for the butterflies and more rewarding for you.

Some stores also sell overwintering boxes for butterflies, some of which are quite ornate and can be attractive additions to the home garden. But little to no evidence exists that these boxes work for butterflies, even though they may provide homes to spiders and other beneficial invertebrates. More effective ways to help adult butterflies survive the winter include leaving dead vegetation and wood-piles, and not disturbing rocks and logs in the garden landscape.

Fruit feeders, like this one consisting of a hanging dish, can attract butterflies and moths that may be looking for something besides flower nectar.

This common buckeye (*Junonia coenia*), like most butterflies and moths, has a long tubular mouthpart called a proboscis that it unfurls and inserts into flowers to sip nectar.

plants within the landscape is remarkable. Species of fritillary can locate violets that have senesced (dried) and are not visible. They lay eggs on or near these dried-up plants. The larvae hatch and immediately go into a period of suspended development (diapause), not feeding until the next spring when the plants are young and green.

Leaves are the primary source of caterpillar food, but these voracious animals also sometimes eat stems, flowers, and immature fruits. Although some butterfly larvae are generalists and feed on a variety of plant parts, others feed on just one or a few parts of their host plant.

## NECTAR PLANTS

Energy-rich nectar is the primary food source for most adult butterflies and moths, and is thus the major attractant to flowers. Butterflies can access either shallow or deep reservoirs of nectar, from a variety of flower shapes and sizes, with a long, tubular mouthpart called a proboscis. Nectar typically consists of fructose, glucose, and sucrose in varying proportions and also includes amino acids. Some nectar also includes secondary compounds such as lipids, antioxidants, and alkaloids. Both the volume of nectar produced and its sugar concentration vary widely across flowering plant species.

Many native plants such as Joe Pye weed provide plentiful nectar and will help attract butterflies to your garden.

Both native and nonnative plants attract butterflies with their nectar, but we believe native plants should always be your first choice. They often grow well because they are adapted to a particular area, and they are not likely to be invasive and crowd out other plants. Many native plants that provide high-quality nectar are also host plants for caterpillars. Such groups of plants include buckwheats (*Eriogonum* species), milkweeds (*Asclepias* species), thistles (*Cirsium* species), wild indigos (*Baptisia* species), and wild lilacs (*Ceanothus* species).

## SAFE PLACES TO TAKE SHELTER

Butterflies are particularly vulnerable to predators during pupation, and safe places of refuge are critical. They also need places to overwinter, whether as eggs, caterpillars, chrysalises, or adults. And they need places to spend the night or to escape storms, especially as adults. The type of shelter varies depending upon the habitat in which the butterfly lives and the particular species of butterfly. Many species that live in prairies and meadows crawl down into the bases of grasses. Woodland butterflies may seek shelter under tree leaves, and alpine butterflies may take advantage of rock crevices. Most butterflies spend the night on

Knowing butterflies and what they need

# Sheltering Habitat

Depending on the species and the location, butterflies may use a variety of features in the garden for shelter.

Chrysalises or cocoons are suspended from branches and twigs

Adults shelter in tree cavities

Adults and pupae sometimes overwinter in man-made structures

Multiple life stages take refuge in brush piles or woodpiles

Adults shelter behind loose bark

Eggs, larvae, and adults shelter in leaf litter

Adults shelter under rocks

Eggs, larvae, and adults shelter in the bases of bunchgrasses

Eggs and larvae overwinter near their wildflower host plants

Caterpillars seek out many different places to pupate in gardens, including structures such as buildings and fences.

their own, but some species, such as zebra longwings (*Heliconius charithonia*), can form large communal roosts in trees.

All butterflies must pupate. Caterpillars often pupate on or near their host plants. Chrysalises can be hidden away and hard to find—under duff or leaf litter, in a tree crevice, in tall grasses or bushes, or attached to a shrub, fence post, or building—but they have also been found in exposed places such as the strands of a barbed wire fence.

Many butterflies undergo a period of suspended development known as diapause, which enables them to survive stretches of inclement weather. During diapause, no growth or development occurs, and most feeding is also halted. Usually this happens during the cold winter months (overwintering or hibernation) or during the summer dry season (aestivation), when vegetation is no longer succulent or nectar-producing flowers are scarce. Strict summer aestivation is uncommon in North American butterflies and usually precedes an overwintering period (for example, a species goes into diapause during the summer dry period and remains in this state until the following spring).

Multiple periods of diapause can happen within one generation. This is the case for butterflies in many high-latitude or high-altitude locations that require two to three years to fully develop due to the short growing season and long winters. Living at elevations above 13,000 feet in the mountains of southern Colorado, the Uncompahgre fritillary (*Boloria acrocnema*) makes a good example. Eggs hatch in the summer and the caterpillars feed for a while before hibernating through the winter. In the second summer, they feed as caterpillars. Some may complete development, pupate, and emerge as adults; others will enter hibernation for a second time. When the third summer arrives, the overwintered caterpillars finish feeding, pupate, and finally emerge as adults.

Gardeners will not encounter this species but may still need to consider butterflies that go through a single period of prolonged diapause, up to a year or longer. The chrysalis of the anise swallowtail (*Papilio zelicaon*), a butterfly that is widespread in western North America, may remain in diapause through two winters and the seasons in between.

The majority of butterflies pass through diapause as a caterpillar or chrysalis, but some overwinter as eggs or adults. Species that go through diapause in the egg stage usually hatch in the spring and feed rapidly on tender new foliage. The adults that emerge then lay eggs that remain dormant from summer to the following spring. Groups of closely related butterflies often employ similar strategies when it comes to diapause, with some exceptions in each group. Many hairstreaks overwinter as eggs, while checkerspots often hibernate as partially grown larvae. White admirals and viceroys do the same but often wrap leaves around themselves and secure the leaves to twigs with silk to provide a secluded location. Duskywing skippers overwinter as fully developed caterpillars, pupating in the spring and emerging shortly thereafter.

Butterflies that overwinter as adults include anglewings, tortoiseshells, and the monarch butterfly. Anglewings and tortoiseshells tend to take shelter

Some butterflies like this mourning cloak (*Nymphalis antiopa*) overwinter as adults. They tuck themselves into tree cavities, logs, brush piles, old rock walls, and buildings for shelter against the winter.

in both natural and manmade areas, including tree cavities, under logs or rocks, behind loose bark, within evergreen foliage, or tucked into stone walls, buildings, and fences. Most butterflies overwinter in or near the same place they were born. The most famous exception to this is the monarch, which may travel hundreds or thousands of miles each fall to overwintering sites along the California coast or in fir forests in Mexico. Other migrant species include cloudless sulphur (*Phoebis sennae*), painted lady (*Vanessa cardui*), and buckeye (*Junonia coenia*). Some migrant species do not make a return journey; individuals in the northern parts of their range die with the arrival of winter. While some of these species are known to lay eggs throughout their journey, these northern regions are often repopulated by new migrants the following year.

No matter which family they belong to, butterflies need larval host plants, nectar plants, and sheltering habitat to support the various stages of their life cycle. We turn next to how to design a garden that will meet their needs.

Monarchs are not the only butterflies that migrate. Other migrants include the cloudless sulphur (*Phoebis sennae*).

Many people do not realize that monarch butterflies overwinter in California, like these clustering on a Monterey pine at Point Lobos Nature Reserve in Carmel.

# Monarch migration

**OF ALL THE ADAPTATIONS** butterflies have evolved for dealing with winter, migration may be the most extreme. The monarch butterflies that roost by the millions in Mexico and coastal California are our most recognizable winter migrants.

Spring- and summer-born monarchs tend to live only a few weeks as adults, but monarchs born in late summer and fall may live up to eight months in order to make an epic migration from summer breeding areas to overwintering sites. The vast majority of monarchs seek winter refuge in a few remnant high-altitude oyamel fir forests in Mexico's Sierra Madre. An individual monarch may have flown up to 2500 miles from southern Canada to these mountains of central Mexico. Other monarchs fly a much shorter journey of only several hundred miles from breeding sites in western U.S. states to the California coast, gathering at more than two hundred groves of eucalyptus, Monterey cypress, and Monterey pine from Mendocino to San Diego counties.

Migrating monarchs require nectar to sustain them on their journeys, and on their subsequent return north they also need native milkweeds on which to lay their eggs. Although the southward migration is made as a single journey, the return is completed over several generations. The butterflies that reach the northern breeding areas are not the ones that left the previous fall. Both nectar and host plant needs can be met with stepping-stone habitat patches, which in some cases may be the "weeds" growing in a field margin or alongside a road. Gardeners can help these migrating pollinators by nurturing a plot of milkweed and other nectar plants and encouraging friends and neighbors to do the same. If these beautiful animals and their incredible migration are to survive, we need to protect not only their overwintering sites but also their summer breeding locations and migration routes—something in which gardeners can play an active role.

Flowers provide beauty for people as well as sustenance for butterflies.

In addition to a diversity of nectar and host plant species, butterfly gardens should strive to offer a range of vegetative structure, including plants of varying heights and stem densities.

# Designing your butterfly garden

**T**O ATTRACT A VARIETY of butterflies and provide the habitats they need to complete their life cycle, an optimal garden design includes regionally appropriate larval host plants, multiple nectar plant species, and sheltered sites that provide safe places to pupate and overwinter. Additionally, good butterfly habitat tends to consist of open, sunny landscapes protected from strong winds. And of course, to sustain both butterflies and other wildlife, these habitats must be free of insecticides.

Due to the clear ecological benefits of using native plants, our garden design recommendations focus mainly on these. Nonnative host plants can be beneficial in certain situations, but you should exercise care never to use invasive plants even if they attract butterflies. Before delving into the key principles of butterfly garden design and offering sample plans for various types of butterfly gardens, we give a brief overview of the main plant groups and the roles they can play in a butterfly garden.

## NATIVE PLANTS AS ELEMENTS OF GARDEN DESIGN

As you learned in the previous chapter, the life cycles of butterflies and moths are intimately connected to the plants that share their home ranges, especially the native plants with which they have coevolved over thousands of years. Collectively, native wildflowers, grasses, vines, shrubs, and trees provide a wealth of essential resources to butterflies, moths, and other insects. Beyond the food and shelter that native plants provide for wildlife, they are typically well adapted to local soils and climates, often require less water than nonnatives, offer increased stormwater filtration, and do not require fertilizers.

Wildflowers (often called forbs by ecologists) should be the foundation of a butterfly garden.

## WILDFLOWERS

Wildflowers (often called forbs by ecologists) are the foundation of every butterfly garden. They can potentially serve as larval hosts, nectar sources, or both. Using native wildflowers to offer food throughout the growing season is a simple, sublime, and effective way of attracting most of the common butterfly species found in your area.

Wildflowers have an annual, biennial, or perennial life cycle. Forbs that offer high-quality nectar to butterflies often have colorful, showy flowers. For maximum visual effect you can choose complementary flower colors, and to provide a consistent source of nectar you can select a group of companion species that bloom sequentially through the seasons. In contrast to shrubs and trees, forbs may vary in vigor and abundance across years due to fluctuations in seasonal temperature and precipitation, which affect seedling survival.

The flowers of many native succulents are likely to attract interesting moth and butterfly visitors. Within their native range, yuccas are always worthy of landscape consideration, both for their association with yucca moths and various skippers and also for their unique architectural form.

# In praise of thistles

**NATIVE THISTLES** (of the genus *Cirsium*) are an undervalued and often misunderstood group of plants. Thistle flowers attract a wide diversity of butterflies and moths, including the monarch (*Danaus plexippus*), the painted lady (*Vanessa cardui*), the hummingbird clearwing moth (*Hemaris thysbe*), and various species of skippers, swallowtails, and sphinx moths. Some native thistles are larval hosts for butterflies including the painted lady, mylitta crescent (*Phyciodes mylitta*), California crescent (*Phyciodes orseis*), and swamp metalmark (*Calephelis muticum*). Thistles are also highly attractive to bumble bees and other native pollinators. Later in the season after the flowers have faded, thistle seeds are an important food source for birds such as the American goldfinch.

Yet, despite the enormous benefits they provide to wildlife, native thistles are often perceived or mis-identified as problem plants. This largely results from confusion with introduced thistle species such as Canada and bull thistle (*Cirsium arvense*, *C. vulgare*) that are classified as noxious weeds in many regions. Eradication efforts targeting nonnative thistles, as well as loss of prairie and grass-land habitats, have made native thistles increasingly rare in our landscapes.

The first step in combatting native thistle declines is to increase awareness about their value. Several counties and states have produced easy-to-use iden-tification guides to help people distinguish between native and nonnative thistles. Another important conservation action is to include thistles in butter-fly and pollinator gardens and other wildlife habitat plantings. Native thistles are not easy to find at plant nurseries, and their seed is rarely available for purchase, but you can help demonstrate demand for the plants by encouraging your local nurseries and seed companies to begin offering them.

Examples of attractive, regionally native thistles for gardens include pasture thistle (*Cirsium discolor*) and swamp thistle (*C. muticum*) for the northeastern United States and eastern Canada, Flodman's thistle (*C. flodmanii*) for the north-central United States and central Canada, yellow thistle (*C. horridulum*) and wavyleaf thistle (*C. undulatum*) for the southern United States, western thistle (*C. occidentale*) for the western United States, and edible thistle (*C. edule*) for the western United States and British Columbia.

Pasture thistle (*Cirsium discolor*), like many other native wildflowers, is a fantastic nectar plant visited by many species of butterflies, including this cloudless sulphur (*Phoebis sennae*).

# Keystone trees: Oaks, willows, and chokecherry

**WE HAVE SUGGESTED** that you select plants for your garden that attract multiple species of butterflies. The top trees that do this include chokecherry (*Prunus virginiana*), willow (*Salix* species), and oak (*Quercus* species).

Among these trees, oaks are well known for supporting many hairstreak and duskywing species, as well as many of the showier moth species, such as the imperial moth (*Eacles imperialis*), the polyphemus moth (*Antheraea polyphemus*), the blind-eye sphinx moth (*Paonias excaecata*), the rosy maple moth (*Dryocampa rubicunda*), and many others. Beyond providing for these more glamorous butterfly and moth species, oaks are also known for supporting countless small, less showy moths that feed other wildlife such as songbirds, tree frogs, and larger insects. Because of the incredible diversity of oak species, locally native species exist across the entire continental United States and most of southern Canada, and these include shrub and scrub oak species that remain quite small in size. Species such as the California scrub oak (*Quercus berberidifolia*), the Gambel oak (*Quercus gambelii*) found from the desert Southwest into the Great Plains, the bear oak (*Quercus ilicifolia*) of southeastern Canada and the northeastern United States, and the turkey oak (*Quercus laevis*) of the Southeast are all attractive small trees that are widely underused in typical garden landscapes.

As a lucky coincidence, chokecherry, which also supports many showy and widespread species—such as tiger swallowtails (*Papilio glaucus*), spring azures (*Celastrina ladon*), coral hairstreaks (*Satyrium titus*),

Chokecherry (*Prunus virginiana*) is among the top trees for supporting numerous butterfly species.

and Weidemeyer's admiral (*Limenitis weidemeyerii*)—is distributed throughout much of the United States and southern Canada. Within that range, chokecherry is also remarkably adaptable to various soil types and planting conditions.

Similarly, various willows—host plants for viceroys (*Limenitis archippus*), mourning cloaks (*Nymphalis antiopa*), red-spotted purples (*Limenitis arthemis*), tiger swallowtails (*Papilio glaucus*), and many others—are found in every part of the United States and Canada, with locally appropriate native species available to any butterfly gardener with a slightly damp area, such as a rain garden.

## GRASSES AND SEDGES

Native grasses and grasslike plants such as sedges offer an important dimension to the butterfly garden. They are larval hosts for many butterflies and moths, especially many skippers. The clumping bases of native

Some butterflies, including many skippers, use grasses as their larval host plants. Native grasses provide other benefits in the garden, too, including serving as pupation and overwintering sites.

perennial bunchgrasses provide shelter and pupation and overwintering sites for various butterfly life stages as well as shelter and nesting areas for beneficial insects such as bumble bees and beetles. Owing to their extensive, fibrous root systems, many native bunchgrasses have low water needs once established, and they can occupy spaces in the root zone that would otherwise be invaded by weeds (especially by weedy or invasive grasses). Additionally, they bring a unique aesthetic to the garden.

Sedges, which typically have a growth habit similar to bunchgrasses, are usually found in natural wetlands or along rivers. In the home garden and urban landscape, sedges are often an excellent sub-stitute for bunchgrasses in rain gardens, bioswales, and other areas that experience temporary flooding and water runoff. As a garden design element, rows of grasses or sedges can be used to form borders, delineate distinct areas, and provide physical support for tall, lanky wildflowers.

## VINES

While relatively few vines support the larval food or nectar requirements of butterflies, those that do can be exceptionally interesting additions to the butterfly garden. The pipevines (*Aristolochia* species) are the best example of this, offering an unusual plant feature for the garden and attracting some of the largest and showiest butterflies, the pipevine swallowtails (*Battus philenor*). Other vining species that are larval hosts include passionflower (*Passiflora* species) and coral honeysuckle (*Lonicera sempervirens*). Within their

Coral honeysuckle (*Lonicera sempervirens*) and other vines can give the butterfly garden a vertical dimension while at the same time attracting some of the showiest butterflies.

Ten times more butterfly and moth species in their larval stage feed upon shrubs and trees than feed upon wildflowers or grasses. Oaks (*Quercus* species) in particular support huge numbers of butterflies and moths.

native ranges, these can be planted along fences or supported by an arbor or trellis. Passionflower and coral honeysuckle, along with some native *Clematis* species, are also attractive nectar sources.

It should be noted that some passionflower and clematis species have the potential to grow aggressively and crowd out other plants. Special caution is warranted when selecting vines for the butterfly garden to ensure that they provide the intended benefits.

For example, while some native clematis species are excellent nectar plants, many cultivated varieties seem to be much less attractive nectar sources than their wild counterparts. Similarly, unlike native pipevine species, the ornamental species *Aristolochia gigantean* introduced from Brazil cannot be eaten by pipevine swallowtail caterpillars.

Designing your butterfly garden

Butterfly bush (*Buddleja davidii*) is attractive to butterflies but can escape the garden and become invasive in some regions.

# Beware of butterfly bush

**BUTTERFLY BUSH** (*Buddleja davidii*), also known as summer lilac or orange-eyed butterfly bush, is a shrub native to Asia that has been introduced to multiple regions of the world for its ornamental value. Butterfly bush is notable for its attractiveness to butterflies and has been a popular garden and landscape plant for many years because it is easy to grow, blooms profusely, and grows rapidly. However, butterfly bush has escaped from U.S. gardens through seed dispersal and now grows wild in several states.

Butterfly bush is listed as a noxious weed in Oregon and Washington, where it colonizes disturbed areas such as roadsides and vacant lots and has invaded floodplains, riparian areas, and recently burned forested areas. Oregon State University has documented that once butterfly bush gets a foothold, it can spread aggressively and crowd out native vegetation. The potential for butterfly bush to behave invasively in other regions is unknown, but lessons learned in the Pacific Northwest suggest that caution with this plant is warranted.

If you already have butterfly bush on your property, cutting off the spent blooms at the end of the season will prevent seed dispersal. Some butterfly bush cultivars have been developed to be sterile or of low fertility, but it is hard to know whether the majority of buddleia plants available from nurseries meet that criterion. Please do your part to limit the spread of this species and instead include native, noninvasive plants in your garden and landscape design. Other summer-blooming shrubs to consider planting, within their native ranges, are buttonbush (*Cephalanthus occidentalis*), false indigo bush (*Amorpha fruticosa*), and New Jersey tea (*Ceanothus americanus*).

Nonnative plants such as lavender, shown here paired with coreopsis, can be attractive to butterflies and fit well with native plants. When planting a nonnative, you should confirm that it is both adapted to your location and not likely to become a weed.

## SHRUBS AND TREES

Trees represent some of the most important caterpillar host plants, with a few groups such as oaks, willows, and wild cherries supporting dozens or even hundreds of butterfly and moth species. Research conducted by Douglas Tallamy at the University of Delaware has demonstrated that, at least in the eastern United States, ten times more butterfly and moth species in their larval stage feed upon shrubs and trees than feed upon forbs or grasses. While we do not know whether this holds true in other parts of the country, we do know that woody plants are of significant value in the butterfly garden. Moreover, a number of native shrubs and trees are also notable nectar plants, and a few—such as buttonbush (*Cephalanthus occidentalis*), chokecherry (*Prunus virginiana*), and wild lilac (*Ceanothus* species)— can fill the roles of both larval hosts and nectar sources.

Beyond providing food for butterflies and moths, trees and shrubs in the garden can offer landscaping benefits that grasses and wildflowers cannot, such as screening and summer shade, although they need to be placed carefully to prevent direct shading of wildflowers. They can attract songbirds with fruit, serve as windbreaks, offer aesthetic value during winter, and provide shelter or roosting sites for butterflies in the evenings or during bad weather.

## NONNATIVE PLANTS IN THE BUTTERFLY GARDEN

Many established home gardens include plants that were chosen for their ornamental value or ease of establishment and that may not be native to the region or even the country. Nonnative plants can certainly provide resources for butterflies. For example, varieties of coneflower, coreopsis, lavender, and salvia are beautiful, butterfly-attractive features of gardens everywhere. Many butterfly species readily draw nectar from nonnatives such as cosmos, zinnia, and Mexican sunflower. And common garden herbs, in addition to their culinary appeal, can support butterflies. For example, chives, thyme, mint, and rosemary offer nectar; and dill, fennel, and parsley are larval hosts for black swallowtails.

When you select nonnative nectar plants for butterflies, choose heirloom varieties rather than hybrids and cultivars if you can. Some ornamental varieties such as double-flowered cultivars have been bred to have very showy flowers but as a consequence may have reduced, lower-quality, or inaccessible nectar. Please make sure the plants you choose for your garden are not classified as noxious or invasive in your region.

# BEST BUTTERFLY GARDEN PLANTS BY REGION

**THE AMAZING DIVERSITY** of butterfly species is almost matched by the diversity of their host and nectar plant requirements. Given this diversity, selecting species for your garden can seem like a daunting process. In general, a good bet is to choose native plants that attract multiple species of butterflies to maximize your garden's chances of success. This table lists such plants by region to help you make appropriate selections. More detailed descriptions of each species are in the next chapter.

| PACIFIC NORTHWEST AND BRITISH COLUMBIA | | | |
|---|---|---|---|
| COMMON NAME | SCIENTIFIC NAME | BLOOM TIME | FLOWER COLOR |
| **TALLER WILDFLOWERS (4 FEET PLUS)** | | | |
| fireweed | *Chamerion angustifolium* | summer | pink |
| edible thistle | *Cirsium edule* | summer | pink |
| **SHORTER WILDFLOWERS (4 FEET OR SHORTER)** | | | |
| wild strawberry | *Fragaria vesca* | spring | white |
| globe gilia | *Gilia capitata* | spring | blue |
| broadleaf lupine | *Lupinus latifolius* | spring | purple |
| seablush | *Plectritis congesta* | spring | pink |
| Oregon sunshine | *Eriophyllum lanatum* | spring and summer | yellow |
| Oregon checkermallow | *Sidalcea oregana* | spring and summer | pink |
| western yarrow | *Achillea millefolium* | summer | white |
| pearly everlasting | *Anaphalis margaritacea* | summer | white |
| showy milkweed | *Asclepias speciosa* | summer | pink and white |
| sulphur buckwheat | *Eriogonum umbellatum* | summer | yellow |
| blanketflower | *Gaillardia aristata* | summer | red and yellow |
| Puget Sound gumweed | *Grindelia integrifolia* | summer | yellow |
| slender cinquefoil | *Potentilla gracilis* | summer | yellow |
| Douglas aster | *Symphyotrichum subspicatum* | fall | purple |

| PACIFIC NORTHWEST AND BRITISH COLUMBIA (continued) | | | |
|---|---|---|---|
| **COMMON NAME** | **SCIENTIFIC NAME** | **BLOOM TIME** | **FLOWER COLOR** |
| **GRASSES** | | | |
| Idaho fescue | *Festuca idahoensis* | spring and summer | n/a |
| Roemer's fescue | *Festuca roemeri* | spring and summer | n/a |
| tufted hairgrass | *Deschampsia cespitosa* | summer | n/a |
| **SHRUBS AND TREES** | | | |
| Saskatoon serviceberry | *Amelanchier alnifolia* | spring | white |
| black hawthorn | *Crataegus douglasii* | spring | white |
| Oregon cherry | *Prunus emarginata* | spring | white |
| Scouler's willow | *Salix scouleriana* | spring | yellow |
| oceanspray | *Holodiscus discolor* | summer | white |
| black elderberry | *Sambucus nigra* | summer | white |
| rose spirea | *Spiraea douglasii* | summer | pink |

| COMMON NAME | SCIENTIFIC NAME | BLOOM TIME | FLOWER COLOR |
|---|---|---|---|
| **DESERT SOUTHWEST** | | | |
| **TALLER WILDFLOWERS (4 FEET PLUS)** | | | |
| Palmer's penstemon | *Penstemon palmeri* | spring and summer | pink |
| prince's plume | *Stanleya pinnata* | spring and summer | yellow |
| scarlet gilia | *Ipomopsis aggregata* | summer | red |
| Rocky Mountain bee plant | *Peritoma serrulata* | summer | purple |
| **SHORTER WILDFLOWERS (4 FEET OR SHORTER)** | | | |
| southwestern mock vervain | *Glandularia gooddingii* | spring | pink |
| desert mallow | *Sphaeralcea ambigua* | spring | orange |
| spider or antelope horn milkweed | *Asclepias asperula* | spring and summer | purple and green |
| Indian blanket | *Gaillardia pulchella* | spring and summer | red and yellow |
| white-tufted evening primrose | *Oenothera caespitosa* | spring and summer | white |
| Spanish bayonet | *Yucca baccata* | spring and summer | white |
| prairie zinnia | *Zinnia grandiflora* | late spring to early fall | yellow |
| white prairie clover | *Dalea candida* | summer | white |
| golden crownbeard | *Verbesina encelioides* | summer | yellow |
| **GRASSES** | | | |
| blue grama | *Bouteloua gracilis* | summer | n/a |
| vine mesquite | *Panicum obtusum* | summer | n/a |
| **VINES** | | | |
| desert pipevine | *Aristolochia watsonii* | spring and summer | green and red |
| **SHRUBS AND TREES** | | | |
| chokecherry | *Prunus virginiana* | spring | white |
| purple sage | *Salvia dorrii* | spring and summer | blue |
| false indigo bush | *Amorpha fruticosa* | summer | purple |
| sulphur buckwheat | *Eriogonum umbellatum* | summer | yellow |
| yellow rabbitbrush | *Chrysothamnus viscidiflorus* | late summer and fall | yellow |

## CALIFORNIA

| COMMON NAME | SCIENTIFIC NAME | BLOOM TIME | FLOWER COLOR |
|---|---|---|---|
| **TALLER WILDFLOWERS (4 FEET PLUS)** | | | |
| showy milkweed | *Asclepias speciosa* | summer | pink and white |
| cobweb thistle | *Cirsium occidentale* | summer | red |
| Pacific aster | *Symphyotrichum chilense* | fall | purple |
| **SHORTER WILDFLOWERS (4 FEET OR SHORTER)** | | | |
| meadow checkermallow | *Sidalcea malviflora* | spring | pink |
| golden yarrow | *Eriophyllum confertiflorum* | spring and summer | yellow |
| deerweed | *Lotus scoparius* | spring and summer | yellow |
| foothill penstemon | *Penstemon heterophyllus* | spring and summer | blue |
| summer lupine | *Lupinus formosus* | summer | purple |
| coyote mint | *Monardella villosa* | summer | purple |
| hummingbird trumpet | *Epilobium canum* | late summer | red |
| California goldenrod | *Solidago californica* | fall | yellow |
| **GRASSES** | | | |
| Idaho fescue | *Festuca idahoensis* | spring and summer | n/a |
| blue wild rye | *Elymus glaucus* | summer | n/a |
| purple needlegrass | *Nassella pulchra* | summer | n/a |
| **VINES** | | | |
| California pipevine | *Aristolochia californica* | winter and spring | green and red |
| **SHRUBS AND TREES** | | | |
| hollyleaf cherry | *Prunus ilicifolia* | spring | white |
| oak | *Quercus* species | spring | brown |
| narrowleaf willow | *Salix exigua* | spring | yellow |
| purple sage | *Salvia dorrii* | spring and summer | blue |
| buckbrush | *Ceanothus cuneatus* | summer | white |
| California buckwheat | *Eriogonum fasciculatum* | summer | white and pink |

## MIDWEST AND GREAT PLAINS

| COMMON NAME | SCIENTIFIC NAME | BLOOM TIME | FLOWER COLOR |
|---|---|---|---|
| **TALLER WILDFLOWERS (4 FEET PLUS)** | | | |
| pasture thistle | *Cirsium discolor* | summer | purple |
| swamp thistle | *Cirsium muticum* | summer | pink |
| sweet Joe Pye weed | *Eupatoriadelphus purpureus* | summer | pink |
| Rocky Mountain blazing star | *Liatris ligulistylis* | summer | purple |
| evening primrose | *Oenothera biennis* | summer | yellow |
| Maryland senna | *Senna marilandica* | summer | yellow |
| cup plant | *Silphium perfoliatum* | summer | yellow |
| blue vervain | *Verbena hastata* | summer | purple |
| **SHORTER WILDFLOWERS (4 FEET OR SHORTER)** | | | |
| wild lupine | *Lupinus perennis* | spring | purple |
| foxglove beardtongue | *Penstemon digitalis* | spring | white |
| golden Alexanders | *Zizia aurea* | spring | yellow |
| butterfly milkweed | *Asclepias tuberosa* | summer | orange |
| small spike false nettle | *Boehmeria cylindrica* | summer | green |
| purple prairie clover | *Dalea purpurea* | summer | purple |
| pale purple coneflower | *Echinacea pallida* | summer | purple |
| round-headed bush clover | *Lespedeza capitata* | summer | white |
| prairie blazing star | *Liatris pycnostachya* | summer | purple |
| wild bergamot | *Monarda fistulosa* | summer | purple |
| prairie phlox | *Phlox pilosa* | summer | pink |
| Virginia mountain mint | *Pycnanthemum virginianum* | summer | white and purple |

| COMMON NAME | SCIENTIFIC NAME | BLOOM TIME | FLOWER COLOR |
|---|---|---|---|
| **GRASSES** | | | |
| big bluestem | *Andropogon gerardii* | summer | n/a |
| prairie dropseed | *Sporobolus heterolepis* | summer | n/a |
| little bluestem | *Schizachyrium scoparium* | summer and fall | n/a |
| Indian grass | *Sorghastrum nutans* | summer and fall | n/a |
| **SHRUBS AND TREES** | | | |
| spicebush | *Lindera benzoin* | spring | yellow |
| chokecherry | *Prunus virginiana* | spring | white |
| oak | *Quercus* species | spring | brown |
| pussy willow | *Salix discolor* | spring | yellow |
| false indigo bush | *Amorpha fruticosa* | summer | purple |
| New Jersey tea | *Ceanothus americanus* | summer | white |

| NORTHEAST AND MID-ATLANTIC | | | |
|---|---|---|---|
| **COMMON NAME** | **SCIENTIFIC NAME** | **BLOOM TIME** | **FLOWER COLOR** |
| **TALLER WILDFLOWERS (4 FEET PLUS)** | | | |
| swamp thistle | *Cirsium muticum* | summer | pink |
| spotted Joe Pye weed | *Eupatoriadelphus maculatus* | summer | pink |
| evening primrose | *Oenothera biennis* | summer | yellow |
| blue vervain | *Verbena hastata* | summer | purple |
| New England aster | *Symphyotrichum novae-angliae* | fall | purple |
| **SHORTER WILDFLOWERS (4 FEET OR SHORTER)** | | | |
| common blue violet | *Viola sororia* | spring | purple |
| golden Alexanders | *Zizia aurea* | spring | yellow |
| pearly everlasting | *Anaphalis margaritacea* | summer | white |
| butterfly milkweed | *Asclepias tuberosa* | summer | orange |
| small spike false nettle | *Boehmeria cylindrica* | summer | green |
| round-headed bush clover | *Lespedeza capitata* | summer | white |
| scarlet beebalm | *Monarda didyma* | summer | red |
| Virginia mountain mint | *Pycnanthemum virginianum* | summer | white and purple |
| black-eyed Susan | *Rudbeckia hirta* | summer | yellow |
| wrinkleleaf goldenrod | *Solidago rugosa* | fall | yellow |

| NORTHEAST AND MID-ATLANTIC (continued) | | | |
|---|---|---|---|
| COMMON NAME | SCIENTIFIC NAME | BLOOM TIME | FLOWER COLOR |
| **GRASSES AND SEDGES** | | | |
| tussock sedge | *Carex stricta* | spring | n/a |
| big bluestem | *Andropogon gerardii* | summer | n/a |
| bottlebrush grass | *Elymus hystrix* | summer | n/a |
| switchgrass | *Panicum virgatum* | summer | n/a |
| Indian grass | *Sorghastrum nutans* | summer and fall | n/a |
| purpletop | *Tridens flavus* | summer and fall | n/a |
| **SHRUBS AND TREES** | | | |
| black huckleberry | *Gaylussacia baccata* | spring | white or pinkish red |
| spicebush | *Lindera benzoin* | spring | yellow |
| chokecherry | *Prunus virginiana* | spring | white |
| oak | *Quercus* species | spring | brown |
| pussy willow | *Salix discolor* | spring | yellow |
| New Jersey tea | *Ceanothus americanus* | summer | white |

| SOUTHEAST | | | |
|---|---|---|---|
| **COMMON NAME** | **SCIENTIFIC NAME** | **BLOOM TIME** | **FLOWER COLOR** |
| **TALLER WILDFLOWERS (4 FEET PLUS)** | | | |
| hollow Joe Pye weed | *Eupatoriadelphus fistulosus* | summer | pink |
| Maryland senna | *Senna marilandica* | summer | yellow |
| starry rosinweed | *Silphium asteriscus* | summer | yellow |
| **SHORTER WILDFLOWERS (4 FEET OR SHORTER)** | | | |
| lanceleaf coreopsis | *Coreopsis lanceolata* | spring | yellow |
| butterfly milkweed | *Asclepias tuberosa* | summer | orange |
| small spike false nettle | *Boehmeria cylindrica* | summer | green |
| yellow thistle | *Cirsium horridulum* | summer | yellow and purple |
| rattlesnake master | *Eryngium yuccifolium* | summer | white |
| hairy bush clover | *Lespedeza hirta* | summer | white |
| dense blazing star | *Liatris spicata* | summer | purple |
| Virginia mountain mint | *Pycnanthemum virginianum* | summer | white and purple |
| black-eyed Susan | *Rudbeckia hirta* | summer | yellow |
| wingstem | *Verbesina alternifolia* | summer | yellow |
| giant ironweed | *Vernonia gigantea* | summer | purple |
| blue mistflower | *Conoclinium coelestinum* | summer and fall | purple |
| wrinkleleaf goldenrod | *Solidago rugosa* | fall | yellow |

| SOUTHEAST (continued) | | | |
|---|---|---|---|
| COMMON NAME | SCIENTIFIC NAME | BLOOM TIME | FLOWER COLOR |
| **GRASSES** | | | |
| bottlebrush grass | *Elymus hystrix* | summer | n/a |
| big bluestem | *Andropogon gerardii* | summer and fall | n/a |
| little bluestem | *Schizachyrium scoparium* | summer and fall | n/a |
| purpletop | *Tridens flavus* | summer and fall | n/a |
| **VINES** | | | |
| Virginia snakeroot | *Aristolochia serpentaria* | spring and summer | green and red |
| butterfly pea | *Clitoria mariana* | summer | purple |
| maypops | *Passiflora incarnata* | summer | purple |
| **SHRUBS AND TREES** | | | |
| spicebush | *Lindera benzoin* | spring | yellow |
| Chickasaw plum | *Prunus angustifolia* | spring | white |
| oak | *Quercus* species | spring | brown |
| coastal plain willow | *Salix caroliniana* | spring | green |
| false indigo bush | *Amorpha fruticosa* | summer | purple |
| buttonbush | *Cephalanthus occidentalis* | summer | white |
| rose mallow | *Hibiscus moscheutos* | summer | white and pink |

Grouping plants of the same species such as this wild blue indigo (*Baptisia australis*) into clusters to create large blocks of color will ultimately make them more visible to passing insects and potentially more attractive to butterflies.

## PRINCIPLES OF BUTTERFLY GARDEN DESIGN

How do you decide how to arrange the palette of local trees, grasses, and wildflowers in your garden? Your priority should be to create a garden that is mostly open, sunny, and filled with wildflowers. While many trees are important for butterflies, open, meadowlike habitat consistently attracts the greatest variety and number of butterflies. Besides that general guideline, a few basic principles can help you create the best possible butterfly habitat.

## CREATE LARGE BLOCKS OF VARIOUS COLORS

Butterflies' preferences for nectar plants are based on several features, including flower color, nectar quality and abundance, flower shape, and sometimes flower fragrance. Butterflies will potentially visit flowers of any color, but they generally prefer white, yellow, pink, orange, red, and purple flowers. Some evidence

indicates that butterflies use color as a visual cue when hunting for plants to land on because they have learned which color flowers tend to produce their favorite types of nectar.

Butterflies have compound eyes, meaning that their eyes are composed of thousands of image-forming lenses (called ommatidia). This arrangement allows the butterfly eye to see many individual images in all directions at the same time. These individual images form an entire picture. Butterflies see a wide range of colors but only see the rough shapes of things—not the details that are distinguished by the human eye.

To attract butterflies as they move through the landscape and allow them to forage more efficiently, create massed plantings of individual species (such as groupings of five or more of the same plants in proximity) to present large splashes of color. Incorporate a wide variety of colors into your garden design to increase your chances of attracting a broad diversity of butterflies and other flower visitors.

## AIM FOR CONTINUOUS BLOOM

Although you generally see the most butterflies in the summer, some species are spring residents and some may visit only in the fall. If you are hoping to provide for the greatest number of species of butterflies in your garden, be sure to plant nectar plants that bloom all across the growing season (which includes winter in some warm climates). It is usually not difficult to find plants that bloom in the summer, but in some regions, choices of spring- and fall-blooming plants may be fewer. Butterfly-attractive shrubs and trees that bloom in the spring include wild lilac (*Ceanothus* species), cherry (*Prunus* species), hawthorn (*Crataegus* species), and serviceberry (*Amelanchier* species). Important late-blooming nectar plants include asters (*Symphyotrichum* species), goldenrods (*Solidago* species), and sunflowers (*Helianthus* species).

Goldenrods (*Solidago* species) are a reliable late-season source of nectar in many areas. A few goldenrods in eastern and midwestern states bloom at the exact time monarch butterflies are migrating south to Mexico, helping to fuel the journey of those butterflies.

## MAKE THE MOST OF SUNNY SPOTS IN YOUR GARDEN

Butterflies need warm temperatures and sunshine in order to fly and forage. Coincidentally, many of the plants that butterflies visit for nectar grow best in areas that receive full sun throughout most of the day. These combined factors mean that butterflies typically forage in open, sunlit habitats. With this in mind, it is ideal to situate your butterfly garden in an area that receives six to eight hours of direct sunlight each day. If you have the option, establishing your garden on a southern exposure will maximize the amount of sun received.

On sunny days when air temperatures are not warm enough for butterflies to become fully active, they commonly bask in the sun to raise their body temperature. Basking sites include leaves and branches, exposed soil, rocks, bricks, gravel paths, and pavement. To increase the availability of basking sites, consider adding large, flat rocks to areas of the garden that receive direct sun.

While most butterflies and their food plants prefer sun, several butterfly plants tolerate full or partial

Planting your butterfly garden in an area that receives plenty of direct sunlight will ensure that butterflies find the warmth they need.

Designing your butterfly garden

Butterflies tend to be creatures of open sunny meadows, but even shaded gardens can attract them if flowers are present.

shade, so take heart if your garden space is restricted to shade. Larval host plants that tolerate at least partial shade include broadleaf lupine (*Lupinus latifolius*) and oceanspray (*Holodiscus discolor*) for the western United States and western Canada; and common blue violet (*Viola sororia*), golden Alexanders (*Zizia aurea*), Joe Pye weed (*Eupatoriadelphus* species), and small spike false nettle (*Boehmeria cylindrica*) for the eastern United States and eastern Canada. Additionally, pipe-vines (*Aristolochia* species), native to several regions of the country, prefer to grow in partial shade.

## PROVIDE BRUSH PILES AND UNKEMPT AREAS FOR SHELTER

Along with needing food plants and basking areas, butterflies and moths need secure dry places to pupate, spend the winter, and seek cover during bad weather. While wooden "butterfly boxes" are marketed for this purpose, they unfortunately are rarely occupied by most species (although spiders, earwigs, and other common garden invertebrates may find them perfectly cozy). Instead, the types of shelter that are most used by butterflies and moths include brush piles, the rough shedding bark of some trees, thick grass tussocks, leaf litter, and other natural features. While some of these items may seem untidy, it is exactly that quality that tends to support the greatest garden biodiversity.

If neatness is a concern, we recommend surrounding your garden with clean, distinct borders so that the chaos at least looks contained. Within the garden itself, features such as brush piles or basking stones can be arranged in distinct piles and delineated with some type of edging or marked with attractive signage explaining what the feature provides to wildlife. For example, the Xerces Society offers Pollinator Habitat signs that gardeners across the United States and Canada are using to help delineate and call attention to their bee and butterfly gardens. Similarly, the National Wildlife Federation offers Certified Wildlife Habitat signs to gardeners who create diverse native-plant landscapes.

## SAMPLE DESIGNS FOR BUTTERFLY GARDENS

The sample landscape plans that follow illustrate how you might put the butterfly garden design principles into practice using the palette of regionally appropriate native plants you select. These plans represent only a small fraction of the variations possible when creating a butterfly garden. In general, the plans include relatively open and unshaded spaces, mass wildflower plantings, and a diversity of flower species to provide food for butterflies throughout the growing season. Some include basking structures such as large rocks. Use one of these plans as a model or mix and match the ideas you see here as you create a plan for a butterfly garden that fits your own landscape.

## A BUTTERFLY RAIN GARDEN

A rain garden is a vegetated depression that collects rainfall and storm water runoff and allows it to percolate back into the ground. Rain gardens typically include diverse native shrub, wildflower, and grass plantings that do not mind getting their feet wet and function as excellent butterfly habitat. Such gardens can make use of artificial water-holding structures, such as large rain barrels, planted with butterfly-attracting plants, or they can consist of more natural-appearing basins vegetated with species that have extensive root systems (to increase water infiltration) and species with high water demands (to absorb excess soil moisture).

Rain gardens are usually fed by rooftop downspouts, but it is increasingly common to see them fed by surface water runoff from paved areas such as parking lots. (These larger rain gardens that are connected to pavement systems are usually referred to as bioswales.) In most cases, some type of slow, gradual outflow system exists, such as a gradual outflow into a lawn area, in the rare chance that a rain garden might overflow its edges.

A rain garden can be any size that works for the space, but you should ensure that the depression is large enough to catch the rain without overflowing into areas near your home. The Three Rivers Rain Garden Alliance has a web page that can help you calculate the optimal size of a rain garden for your yard (raingardenalliance.org/right/calculator). The recommended size is based on the nonporous surface area feeding into the garden, the soil type, and the slope.

# Butterfly Rain Garden and Upland Habitat

Rain gardens can make use of artificial water-holding structures or more natural-appearing basins and can complement upland butterfly habitat.

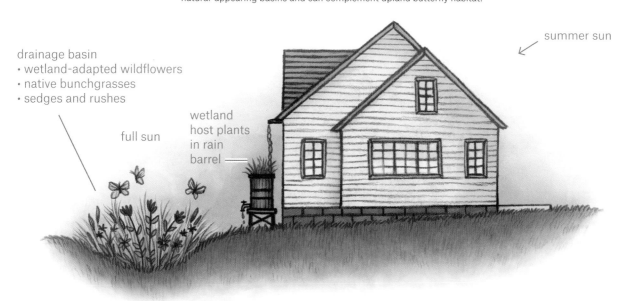

drainage basin
• wetland-adapted wildflowers
• native bunchgrasses
• sedges and rushes

full sun

wetland host plants in rain barrel

summer sun

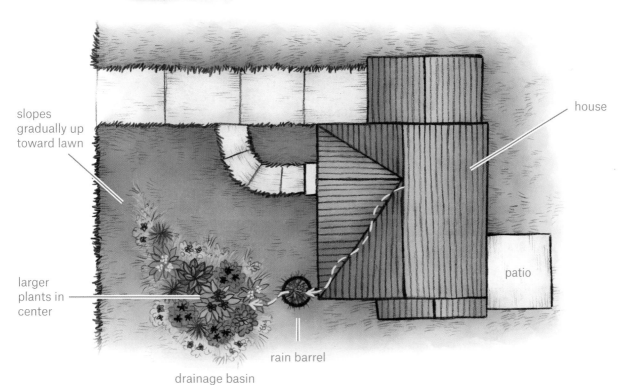

slopes gradually up toward lawn

larger plants in center

house

patio

rain barrel

drainage basin

# Butterfly Xeriscape Garden

For arid conditions, use drought-tolerant locally adapted species, consider incorporating simple water-conserving strategies, and plan for the risk of local wildfires.

To fine-tune a rain garden for butterflies, include as much plant diversity as possible, especially wild-flower diversity. A rain garden's sloping edges offer the opportunity to include damp meadow species on the upper fringes and true wetland plants in the bottom of the basin—a range of habitat types usually unavailable in urban landscapes. This type of landscape can complement other parts of the yard that you might be maintaining as upland habitat consisting of larger trees and shrubs. In combination, such different features can provide multiple benefits for a property such as reduced storm water runoff and summer shade to cool the house and yard and reduce air conditioning bills, while at the same time attracting butterflies.

In some areas, local watershed agencies, conservation districts, and other government agencies offer

Designing your butterfly garden

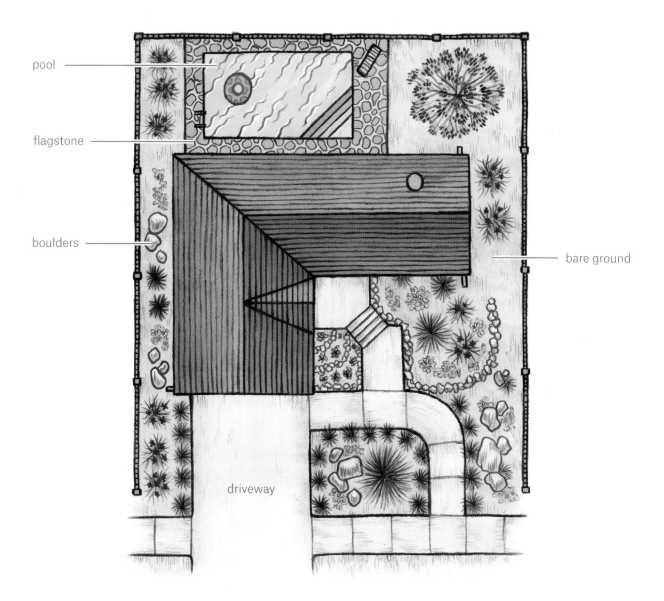

pool

flagstone

boulders

bare ground

driveway

financial and technical assistance for the creation of rain gardens due to their multiple benefits. It is worth checking around to find out if special incentives are available in your locale. A few areas even offer local tax reductions or discounts on your water bill for landscapes that reduce areas of pavement and increase storm water infiltration on your property.

## A XERISCAPE GARDEN FOR BUTTERFLIES

Arid regions are home to some of the greatest butterfly diversity in North America, as well as some of the greatest diversity of other flower visitors, including native bees, hummingbirds, and nectar-feeding bats. Warmer arid regions also offer the opportunity to watch these flower visitors on a nearly year-round

# Multiuse Backyard Garden

In a backyard garden, a balanced plan locates butterfly host, nectar, and shelter plants as well as brush piles at the outer edges and maintains areas of turf or patio closer to the house.

trees

tall wildflowers

stone wall

brush pile

shrubs

various wildflowers

mowed turf

bunchgrasses

basis. Warmer or cooler, arid regions invite butterfly gardening with native plants as a sustainable alternative to more water-intensive landscapes such as lawns.

Xeriscape gardening looks to reduce or eliminate the need for supplemental irrigation by using the most drought-tolerant locally adapted species. Consider simple water-conserving strategies for the garden such as positioning plants with higher water needs near downspouts and incorporating water catchment systems such as rain barrels and cisterns to help retain any available surface runoff and make possible a wider range of plants. In cases where some irrigation water is available, it can be used most efficiently with either new technology such as micro-drip emitter sprinkler systems or very old technology such as ollas—unglazed clay water pots buried in the ground near the root systems of water-hungry plants.

One important consideration for designing a xeriscape garden can be planning for the risk of local wildfires. Where this is a concern, it may be import-

Designing your butterfly garden

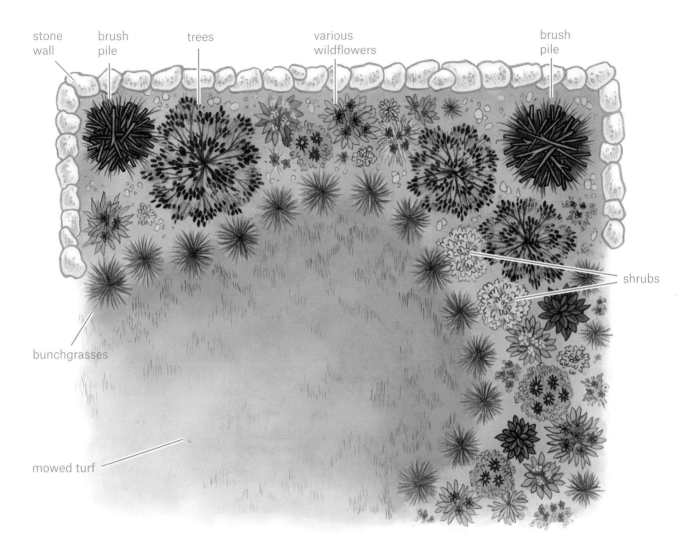

stone wall — brush pile — trees — various wildflowers — brush pile — shrubs — bunchgrasses — mowed turf

ant to locate larger, brushy plant growth away from the house and to create firebreaks between vegetated areas with boulders, stone retaining walls, pavers, and concrete patio areas.

## A MULTIUSE BACKYARD GARDEN

Backyard butterfly gardens often take their cue from ornamental landscaping, using neatly aligned rows of the same species and complementing those with alter-

nating rows or clusters of another species to create a sense of order. Such gardens also typically place taller species farthest away from outdoor living spaces (such as positioning tall plants against fences at the outer edge of the yard) and define the various parts of the garden with edging or border plants. Locating butterfly host, nectar, and shelter plants at the outer edges makes it simple to maintain areas of turf or patio closer to the house so that your backyard offers spaces for relaxation or play while also bringing butterflies in.

# Butterfly Meadow

Larger landscapes such as big backyards, farms, parks, nature centers, botanical gardens, arboretums, and zoos can create striking butterfly gardens with large meadow-type plantings.

Backyard butterfly gardening mostly differs from normal ornamental gardening in the matter of plant selection—specifically the selection first and foremost of plants that are attractive to butterflies instead of only to people. Hence, rather than hydrangeas and peonies, a backyard butterfly garden might consist of clumping goldenrods or Joe Pye weed. If your backyard garden has some hidden areas, you can carefully position a few brush piles to offer real wildlife habitat.

## A BUTTERFLY MEADOW FOR LARGER SPACES

Where space allows, wildflower-rich meadow plantings are typically the best landscapes for attracting and

Designing your butterfly garden

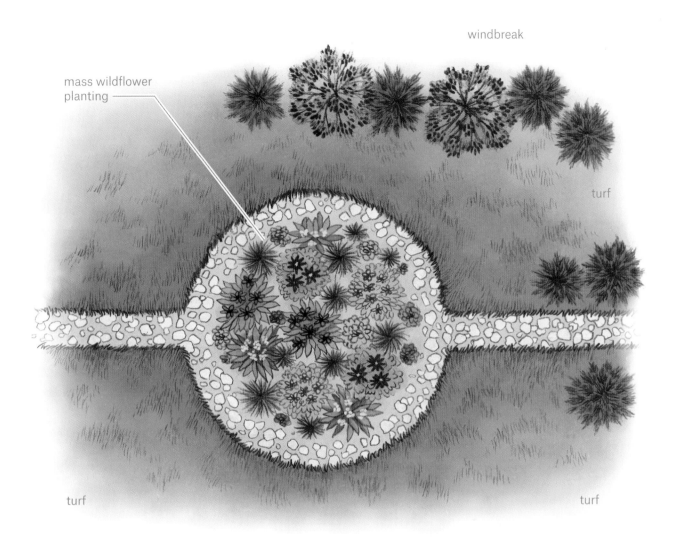

windbreak

mass wildflower planting

turf

turf

turf

sustaining an abundance and diversity of butterflies. Such meadows can be any shape from round to square and range in size from relatively small, beginning at perhaps 100 square feet, to much larger meadows (more than 10,000 square feet). Of course, the larger the meadow, the more butterflies it will attract. Large backyards, rural properties, farms, arboretums, botani-

cal gardens, parks, zoos, and other larger landscapes all can incorporate butterfly meadows.

A typical approach for designing butterfly meadows is to create large, contiguous areas of habitat, with walking trails that either snake through the meadow or encircle it. If the meadow is in a public setting, interpretive signage about the plants or common butterflies

# Roadside Butterfly Habitat

Whether an urban parking strip or a highway right of way, almost any type of roadside can incorporate butterfly habitat.

of the area can educate visitors and inspire them to create their own butterfly-friendly landscapes at home.

The best locations for these meadows are buffered by some kind of surrounding windbreak and linked to other adjacent natural habitat. Due to the cost of plants, large meadow plantings are usually established from seed. Most meadow plantings are maintained through occasional mowing or, for larger areas, burning. Mowing should be done only in the late fall after butterflies have gone into diapause. If you are burning the site, only portions (up to one third) should be burned at any one time. Remember that butterflies are likely to be living on the site at all times of the year even though you might not be able to see them.

## PARKING STRIP GARDENS AND ROADSIDE PRAIRIES

Roadsides cover more than 17 million acres of land in the United States, a figure that does not even include residential street parking strips, driveway edges, and parking lot islands. While these landscapes are typically mowed due to both real and sometimes

Designing your butterfly garden

mowed grass

shrubs and trees on backslope

taller wildflowers in ditch

simply perceived safety concerns, when planted and maintained as wildflower meadows they offer prime butterfly habitat.

A few considerations enter into planning for gardens along streets and roadsides. First, especially along busy streets and roads, a mowed setback is typically needed closest to the road to maintain clear visibility for drivers and an emergency stopping area. Farther away from the road, along ditch bottoms and the ditch backslope farthest from the road, taller native grasses and wildflowers are usually fine. In fact, such species

in some cases have been documented to help reduce encroachment by tree seedlings, thus reducing the need for frequent mowing and decreasing long-term maintenance costs. Within the mowed area next to the road, low-growing native grasses such as blue grama or buffalo grass can often be established. The habitat benefits these offer may be minimal, but they are likely greater than those of introduced turfgrasses.

Two other considerations are avoiding plants that are a potential fuel source in areas at risk of wildfires and avoiding any plants that are known to be intolerant of salt in areas where salts are used to de-ice roads. In parking strips along residential streets, these concerns may be less significant, but it is still important to develop a design consistent with the surrounding landscape. For example, in cities with tall-vegetation ordinances, it might be necessary to plan parking strip gardens as low-growing, more manicured assemblages.

Finally, there is often a concern about planting butterfly habitat near roads due to the potential for butterfly and car collisions. In fact, research suggests that there are actually fewer car strikes when an abundance of habitat is present along roads since butterflies spend more time occupying that habitat than moving back and forth across roads in search of flowers.

## INVITING KIDS INTO YOUR BUTTERFLY GARDEN

Many of us have childhood memories of butterflies. Whether it was watching a monarch or swallowtail soar through the sky or seeing large moths come to the porch light at night, these memories stay with us for a lifetime. With a little effort, you can make your butterfly garden kid friendly and provide enjoyment to people of all ages.

One key to having a child-friendly butterfly garden is to make it easy for them to see the butterflies without stepping on or pushing over the very flowers that attract these animals. Having lots of paths through your garden will allow access for people of all ages and will facilitate close inspection of these winged visitors. Another important part of gardening for kids is to think about size. Many of the plants that we look down on, a child needs to look up at. Having plantings of various sizes (some shorter and some taller) will allow young visitors to see the landscape and its inhabitants.

A successful kids' garden will have activities for young people other than just butterfly watching. Having places to hide is a favorite with most kids.

Sculptures and other features like ponds or fountains will enhance the garden for kids, adding a note of wonder to the landscape. Also having the garden next to a play area with a fort, slide, and swings will provide for hours of play. The play structure will allow kids to look down on the garden and its visitors from "way up high."

If you invite kids into your garden, try not to be too worried if plants get damaged. Kids at play will likely damage some plants as they try to get a better look at a garden visitor. You might not want to have them catching butterflies in your garden, though. One of the authors let his child loose with a net to chase a butterfly in the garden. The butterfly eluded capture but several plants were flattened as the youngster ran vigorously while swiping the net.

Including children in your garden plans will also help them learn the importance of maintaining a place for all animals, which in the end will benefit us all.

Butterflies are among the most accessible wildlife groups available to kids and can serve as a bridge to better understanding the natural world.

Designing your butterfly garden

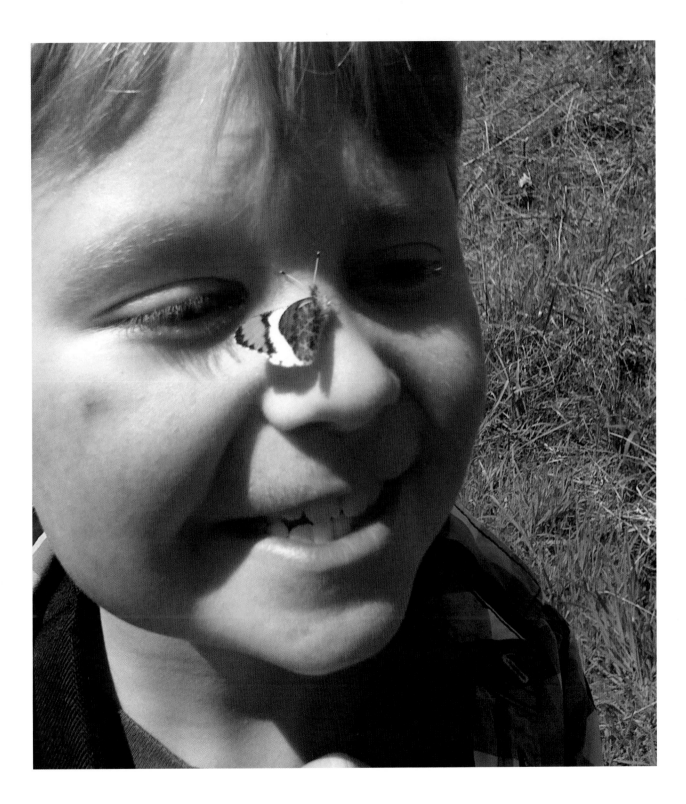

Careful choice of plants will ensure that butterflies will find both nectar and host plants in your garden. Here an American lady (*Vanessa virginiensis*) feeds on the nectar of narrow-leaved purple coneflower (*Echinacea angustifolia*).

# Butterfly garden plants of North America

**B**UTTERFLY GARDENING BEGINS with plants, especially native plants. The species described here represent some of the best plant options for supporting butterflies in garden settings in various parts of the United States and Canada. Included are more than one hundred wildflowers, perennial grasses and sedges, vines, and trees and shrubs known to produce an abundance of nectar and/ or to be the preferred larval host plants of our more common butterflies. The flowering species also attract a marvelous diversity of other pollinators, including mason bees, flower flies, and beneficial insects that prey on garden pests.

The species in this directory tolerate a range of soil conditions and are typically available from native plant nurseries. If individual species for your region are difficult to find, look for closely related ones, ideally within the same genus. Bloom time is given to help you design a garden with something blooming throughout the year. For each plant, we also specify the life cycle as annual, biennial, or perennial. Where two or three possibilities are given, the life cycle may be variable within the species due to genetic and climate factors. If the plant is a larval host, the species of butterflies or moths that lay their eggs on the plant are listed.

# Black-eyed Susan

*Rudbeckia hirta*

Showy, profuse flowers attract some butterflies and bees. Prefers full sun and is heat and drought tolerant.

**BLOOM TIME** summer

**FLOWER COLOR** yellow

**MAXIMUM HEIGHT** 3 feet

**LIFE CYCLE** annual, biennial, or perennial

**SOIL MOISTURE** dry to wet

**NECTAR VALUE** limited

**LARVAL HOST TO** bordered patch (*Chlosyne lacinia*), gorgone checkerspot (*Chlosyne gorgone*), silvery checkerspot (*Chlosyne nycteis*)

**NATIVE RANGE** eastern United States, Midwest, parts of the Great Plains, southern Canada

# Blanketflower

*Gaillardia aristata*

Vibrant, typically two-toned flowers have highly variable color patterns. Prefers well-drained soils and is easily established from seed.

**BLOOM TIME** summer

**FLOWER COLOR** red, yellow

**MAXIMUM HEIGHT** 3 feet

**LIFE CYCLE** perennial

**SOIL MOISTURE** dry

**NECTAR VALUE** yes

**LARVAL HOST TO** gaillardia flower moth (*Schinia masoni*)

**NATIVE RANGE** mountain and inland Northwest regions, western Canada

# Blue mistflower

*Conoclinium coelestinum*

Fluffy flowers borne in dense clusters are a favored nectar source of many butterflies. Has the potential to spread outside of its planted area.

**BLOOM TIME** summer and fall

**FLOWER COLOR** purple

**MAXIMUM HEIGHT** 3 feet

**LIFE CYCLE** perennial

**SOIL MOISTURE** average to wet

**NECTAR VALUE** yes

**LARVAL HOST TO** unknown

**NATIVE RANGE** Mid-Atlantic and Southeast regions

# Blue vervain

*Verbena hastata*

Small flowers ringed around slender, branched spikes attract butterflies and bees. Seeds support songbirds.

**BLOOM TIME** summer

**FLOWER COLOR** purple

**MAXIMUM HEIGHT** 5 feet

**LIFE CYCLE** biennial or perennial

**SOIL MOISTURE** wet

**NECTAR VALUE** yes

**LARVAL HOST TO** common buckeye (*Junonia coenia*)

**NATIVE RANGE** northeastern United States west to the eastern Great Plains

# Broadleaf lupine

*Lupinus latifolius*

Large, showy flower stalks rise above attractive foliage. Adaptable to most soil types and tolerates some shade.

**BLOOM TIME** spring

**FLOWER COLOR** purple

**MAXIMUM HEIGHT** 4 feet

**LIFE CYCLE** perennial

**SOIL MOISTURE** average

**NECTAR VALUE** no

**LARVAL HOST TO** Boisduval's blue (*Plebejus icarioides*), clouded sulphur (*Colias philodice*), orange sulphur (*Colias eurytheme*), Persius duskywing (*Erynnis persius*), silvery blue (*Glaucopsyche lygdamus*)

**NATIVE RANGE** California and the Pacific Northwest

# Butterfly milkweed

*Asclepias tuberosa*

Brilliant blooms arranged in clusters are a favored nectar source of many insects. In contrast to other milkweeds, has clear rather than milky sap. Prefers sandy soils.

**BLOOM TIME** summer

**FLOWER COLOR** orange

**MAXIMUM HEIGHT** 3 feet

**LIFE CYCLE** perennial

**SOIL MOISTURE** dry

**NECTAR VALUE** yes

**LARVAL HOST TO** dogbane tiger moth (*Cycnia tenera*), milkweed tussock moth (*Euchaetes egle*), monarch (*Danaus plexippus*), queen (*Danaus gilippus*), unexpected cycnia (*Cycnia inopinatus*)

**NATIVE RANGE** eastern United States and desert Southwest, Ontario and Quebec

# California goldenrod

*Solidago californica*

Small yet abundant flowers are an important late-season nectar source for butterflies and many other insects.

**BLOOM TIME** fall

**FLOWER COLOR** yellow

**MAXIMUM HEIGHT** 3 feet

**LIFE CYCLE** perennial

**SOIL MOISTURE** average

**NECTAR VALUE** yes

**LARVAL HOST TO** unknown

**NATIVE RANGE** California and Oregon

# Cobweb thistle

*Cirsium occidentale*

This native, noninvasive thistle has densely hairy foliage, stems and bracts, and large showy flowers that attract butterflies, bees, and hummingbirds. Prefers well-drained soils.

**BLOOM TIME** summer

**FLOWER COLOR** red

**MAXIMUM HEIGHT** 6 feet

**LIFE CYCLE** biennial, sometimes perennial

**SOIL MOISTURE** average to dry

**NECTAR VALUE** yes

**LARVAL HOST TO** California crescent (*Phyciodes orseis*), mylitta crescent (*Phyciodes mylitta*), painted lady (*Vanessa cardui*)

**NATIVE RANGE** California, southern Oregon, and western Nevada

# Common blue violet
*Viola sororia*

Low-growing plant has delicate flowers and attractive, heart-shaped leaves. Tolerates partial shade and self-seeds under favorable conditions.

**BLOOM TIME** spring

**FLOWER COLOR** purple

**MAXIMUM HEIGHT** 1 foot

**LIFE CYCLE** annual

**SOIL MOISTURE** wet

**NECTAR VALUE** yes

**LARVAL HOST TO** Aphrodite fritillary (*Speyeris aphrodite*), great spangled fritillary (*Speyeria cybele*), meadow fritillary (*Boloria bellona*), silver-bordered fritillary (*Boloria selene*), variegated fritillary (*Euptoieta claudia*)

**NATIVE RANGE** eastern United States and southeastern Canada

# Coyote mint
*Monardella villosa*

Showy, abundant blooms decorate aromatic gray-green foliage. Prefers good drainage and minimal summer water.

**BLOOM TIME** summer

**FLOWER COLOR** purple

**MAXIMUM HEIGHT** 2 feet

**LIFE CYCLE** perennial

**SOIL MOISTURE** average to dry

**NECTAR VALUE** yes

**LARVAL HOST TO** unknown

**NATIVE RANGE** California and Oregon

# Cup plant

*Silphium perfoliatum*

This tall, robust plant has large sunflower-like flowers. Birds are attracted to its seeds and the water that accumulates in the cup-shaped structures formed by the leaves.

**BLOOM TIME** summer

**FLOWER COLOR** yellow

**MAXIMUM HEIGHT** 6 feet+

**LIFE CYCLE** perennial

**SOIL MOISTURE** average to wet

**NECTAR VALUE** yes

**LARVAL HOST TO** unknown

**NATIVE RANGE** Midwest and Great Lakes region, southeastern Canada

# Deerweed

*Lotus scoparius*

This vital host plant for California butterflies has small but abundant flowers that also attract bees. Very drought tolerant.

**BLOOM TIME** spring and summer

**FLOWER COLOR** yellow

**MAXIMUM HEIGHT** 3 feet

**LIFE CYCLE** perennial

**SOIL MOISTURE** average to dry

**NECTAR VALUE** yes

**LARVAL HOST TO** Acmon blue (*Plebejus acmon*), Afranius duskywing (*Erynnis afranius*), Avalon scrub hairstreak (*Strymon avalona*), bramble hairstreak (*Callophrys dumetorum*), funereal duskywing (*Erynnis funeralis*), northern cloudywing (*Thorybes pylades*)

**NATIVE RANGE** California and Baja California

# Dense blazing star

*Liatris spicata*

This magnet for butterflies and bees has tall, showy flower spikes and grasslike leaves. Plants grow in discrete clumps and have a very tidy appearance.

**BLOOM TIME** late summer

**FLOWER COLOR** purple

**MAXIMUM HEIGHT** 4 feet

**LIFE CYCLE** perennial

**SOIL MOISTURE** average to wet

**NECTAR VALUE** yes

**LARVAL HOST TO** unknown

**NATIVE RANGE** eastern United States, excluding most of New England; southern Ontario and Quebec

# Desert mallow

*Sphaeralcea ambigua*

Large flowers cluster at the ends of stems, and woolly gray-green foliage remains evergreen. Drought tolerant.

**BLOOM TIME** variable and extended; peak bloom usually in spring

**FLOWER COLOR** orange

**MAXIMUM HEIGHT** 3 feet

**LIFE CYCLE** perennial

**SOIL MOISTURE** dry

**NECTAR VALUE** yes

**LARVAL HOST TO** common checkered skipper (*Pyrgus communis*), northern white skipper (*Heliopetes ericetorum*), painted lady (*Vanessa cardui*), small checkered skipper (*Pyrgus scriptura*), West Coast lady (*Vanessa annabella*)

**NATIVE RANGE** southwestern United States and northwestern Mexico

# Douglas aster

*Symphyotrichum subspicatum*

This is an important late-season nectar source. Prefers damp or occasionally flooded soils.

**BLOOM TIME** fall

**FLOWER COLOR** purple

**MAXIMUM HEIGHT** 4 feet

**LIFE CYCLE** perennial

**SOIL MOISTURE** average to wet

**NECTAR VALUE** yes

**LARVAL HOST TO** unknown

**NATIVE RANGE** northwestern United States and western Canada

# Edible thistle

*Cirsium edule*

This native, noninvasive thistle is frequently visited by butterflies and bees. Seeds are attractive to songbirds.

**BLOOM TIME** summer

**FLOWER COLOR** pink

**MAXIMUM HEIGHT** 6 feet

**LIFE CYCLE** biennial or perennial

**SOIL MOISTURE** average to wet

**NECTAR VALUE** yes

**LARVAL HOST TO** mylitta crescent (*Phyciodes mylitta*), painted lady (*Vanessa cardui*)

**NATIVE RANGE** Pacific Northwest, including British Columbia

# Evening primrose

*Oenothera biennis*

Showy, fragrant flowers typically bloom at night and into the morning. Seeds are attractive to birds.

**BLOOM TIME** summer

**FLOWER COLOR** yellow

**MAXIMUM HEIGHT** 6 feet

**LIFE CYCLE** biennial

**SOIL MOISTURE** average to dry

**NECTAR VALUE** yes

**LARVAL HOST TO** primrose moth (*Schinia florida*), white-lined sphinx moth (*Hyles lineata*)

**NATIVE RANGE** eastern United States from the Great Lakes and New England south to the Gulf Coast

# Fireweed

*Chamerion angustifolium*

This very tall plant with willowlike leaves is topped with large flower clusters. Thrives in moist soil and can potentially spread either by rhizomes or seed dispersal.

**BLOOM TIME** summer

**FLOWER COLOR** pink

**MAXIMUM HEIGHT** 6 feet

**LIFE CYCLE** perennial

**SOIL MOISTURE** average to wet

**NECTAR VALUE** yes

**LARVAL HOST TO** bedstraw moth (*Hyles gallii*), white-lined sphinx moth (*Hyles lineata*)

**NATIVE RANGE** northern tier of the United States into Canada

# Foothill penstemon

*Penstemon heterophyllus*

Iridescent blooms attract butterflies, bees, and hummingbirds. Requires good drainage and is heat and drought tolerant.

**BLOOM TIME** spring and early summer

**FLOWER COLOR** blue

**MAXIMUM HEIGHT** 3 feet

**LIFE CYCLE** perennial

**SOIL MOISTURE** dry

**NECTAR VALUE** yes

**LARVAL HOST TO** unknown

**NATIVE RANGE** California

# Foxglove beardtongue

*Penstemon digitalis*

This prolific nectar producer is visited by a huge diversity of butterflies, moths, and bees. Often grows in clumps; foliage remains semi-evergreen at southern latitudes.

**BLOOM TIME** spring

**FLOWER COLOR** white

**MAXIMUM HEIGHT** 3 feet

**LIFE CYCLE** perennial

**SOIL MOISTURE** average

**NECTAR VALUE** yes

**LARVAL HOST TO** unknown

**NATIVE RANGE** eastern United States and Canada, although uncommon in the southeastern states

# Giant ironweed

*Vernonia gigantea*

This tall, robust plant has showy flower clusters. Hardy and adaptable.

**BLOOM TIME** late summer

**FLOWER COLOR** purple

**MAXIMUM HEIGHT** 7 feet

**LIFE CYCLE** perennial

**SOIL MOISTURE** average to wet

**NECTAR VALUE** yes

**LARVAL HOST TO** ironweed borer moth (*Papaipema cerussata*), red groundling moth (*Perigea xanthioides*)

**NATIVE RANGE** central Great Lakes south to the Gulf Coast

# Globe gilia

*Gilia capitata*

Giobe-shaped, periwinkle-blue flowers attract butterflies and bees. Easy to establish from seed; may require periodic reseeding.

**BLOOM TIME** spring

**FLOWER COLOR** blue

**MAXIMUM HEIGHT** 1 foot

**LIFE CYCLE** annual

**SOIL MOISTURE** average

**NECTAR VALUE** yes

**LARVAL HOST TO** unknown

**NATIVE RANGE** western United States and Baja California

# Golden Alexanders

*Zizia aurea*

The small flowers of this early-blooming member of the carrot family offer nectar. Prefers poorly drained and wet soils and tolerates some shade.

**BLOOM TIME** spring

**FLOWER COLOR** yellow

**MAXIMUM HEIGHT** 3 feet

**LIFE CYCLE** perennial

**SOIL MOISTURE** wet

**NECTAR VALUE** yes

**LARVAL HOST TO** black swallowtail (*Papilio polyxenes*)

**NATIVE RANGE** eastern United States and eastern Canada

# Golden crownbeard

*Verbesina encelioides*

An important late-season nectar source for butterflies and many other insects, this plant flowers prolifically with an extended bloom period.

**BLOOM TIME** summer

**FLOWER COLOR** yellow

**MAXIMUM HEIGHT** 3 feet

**LIFE CYCLE** annual

**SOIL MOISTURE** dry

**NECTAR VALUE** yes

**LARVAL HOST TO** bordered patch (*Chlosyne lacinia*)

**NATIVE RANGE** southwestern United States and northern Mexico

# Golden yarrow

*Eriophyllum confertiflorum*

This drought-tolerant plant has abundant clusters of bright yellow flowers. Prefers full sun and good drainage; may need summer water.

**BLOOM TIME** spring and summer

**FLOWER COLOR** yellow

**MAXIMUM HEIGHT** 2 feet

**LIFE CYCLE** perennial

**SOIL MOISTURE** dry

**NECTAR VALUE** yes

**LARVAL HOST TO** unknown

**NATIVE RANGE** California and Baja California

# Hairy bush clover

*Lespedeza hirta*

The small, inconspicuous flowers of this broadly used host plant also attract some bees. Prefers partial rather than full sun.

**BLOOM TIME** summer

**FLOWER COLOR** white

**MAXIMUM HEIGHT** 3 feet

**LIFE CYCLE** perennial

**SOIL MOISTURE** average to dry

**NECTAR VALUE** no

**LARVAL HOST TO** bella moth (*Utetheisa ornatrix*), black-spotted prominent moth (*Dasylophia anguina*), cloudless sulphur (*Phoebis sennae*), confused cloudywing (*Thorybes confusis*), eastern tailed blue (*Cupido comyntas*), gray hairstreak (*Strymon melinus*), southern cloudywing (*Thorybes bathyllus*), Zarucco duskywing (*Erynnis zarucco*)

**NATIVE RANGE** eastern United States, excluding the western Great Lakes region; Ontario

# Hollow Joe Pye weed

*Eupatoriadelphus fistulosus*

This prolific nectar producer does well in either full sun or part shade.

**BLOOM TIME** late summer

**FLOWER COLOR** pink

**MAXIMUM HEIGHT** 6 feet+

**LIFE CYCLE** perennial

**SOIL MOISTURE** wet

**NECTAR VALUE** yes

**LARVAL HOST TO** Clymene moth (*Haploa clymene*), Eupatorium borer moth (*Carmenta bassiformis*), ruby tiger moth (*Phragmatobia fuliginosa*), three-lined flower moth (*Schinia trifascia*)

**NATIVE RANGE** eastern United States, excluding the western Great Lakes region; Ontario

# Hummingbird trumpet

*Epilobium canum*

This very attractive plant with abundant scarlet flowers and soft gray foliage is a critical late-season nectar source for butterflies, bees, and hummingbirds. Drought tolerant.

**BLOOM TIME** late summer

**FLOWER COLOR** red

**MAXIMUM HEIGHT** 3 feet

**LIFE CYCLE** perennial

**SOIL MOISTURE** dry

**NECTAR VALUE** yes

**LARVAL HOST TO** unknown

**NATIVE RANGE** southwestern United States and northern Mexico

# Indian blanket

*Gaillardia pulchella*

Vivid, usually two-toned flowers have color patterns that vary across ecotypes and cultivars. Easily established from seed and drought tolerant.

**BLOOM TIME** spring and summer

**FLOWER COLOR** red, yellow

**MAXIMUM HEIGHT** 2 feet

**LIFE CYCLE** annual, biennial, or perennial

**SOIL MOISTURE** dry

**NECTAR VALUE** yes

**LARVAL HOST TO** bordered patch (*Chlosyne lacinia*), painted schinia moth (*Gaillardia pulchella*)

**NATIVE RANGE** southern United States, excluding California; northern Mexico

# Lanceleaf coreopsis

*Coreopsis lanceolata*

This early bloomer often reseeds itself and can spread by rhizomes, forming small clonal colonies. Drought tolerant and prefers well-drained soils.

**BLOOM TIME** spring

**FLOWER COLOR** yellow

**MAXIMUM HEIGHT** 3 feet

**LIFE CYCLE** perennial

**SOIL MOISTURE** dry

**NECTAR VALUE** yes

**LARVAL HOST TO** unknown

**NATIVE RANGE** eastern United States and Ontario

# Maryland senna

*Senna marilandica*

This larval host has attractive yellow flowers and conspicuous seedpods. Prefers moist, well-drained soils.

**BLOOM TIME** summer

**FLOWER COLOR** yellow

**MAXIMUM HEIGHT** 6 feet

**LIFE CYCLE** perennial

**SOIL MOISTURE** average to wet

**NECTAR VALUE** no

**LARVAL HOST TO** cloudless sulphur (*Phoebis sennae*), orange-barred sulphur (*Phoebis philea*), sleepy orange (*Abaeis nicippe*)

**NATIVE RANGE** southeastern United States, north to the southern Great Lakes region

# Meadow checkermallow

*Sidalcea malviflora*

Has attractive basal foliage and striking blooms borne on tall stems. Often reseeds itself.

**BLOOM TIME** spring

**FLOWER COLOR** pink

**MAXIMUM HEIGHT** 3 feet

**LIFE CYCLE** perennial

**SOIL MOISTURE** average to wet

**NECTAR VALUE** yes

**LARVAL HOST TO** West Coast lady (*Vanessa annabella*)

**NATIVE RANGE** Washington, Oregon, California, and Baja California

# New England aster

*Symphyotrichum novae-angliae*

As one of the latest fall-blooming plants, offers an essential source of nectar to many butterflies and bees.

**BLOOM TIME** fall

**FLOWER COLOR** purple

**MAXIMUM HEIGHT** 6 feet+

**LIFE CYCLE** perennial

**SOIL MOISTURE** average

**NECTAR VALUE** yes

**LARVAL HOST TO** pearl crescent (*Phyciodes tharos*)

**NATIVE RANGE** northeastern United States west to the Great Plains; eastern Canada

# Oregon checkermallow

*Sidalcea oregana*

Large pink flowers bloom in sequence atop tall stems. Does well in moist or dry soils.

**BLOOM TIME** spring and summer

**FLOWER COLOR** pink

**MAXIMUM HEIGHT** 4 feet

**LIFE CYCLE** perennial

**SOIL MOISTURE** wet to dry

**NECTAR VALUE** yes

**LARVAL HOST TO** West Coast lady (*Vanessa annabella*)

**NATIVE RANGE** western United States and British Columbia

# Oregon sunshine

*Eriophyllum lanatum*

With profuse yellow blooms and woolly gray-green foliage, this plant sometimes exhibits a shrubby growth form. Prefers well-drained soils and often reseeds itself.

**BLOOM TIME** spring and summer

**FLOWER COLOR** yellow

**MAXIMUM HEIGHT** 3 feet

**LIFE CYCLE** annual or perennial

**SOIL MOISTURE** dry

**NECTAR VALUE** yes

**LARVAL HOST TO** unknown

**NATIVE RANGE** western United States and British Columbia

Butterfly garden plants of North America

# Pacific aster

*Symphyotrichum chilense*

Serves as an important late-season nectar source for butterflies, bees, and many other insects. Tolerates clay soils.

**BLOOM TIME** fall

**FLOWER COLOR** purple

**MAXIMUM HEIGHT** 5 feet

**LIFE CYCLE** perennial

**SOIL MOISTURE** dry

**NECTAR VALUE** yes

**LARVAL HOST TO** unknown

**NATIVE RANGE** western United States and British Columbia

# Pale purple coneflower

*Echinacea pallida*

Supports a wide diversity of butterflies and bees and is particularly attractive to skippers. Drought tolerant and prefers well-drained soils.

**BLOOM TIME** summer

**FLOWER COLOR** purple

**MAXIMUM HEIGHT** 3 feet

**LIFE CYCLE** perennial

**SOIL MOISTURE** dry

**NECTAR VALUE** yes

**LARVAL HOST TO** silvery checkerspot (*Chlosyne nycteis*)

**NATIVE RANGE** central Midwest south through the Lower Mississippi River Valley

# Palmer's penstemon
*Penstemon palmeri*

This evergreen larval host has showy, fragrant flowers. Heat and drought tolerant and prefers well-drained soils.

**BLOOM TIME** spring and summer

**FLOWER COLOR** pink

**MAXIMUM HEIGHT** 5 feet

**LIFE CYCLE** perennial

**SOIL MOISTURE** dry

**NECTAR VALUE** yes

**LARVAL HOST TO** Arachne checkerspot (*Poladryas arachne*), variable checkerspot (*Euphydryas chalcedona*)

**NATIVE RANGE** Great Basin and desert Southwest

# Pasture thistle

*Cirsium discolor*

This native, noninvasive thistle is highly attractive to butterflies and bees, bumble bees in particular. Seeds provide food for songbirds.

BLOOM TIME late summer

FLOWER COLOR purple

MAXIMUM HEIGHT 6 feet

LIFE CYCLE biennial or perennial

SOIL MOISTURE average

NECTAR VALUE yes

LARVAL HOST TO painted lady (*Vanessa cardui*)

NATIVE RANGE eastern United States, excluding the southern coastal plain; eastern Canada

# Pearly everlasting

*Anaphalis margaritacea*

Has delicate, papery flowers in tightly formed clusters and finely woolly foliage; can be used in dried flower arrangements. Prefers full sun and well-drained soils.

BLOOM TIME summer

FLOWER COLOR white

MAXIMUM HEIGHT 3 feet

LIFE CYCLE perennial

SOIL MOISTURE dry

NECTAR VALUE yes

LARVAL HOST TO American lady (*Vanessa virginiensis*), painted lady (*Vanessa cardui*)

NATIVE RANGE disjunct populations in New England and eastern Canada, the western Great Lakes, the entire western United States, and northern Mexico

# Prairie blazing star

*Liatris pycnostachya*

Provides nectar to a broad community of butterflies including monarchs, swallowtails, skippers, and sulphurs. Heat and drought tolerant.

**BLOOM TIME** summer

**FLOWER COLOR** purple

**MAXIMUM HEIGHT** 4 feet

**LIFE CYCLE** perennial

**SOIL MOISTURE** average to wet

**NECTAR VALUE** yes

**LARVAL HOST TO** bleeding flower moth (*Schinia sanguinea*)

**NATIVE RANGE** Upper Midwest south to eastern Texas, Louisiana, and Mississippi

# Prairie phlox

*Phlox pilosa*

Bright, fragrant flowers vary in color, ranging from white to pink to purple. Prefers well-drained soils.

BLOOM TIME summer

FLOWER COLOR pink

MAXIMUM HEIGHT 3 feet

LIFE CYCLE perennial

SOIL MOISTURE dry

NECTAR VALUE yes

LARVAL HOST TO phlox moth (*Schinia indiana*)

NATIVE RANGE eastern United States, excluding New England and New York; Ontario

# Prairie zinnia

*Zinnia grandiflora*

This low-growing ground cover blooms profusely. Prefers well-drained soils, spreads by rhizomes, and is deer resistant.

BLOOM TIME late spring to early fall

FLOWER COLOR yellow

MAXIMUM HEIGHT 1 foot

LIFE CYCLE perennial

SOIL MOISTURE dry

NECTAR VALUE yes

LARVAL HOST TO unknown

NATIVE RANGE southwestern United States and northern Mexico

# Prince's plume

*Stanleya pinnata*

Features multiple, tall flowering stalks and attractive basal foliage. Needs no water once established.

**BLOOM TIME** spring and summer

**FLOWER COLOR** yellow

**MAXIMUM HEIGHT** 6 feet

**LIFE CYCLE** perennial

**SOIL MOISTURE** dry

**NECTAR VALUE** yes

**LARVAL HOST TO** Becker's white (*Pontia beckerii*), checkered white (*Pyrgus albescens*)

**NATIVE RANGE** Great Basin to the western Great Plains

# Puget Sound gumweed

*Grindelia integrifolia*

Produces bright, long-lasting blooms and sticky, resinous flower heads with curly bracts. Flowers year round in warm weather.

**BLOOM TIME** late summer

**FLOWER COLOR** yellow

**MAXIMUM HEIGHT** 4 feet

**LIFE CYCLE** perennial

**SOIL MOISTURE** average

**NECTAR VALUE** yes

**LARVAL HOST TO** unknown

**NATIVE RANGE** Pacific Northwest, including British Columbia

# Purple prairie clover

*Dalea purpurea*

Pretty golden stamens contrast nicely with vibrant purple blossoms; attracts both butterflies and bees. Contributes nitrogen to the soil and is very heat and drought tolerant.

**BLOOM TIME** summer

**FLOWER COLOR** purple

**MAXIMUM HEIGHT** 3 feet

**LIFE CYCLE** perennial

**SOIL MOISTURE** average to dry

**NECTAR VALUE** yes

**LARVAL HOST TO** southern dogface (*Zerene cesonia*)

**NATIVE RANGE** central United States and Canada

# Rattlesnake master

*Eryngium yuccifolium*

Strikingly unique flowers attract incredible insect diversity. Prefers full sun.

**BLOOM TIME** late summer

**FLOWER COLOR** white

**MAXIMUM HEIGHT** 4 feet

**LIFE CYCLE** perennial

**SOIL MOISTURE** average

**NECTAR VALUE** yes

**LARVAL HOST TO** rattlesnake-master borer moth (*Papaipema eryngii*)

**NATIVE RANGE** Florida to east Texas, north to Minnesota, and east to the Mid-Atlantic

# Rocky Mountain bee plant

*Peritoma serrulata*

Abundant, distinctive flowers attract a broad diversity of butterflies and bees. Pendulous seedpods resemble peas. May grow as wide as it is tall.

**BLOOM TIME** summer

**FLOWER COLOR** purple

**MAXIMUM HEIGHT** 5 feet

**LIFE CYCLE** annual

**SOIL MOISTURE** dry

**NECTAR VALUE** yes

**LARVAL HOST TO** checkered white (*Pyrgus albescens*)

**NATIVE RANGE** western United States and Canada

# Rocky Mountain blazing star

*Liatris ligulistylis*

Incredibly attractive to monarch butterflies. Seeds are eaten by songbirds.

**BLOOM TIME** summer

**FLOWER COLOR** purple

**MAXIMUM HEIGHT** 5 feet

**LIFE CYCLE** perennial

**SOIL MOISTURE** average

**NECTAR VALUE** yes

**LARVAL HOST TO** bleeding flower moth (*Schinia sanguinea*)

**NATIVE RANGE** east of the Rockies to the Upper Midwest

# Round-headed bush clover

*Lespedeza capitata*

This broadly used larval host plant also provides seed for birds. Requires good drainage and is drought tolerant.

**BLOOM TIME** summer

**FLOWER COLOR** white

**MAXIMUM HEIGHT** 4 feet

**LIFE CYCLE** perennial

**SOIL MOISTURE** dry

**NECTAR VALUE** no

**LARVAL HOST TO** eastern tailed blue (*Cupido comyntas*), gray hairstreak (*Strymon melinus*), hoary edge (*Achalarus lyciades*), northern cloudywing (*Thorybes pylades*), orange sulphur (*Colias eurytheme*), silver-spotted skipper (*Epar'gyreus clarus*), southern cloudywing (*Thorybes bathyllus*), spring azure (*Celastrina ladon*)

**NATIVE RANGE** eastern United States, Quebec and New Brunswick

# Scarlet beebalm

*Monarda didyma*

This mint family member has spectacularly showy flowers and fragrant foliage. Also attracts hummingbirds.

**BLOOM TIME** summer

**FLOWER COLOR** red

**MAXIMUM HEIGHT** 3 feet

**LIFE CYCLE** perennial

**SOIL MOISTURE** average to wet

**NECTAR VALUE** yes

**LARVAL HOST TO** hermit sphinx (*Lintneria eremitus*), orange mint moth (*Pyrausta orphisalis*), raspberry pyrausta (*Pyrausta signatalis*)

**NATIVE RANGE** northeastern United States and eastern Canada

# Scarlet gilia

*Ipomopsis aggregata*

Covered with brilliant red, tubular flowers in its second year, this plant attracts butterflies and hummingbirds. Requires well-drained soil and is drought tolerant yet tends to need more water than other desert wildflowers.

**BLOOM TIME** summer

**FLOWER COLOR** red

**MAXIMUM HEIGHT** 5 feet

**LIFE CYCLE** biennial

**SOIL MOISTURE** dry

**NECTAR VALUE** yes

**LARVAL HOST TO** unknown

**NATIVE RANGE** western United States, British Columbia, and northern Mexico

# Seablush

*Plectritis congesta*

Delicate flowers offer an important spring nectar source for butterflies and bees. Easy to establish from seed but may require periodic reseeding.

**BLOOM TIME** spring

**FLOWER COLOR** pink

**MAXIMUM HEIGHT** 2 feet

**LIFE CYCLE** annual

**SOIL MOISTURE** average to wet

**NECTAR VALUE** yes

**LARVAL HOST TO** unknown

**NATIVE RANGE** western United States and British Columbia

# Showy milkweed

*Asclepias speciosa*

Ball-shaped clusters of large, star-shaped flowers are magnets for butterflies, bees, and many other insects. Tall, robust plants typically flower in their second year when started from seed.

BLOOM TIME summer

FLOWER COLOR pink and white

MAXIMUM HEIGHT 5 feet

LIFE CYCLE perennial

SOIL MOISTURE average to wet

NECTAR VALUE yes

LARVAL HOST TO dogbane tiger moth (*Cycnia tenera*), monarch (*Danaus plexippus*), queen (*Danaus gilippus*)

NATIVE RANGE western United States and Canada

# Slender cinquefoil

*Potentilla gracilis*

This rose family member with sunny blooms and broad, dissected leaves tolerates drought and light shade.

BLOOM TIME summer

FLOWER COLOR yellow

MAXIMUM HEIGHT 2 feet

LIFE CYCLE perennial

SOIL MOISTURE average

NECTAR VALUE yes

LARVAL HOST TO two-banded checkered skipper (*Pyrgus ruralis*)

NATIVE RANGE western United States and Canada

# Small spike false nettle

*Boehmeria cylindrica*

Lacks the stinging hairs characteristic of some of its relatives. Flowers are inconspicuous and wind-pollinated. Prefers light shade.

**BLOOM TIME** summer

**FLOWER COLOR** green

**MAXIMUM HEIGHT** 3 feet

**LIFE CYCLE** perennial

**SOIL MOISTURE** average to wet

**NECTAR VALUE** no

**LARVAL HOST TO** eastern comma (*Polygonia comma*), question mark (*Polygonia interrogationis*), red admiral (*Vanessa atalanta*)

**NATIVE RANGE** eastern United States and Canada

# Southwestern mock vervain

*Glandularia gooddingii*

Short-statured evergreen plant has a mounding growth habit. Tends to be short lived but reseeds itself.

**BLOOM TIME** spring

**FLOWER COLOR** pink

**MAXIMUM HEIGHT** 1 foot

**LIFE CYCLE** perennial

**SOIL MOISTURE** dry

**NECTAR VALUE** yes

**LARVAL HOST TO** unknown

**NATIVE RANGE** southwestern United States and northern Mexico

# Spanish bayonet

*Yucca baccata*

Thick clusters of drooping, bell-shaped flowers rise on stalks above the narrow, spine-tipped evergreen leaves of this shrublike succulent. After feeding, skipper larvae pupate in the plants' roots.

**BLOOM TIME** spring and summer

**FLOWER COLOR** white

**MAXIMUM HEIGHT** 4 feet

**LIFE CYCLE** perennial

**SOIL MOISTURE** dry

**NECTAR VALUE** yes

**LARVAL HOST TO** ursine giant skipper (*Megathymus ursus*), yucca giant skipper (*Megathymus yuccae*), various yucca moths (*Proxodus* species)

**NATIVE RANGE** desert Southwest and northern Mexico

# Spider or antelope horn milkweed

*Asclepias asperula*

Low growing and clump forming, this milkweed produces ball-shaped clusters of strikingly unique flowers followed by large, distinctive seedpods.

BLOOM TIME spring and summer

FLOWER COLOR purple and green

MAXIMUM HEIGHT 2 feet

LIFE CYCLE perennial

SOIL MOISTURE average

NECTAR VALUE yes

LARVAL HOST TO dogbane tiger moth (*Cycnia tenera*), monarch (*Danaus plexippus*), queen (*Danaus gilippus*), unexpected cycnia (*Cycnia inopinatus*)

NATIVE RANGE southwestern United States and northern Mexico

# Spotted Joe Pye weed

*Eupatoriadelphus maculatus*

Clusters of small, fragrant flowers attract a large diversity of insects. Often forms small clonal colonies; tolerates part shade.

BLOOM TIME summer

FLOWER COLOR pink

MAXIMUM HEIGHT 5 feet

LIFE CYCLE perennial

SOIL MOISTURE wet

NECTAR VALUE yes

LARVAL HOST TO Clymene moth (*Haploa clymene*), Eupatorium borer moth (*Carmenta bassiformis*), ruby tiger moth (*Phragmatobia fuliginosa*), three-lined flower moth (*Schinia trifascia*)

NATIVE RANGE New England and eastern Canada, west to the Great Lakes

# Starry rosinweed

*Silphium asteriscus*

This tall, robust plant with large, showy flowers attracts butterflies and bees. Drought tolerant once established and often reseeds itself.

**BLOOM TIME** summer

**FLOWER COLOR** yellow

**MAXIMUM HEIGHT** 5 feet

**LIFE CYCLE** perennial

**SOIL MOISTURE** dry

**NECTAR VALUE** yes

**LARVAL HOST TO** unknown

**NATIVE RANGE** Texas east to the Mid-Atlantic region

Butterfly garden plants of North America

# Sulphur buckwheat

*Eriogonum umbellatum*

This low-growing evergreen plant blooms profusely and is attractive to both butterflies and bees. Good candidate for inclusion in rock gardens.

**BLOOM TIME** summer

**FLOWER COLOR** yellow

**MAXIMUM HEIGHT** 3 feet

**LIFE CYCLE** perennial

**SOIL MOISTURE** dry

**NECTAR VALUE** yes

**LARVAL HOST TO** bramble hairstreak (*Callophrys dumetorum*), desert green hairstreak (*Callophrys sheridanii comstocki*), lupine blue (*Plebejus lupini*), Mormon metalmark (*Apodemia mormo*), Rocky Mountain dotted blue (*Euphilotes ancilla*), Sheridan's hairstreak (*Callophrys sheridanii*), Sonoran metalmark (*Apodemia mejicanus*), western green hairstreak (*Callophrys affinis*)

**NATIVE RANGE** western United States and Canada

# Summer lupine

*Lupinus formosus*

This important larval host, shorter statured than most other lupines, is visited by bees for pollen. Drought tolerant.

**BLOOM TIME** summer

**FLOWER COLOR** purple

**MAXIMUM HEIGHT** 2 feet

**LIFE CYCLE** perennial

**SOIL MOISTURE** dry

**NECTAR VALUE** no

**LARVAL HOST TO** Acmon blue (*Plebejus acmon*), arrowhead blue (*Glaucopsyche piasus*), Melissa blue (*Plebejus melissa*), silvery blue (*Glaucopsyche lygdamus*), sooty hairstreak (*Satyrium fuliginosum*)

**NATIVE RANGE** California and Oregon

# Swamp thistle

*Cirsium muticum*

This native, noninvasive thistle is an essential nectar source for butterflies and bees. Seeds are attractive to songbirds.

**BLOOM TIME** summer

**FLOWER COLOR** pink

**MAXIMUM HEIGHT** 7 feet

**LIFE CYCLE** biennial

**SOIL MOISTURE** wet

**NECTAR VALUE** yes

**LARVAL HOST TO** painted lady (*Vanessa cardui*), swamp metalmark (*Calephelis muticum*)

**NATIVE RANGE** eastern United States and Canada, although rare in the south-central and southeastern states

# Sweet Joe Pye weed

*Eupatoriadelphus purpureus*

This Joe Pye weed is an important nectar source for butterflies, moths, and bees. Prefers light shade and poorly drained and wetland edge soils.

**BLOOM TIME** summer

**FLOWER COLOR** pink

**MAXIMUM HEIGHT** 7 feet

**LIFE CYCLE** perennial

**SOIL MOISTURE** wet

**NECTAR VALUE** yes

**LARVAL HOST TO** Eupatorium borer moth (*Carmenta bassiformis*), red groundling moth (*Perigea xanthioides*), ruby tiger moth (*Phragmatobia fuliginosa*), three-lined flower moth (*Schinia trifascia*)

**NATIVE RANGE** eastern United States and Ontario

# Virginia mountain mint

*Pycnanthemum virginianum*

This and other mountain mints have fragrant foliage and are a favored nectar source of many insects.

**BLOOM TIME** summer

**FLOWER COLOR** white and purple

**MAXIMUM HEIGHT** 3 feet

**LIFE CYCLE** perennial

**SOIL MOISTURE** average to wet

**NECTAR VALUE** yes

**LARVAL HOST TO** unknown

**NATIVE RANGE** northeastern United States and eastern Canada

# Western yarrow

*Achillea millefolium*

With feathery, fernlike foliage and flat-topped flower clusters, makes a nice cut flower, either fresh or dried. When buying seeds, look for western yarrow specifically as opposed to non-locally native cultivars.

**BLOOM TIME** summer

**FLOWER COLOR** white

**MAXIMUM HEIGHT** 2 feet

**LIFE CYCLE** perennial

**SOIL MOISTURE** average to dry

**NECTAR VALUE** limited

**LARVAL HOST TO** unknown

**NATIVE RANGE** entire United States and Canada

# White prairie clover

*Dalea candida*

Attracts both butterflies and bees, contributes nitrogen to the soil, and prefers well-drained soils.

BLOOM TIME summer

FLOWER COLOR white

MAXIMUM HEIGHT 2 feet

LIFE CYCLE perennial

SOIL MOISTURE average to dry

NECTAR VALUE yes

LARVAL HOST TO clouded sulphur (*Colias philodice*), marine blue (*Leptotes marina*), Reakirt's blue (*Echinargus isola*), southern dogface (*Zerene cesonia*)

NATIVE RANGE central United States and Canada

# White-tufted evening primrose

*Oenothera caespitosa*

This short-statured plant with large, showy flowers typically blooms overnight and into the morning, attracting nectar-seeking moths. Requires good drainage.

BLOOM TIME spring and summer

FLOWER COLOR white

MAXIMUM HEIGHT 1 foot

LIFE CYCLE perennial

SOIL MOISTURE dry

NECTAR VALUE yes

LARVAL HOST TO white-lined sphinx moth (*Hyles lineata*)

NATIVE RANGE inland Northwest, Mountain region, Great Basin, desert Southwest, south-central Canada, and northern Mexico

# Wild bergamot

*Monarda fistulosa*

Eye-catching, prolific blooms are visited by butterflies, moths, bees, and hummingbirds. Foliage is fragrant.

**BLOOM TIME** summer

**FLOWER COLOR** purple

**MAXIMUM HEIGHT** 4 feet

**LIFE CYCLE** perennial

**SOIL MOISTURE** average

**NECTAR VALUE** yes

**LARVAL HOST TO** hermit sphinx (*Lintneria eremitus*), orange mint moth (*Pyrausta orphisalis*), raspberry pyrausta (*Pyrausta signatalis*)

**NATIVE RANGE** New England and eastern Canada west to the Great Lakes and south to the Gulf Coast

# Wild lupine

*Lupinus perennis*

This widely used larval host plant requires good drainage and prefers dry, sandy soils.

**BLOOM TIME** spring

**FLOWER COLOR** purple

**MAXIMUM HEIGHT** 2 feet

**LIFE CYCLE** perennial

**SOIL MOISTURE** average to dry

**NECTAR VALUE** no

**LARVAL HOST TO** clouded sulphur (*Colias philodice*), eastern tailed blue (*Cupido comyntas*), frosted elfin (*Callophrys irus*), gray hairstreak (*Strymon melinus*), Karner blue (*Plebejus melissa samuelis*), Persius duskywing (*Erynnis persius*), silvery blue (*Glaucopsyche lygdamus*), wild indigo duskywing (*Erynnis baptisiae*)

**NATIVE RANGE** eastern United States and Ontario, with a disjunct distribution

# Wild strawberry

*Fragaria vesca*

This attractive, diminutive plant thrives in partial shade and moist soils. Fruits are edible.

**BLOOM TIME** spring

**FLOWER COLOR** white

**MAXIMUM HEIGHT** 1 foot

**LIFE CYCLE** perennial

**SOIL MOISTURE** wet

**NECTAR VALUE** yes

**LARVAL HOST TO** two-banded checkered skipper (*Pyrgus ruralis*)

**NATIVE RANGE** northern tier United States and across southern Canada, south through the Rocky Mountains; Baja California

# Wingstem

*Verbesina alternifolia*

# Wrinkleleaf goldenrod

*Solidago rugosa*

Uniquely shaped flowers attract both butterflies and bees. Shade tolerant and a great candidate for rain gardens.

This is an important late season nectar source for butterflies, moths, bees, and more. Often grows in clumps.

BLOOM TIME late summer

FLOWER COLOR yellow

MAXIMUM HEIGHT 6 feet

LIFE CYCLE perennial

SOIL MOISTURE wet

NECTAR VALUE yes

LARVAL HOST TO gold moth (*Basilodes pepita*), silvery checkerspot (*Chlosyne nycteis*)

NATIVE RANGE eastern United States and Ontario

BLOOM TIME fall

FLOWER COLOR yellow

MAXIMUM HEIGHT 6 feet

LIFE CYCLE perennial

SOIL MOISTURE average to wet

NECTAR VALUE yes

LARVAL HOST TO unknown

NATIVE RANGE eastern United States and Canada

# Yellow thistle

*Cirsium horridulum*

This native, noninvasive thistle is very prickly but has showy flowers and is an excellent nectar source for butterflies and bumble bees.

**BLOOM TIME** summer

**FLOWER COLOR** yellow or purple

**MAXIMUM HEIGHT** 3 feet

**LIFE CYCLE** annual or biennial

**SOIL MOISTURE** average

**NECTAR VALUE** yes

**LARVAL HOST TO** little metalmark (*Calephelis virginiensis*), painted lady (*Vanessa cardui*)

**NATIVE RANGE** southeastern United States

# Big bluestem

*Andropogon gerardii*

This tall, densely growing warm-season bunchgrass has gray or blue-green foliage that changes color in the fall. Drought tolerant and deer resistant.

BLOOM TIME summer and fall

MAXIMUM HEIGHT 7 feet

SOIL MOISTURE average to wet

LARVAL HOST TO Arogos skipper (*Atrytone arogos*), Byssus skipper (*Problema byssus*), cobweb skipper (*Hesperia metea*), common wood nymph (*Cercyonis pegala*), Delaware skipper (*Anatrytone logan*), dusted skipper (*Atrytonopsis hianna*)

NATIVE RANGE central and eastern United States and Canada

# Blue grama

*Bouteloua gracilis*

This short-statured, warm-season grass can be densely planted to form a shaggy, no-mow lawn that requires little water.

BLOOM TIME summer

MAXIMUM HEIGHT 2 feet

SOIL MOISTURE dry

LARVAL HOST TO Garita skipperling (*Oarisma garita*), green skipper (*Hesperia viridis*), Pahaska skipper (*Hesperia pahaska*), Rhesus skipper (*Polites rhesus*), Simius roadside skipper (*Notamblyscirtes simius*), Uncas skipper (*Hesperia uncas*)

NATIVE RANGE Great Plains west to the Great Basin and southern California; southern Canada

# Blue wild rye

*Elymus glaucus*

This cool-season bunchgrass offers attractive blue-green foliage. Prefers moist soil yet will tolerate drier conditions.

**BLOOM TIME** summer

**MAXIMUM HEIGHT** 4 feet

**SOIL MOISTURE** average

**LARVAL HOST TO** woodland skipper (*Ochlodes sylvanoides*)

**NATIVE RANGE** western United States and Canada

# Bottlebrush grass

*Elymus hystrix*

This cool-season bunchgrass has unique bottlebrush-shaped flower spikes. Tolerates shade.

**BLOOM TIME** summer

**MAXIMUM HEIGHT** 5 feet

**SOIL MOISTURE** average

**LARVAL HOST TO** northern pearly eye (*Lethe anthedon anthedon*)

**NATIVE RANGE** Great Lakes and Northeast regions; eastern Canada

# Idaho fescue

*Festuca idahoensis*

This low-growing bunchgrass with tall flowering stems is highly adaptable and drought tolerant.

**BLOOM TIME** spring and summer

**MAXIMUM HEIGHT** 2 feet

**SOIL MOISTURE** average to dry

**LARVAL HOST TO** Lindsey's skipper (*Hesperia lindseyi*), sandhill skipper (*Polites sabuleti*), Sonora skipper (*Polites sonora*), woodland skipper (*Ochlodes sylvanoides*), western banded skipper (*Hesperia colorado*)

**NATIVE RANGE** western United States and Canada

# Indian grass

*Sorghastrum nutans*

This warm-season bunchgrass offers showy flowers and seed heads and attractive fall color.

**BLOOM TIME** summer and fall

**MAXIMUM HEIGHT** 7 feet

**SOIL MOISTURE** average

**LARVAL HOST TO** pepper-and-salt skipper (*Amblyscirtes hegon*)

**NATIVE RANGE** central and eastern United States and Canada

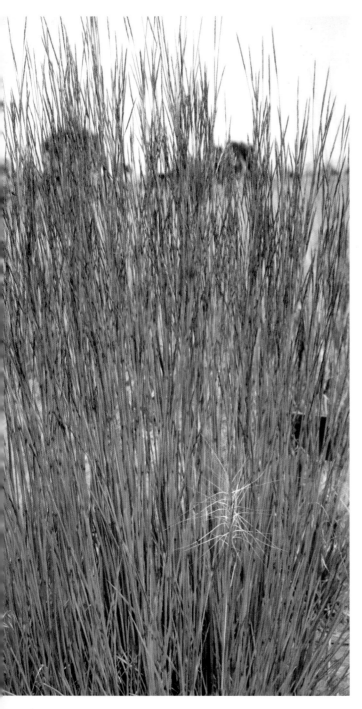

# Little bluestem

*Schizachyrium scoparium*

This clump-forming, drought tolerant bunchgrass has attractive blue-green foliage that turns red in the fall.

**BLOOM TIME** summer and fall

**MAXIMUM HEIGHT** 3 feet

**SOIL MOISTURE** dry

**LARVAL HOST TO** cobweb skipper (*Hesperia metea*), common wood nymph (*Cercyonis pegala*), crossline skipper (*Polites origenes*), Dakota skipper (*Hesperia dacotae*), dusted skipper (*Atrytonopsis hianna*), Indian skipper (*Hesperia sassacus*), Leonard's skipper (*Hesperia leonardus*), Ottoe skipper (*Hesperia ottoe*), swarthy skipper (*Nastra lherminier*)

**NATIVE RANGE** eastern and central United States and Canada

# Prairie dropseed

*Sporobolus heterolepis*

This compact bunchgrass features graceful flowers and attractive fall color. Prefers sandy soils.

**BLOOM TIME** summer

**MAXIMUM HEIGHT** 3 feet

**SOIL MOISTURE** dry

**LARVAL HOST TO** Poweshiek skipper (*Oarisma poweshiek*)

**NATIVE RANGE** Canada and United States except southeastern states

# Purple needlegrass

*Nassella pulchra*

This drought-tolerant, very adaptable bunchgrass has showy flowers with long, sharp spines.

**BLOOM TIME** summer

**MAXIMUM HEIGHT** 3 feet

**SOIL MOISTURE** dry

**LARVAL HOST TO** common branded skipper (*Hesperia comma*), Uncas skipper (*Hesperia uncas*)

**NATIVE RANGE** California and Baja California

# Purpletop

*Tridens flavus*

This warm-season bunchgrass offers attractive purple seed heads. Prefers well-drained soils.

**BLOOM TIME** summer and fall

**MAXIMUM HEIGHT** 7 feet

**SOIL MOISTURE** dry

**LARVAL HOST TO** common wood nymph (*Cercyonis pegala*), crossline skipper (*Polites origenes*), little glassywing (*Pompeius verna*), Zabulon skipper (*Poanes zabulon*)

**NATIVE RANGE** southern Great Plains east to Vermont and Florida

# Roemer's fescue

*Festuca roemeri*

This clump-forming, cool-season bunchgrass with fine-textured foliage sometimes has a bluish cast.

**BLOOM TIME** spring and summer

**MAXIMUM HEIGHT** 2 feet

**SOIL MOISTURE** average

**LARVAL HOST TO** woodland skipper (*Ochlodes sylvanoides*)

**NATIVE RANGE** West Coast of the United States and Canada

# Switchgrass

*Panicum virgatum*

This warm-season bunchgrass forms dense, tidy clumps and sports reddish purple seed heads and bright yellow color in the fall.

**BLOOM TIME** summer

**MAXIMUM HEIGHT** 6 feet

**SOIL MOISTURE** average

**LARVAL HOST TO** Delaware skipper (*Anatrytone logan*), Hobomok skipper (*Poanes hobomok*)

**NATIVE RANGE** southern Great Basin and the desert Southwest; east of the Rockies in both the United States and Canada

# Tufted hairgrass

*Deschampsia cespitosa*

This cool-season bunchgrass has abundant, fine-textured seed heads. Adapts to a variety of growing conditions.

**BLOOM TIME** summer

**MAXIMUM HEIGHT** 3 feet

**SOIL MOISTURE** wet

**LARVAL HOST TO** Juba skipper (*Hesperia juba*), umber skipper (*Poanes melane*)

**NATIVE RANGE** western United States and Canada; northern Mexico

# Tussock sedge

*Carex stricta*

This grasslike plant with attractive foliage sometimes grows in discrete tufts up to a few feet wide. Prefers full sun and damp or occasionally flooded soils.

**BLOOM TIME** spring

**MAXIMUM HEIGHT** 3 feet

**SOIL MOISTURE** wet

**LARVAL HOST TO** black dash (*Euphyes conspicua*), dun skipper (*Euphyes vestris*), eyed brown (*Lethe eurydice eurydice*)

**NATIVE RANGE** New England and eastern Canada west to the Great Lakes

# Vine mesquite

*Panicum obtusum*

This warm-season stoloniferous grass can spread by rhizomes. Prefers moist soils.

**BLOOM TIME** summer

**MAXIMUM HEIGHT** 3 feet

**SOIL MOISTURE** average to wet

**LARVAL HOST TO** dotted roadside skipper (*Amblyscirtes eos*)

**NATIVE RANGE** Utah east to Kansas and south through Mexico

# Butterfly pea
*Clitoria mariana*

This herbaceous plant usually has a vining habit but sometimes grows erect; very showy flowers. Prefers sandy soils.

**BLOOM TIME** summer

**FLOWER COLOR** purple or blue

**LIFE CYCLE** perennial

**SOIL MOISTURE** dry

**NECTAR VALUE** no

**LARVAL HOST TO** long-tailed skipper (*Urbanus proteus*)

**NATIVE RANGE** southeastern United States

# California pipevine

*Aristolochia californica*

This woody vine has unique pipe-shaped flowers and deciduous foliage. Prefers part shade and moist soil.

**BLOOM TIME** winter and spring

**FLOWER COLOR** green and red

**LIFE CYCLE** perennial

**SOIL MOISTURE** average to wet

**NECTAR VALUE** no

**LARVAL HOST TO** pipevine swallowtail (*Battus philenor*)

**NATIVE RANGE** California

# Desert pipevine

*Aristolochia watsonii*

This herbaceous vine has pipe-shaped flowers and elongated, arrow-shaped leaves. Prefers part shade and tolerates drought.

**BLOOM TIME** spring and summer

**FLOWER COLOR** green and red

**LIFE CYCLE** perennial

**SOIL MOISTURE** dry

**NECTAR VALUE** no

**LARVAL HOST TO** pipevine swallowtail (*Battus philenor*)

**NATIVE RANGE** Arizona, New Mexico, and northern Mexico

# Maypops

*Passiflora incarnata*

This herbaceous vine has highly unique flowers, deciduous foliage, and edible fruit. Tolerates drought and can spread by root suckers.

**BLOOM TIME** summer

**FLOWER COLOR** purple

**LIFE CYCLE** perennial

**SOIL MOISTURE** average to dry

**NECTAR VALUE** yes

**LARVAL HOST TO** crimson-patched longwing (*Heliconius erato*), Gulf fritillary (*Agraulis vanillae*), Julia (*Dryas iulia*), Plebeian sphinx (*Paratraea plebeja*), variegated fritillary (*Euptoieta claudia*), zebra longwing (*Heliconius charithonia*)

**NATIVE RANGE** southeastern United States

# Virginia snakeroot

*Aristolochia serpentaria*

This herbaceous vine has pipe-shaped flowers and elongated, heart-shaped leaves; foliage is deciduous. Prefers to grow in shade.

**BLOOM TIME** spring and summer

**FLOWER COLOR** green and red

**LIFE CYCLE** perennial

**SOIL MOISTURE** average to dry

**NECTAR VALUE** no

**LARVAL HOST TO** pipevine swallowtail (*Battus philenor*), polydamas swallowtail (*Battus polydamas*)

**NATIVE RANGE** eastern United States, excluding the Upper Midwest and most of New England

# Black elderberry

*Sambucus nigra*

Grows as a deciduous shrub or small tree with edible berries. Prefers moist soil but can be quite drought tolerant once established.

**BLOOM TIME** summer

**FLOWER COLOR** white

**MAXIMUM HEIGHT** 20 feet

**SOIL MOISTURE** wet

**NECTAR VALUE** limited

**LARVAL HOST TO** spring azure (*Celastrina ladon*)

**NATIVE RANGE** United States and Canada, except some large swaths of the central states and provinces; into southern Mexico

# Black hawthorn

*Crataegus douglasii*

Grows as a deciduous shrub or small tree with edible berries. Prefers full sun but tolerates partial shade.

**BLOOM TIME** spring

**FLOWER COLOR** white

**MAXIMUM HEIGHT** 30 feet

**SOIL MOISTURE** average to wet

**NECTAR VALUE** yes

**LARVAL HOST TO** gray hairstreak (*Strymon melinus*), mourning cloak (*Nymphalis antiopa*), pale tiger swallowtail (*Papilio eurymedon*), western tiger swallowtail (*Papilio rutulus*)

**NATIVE RANGE** northwestern United States and western Canada

# Black huckleberry

*Gaylussacia baccata*

This deciduous colony-forming shrub has nice fall color and edible berries that also attract birds. Tolerates partial shade.

**BLOOM TIME** spring

**FLOWER COLOR** white or pinkish red

**MAXIMUM HEIGHT** 4 feet

**SOIL MOISTURE** average to dry

**NECTAR VALUE** yes

**LARVAL HOST TO** brown elfin (*Callophrys augustinus*), Gordian sphinx (*Sphinx gordius*), Henry's elfin (*Callophrys henrici*), huckleberry sphinx (*Paonias astylus*)

**NATIVE RANGE** northeastern United States and eastern Canada

# Buckbrush

*Ceanothus cuneatus*

This slow-growing evergreen shrub has abundant, fragrant flowers. Highly adaptable and very drought tolerant.

**BLOOM TIME** summer

**FLOWER COLOR** white

**MAXIMUM HEIGHT** 8 feet

**SOIL MOISTURE** dry

**NECTAR VALUE** yes

**LARVAL HOST TO** California hairstreak (*Satyrium californica*), California tortoiseshell (*Nymphalis californica*), ceanothus silkmoth (*Hyalophora euryalus*), echo blue (*Celastrina echo*), hedgerow hairstreak (*Satyrium saepium*), Pacuvius duskywing (*Erynnis pacuvius*), western green hairstreak (*Callophrys affinis*), white-streaked saturnia moth (*Saturnia albofasciata*)

**NATIVE RANGE** Oregon, California, and Baja California

# Buttonbush

*Cephalanthus occidentalis*

Unique, pincushion-like flowers are very attractive to butterflies and bees. Tolerates partial shade, will survive periodic flooding, and is a great candidate for rain gardens. Also tolerates clay soils.

**BLOOM TIME** summer

**FLOWER COLOR** white

**MAXIMUM HEIGHT** 15 feet

**SOIL MOISTURE** wet

**NECTAR VALUE** yes

**LARVAL HOST TO** hydrangea sphinx (*Darapsa versicolor*), royal walnut moth (*Citheronia regalis*), titan sphinx (*Aellopos titan*)

**NATIVE RANGE** eastern United States and Canada; California, Arizona, New Mexico, and northern Mexico

# California buckwheat

*Eriogonum fasciculatum*

This evergreen shrub is a favored nectar source of many butterflies, especially blues and hairstreaks. Very drought tolerant.

**BLOOM TIME** summer

**FLOWER COLOR** white and pink

**MAXIMUM HEIGHT** 3 feet

**SOIL MOISTURE** average to dry

**NECTAR VALUE** yes

**LARVAL HOST TO** Acmon blue (*Plebejus acmon*), blue copper (*Lycaena heteronea*), Electra buckmoth (*Hemileuca electra*), Gorgon copper (*Lycaena gorgon*), lupine blue (*Plebejus lupine*), western green hairstreak (*Callophrys affinis*)

**NATIVE RANGE** southwestern United States and northern Mexico

# Chickasaw plum

*Prunus angustifolia*

This deciduous, thicket-forming shrub or small tree has fragrant flowers and edible fruit and is broadly used as a larval host.

**BLOOM TIME** spring

**FLOWER COLOR** white

**MAXIMUM HEIGHT** 30 feet

**SOIL MOISTURE** average to dry

**NECTAR VALUE** yes

**LARVAL HOST TO** black-waved flannel moth (*Lagoa crispata*), blinded sphinx (*Paonias excaecata*), cecropia moth (*Hyalophora cecropia*), coral hairstreak (*Satyrium titus*), elm sphinx (*Ceratomia amyntor*), hummingbird clearwing moth (*Hemaris thysbe*), imperial moth (*Eacles imperialis*), Io moth (*Automeris io*), polyphemus moth (*Antheraea polyphemus*), promethea moth (*Callosamia promethea*), red-spotted purple (*Limenitis arthemis astyanax*), small-eyed sphinx (*Paonias myops*), spring azure (*Celastrina ladon*), striped hairstreak (*Satyrium liparops*), tiger swallowtail (*Papilio glaucus*)

**NATIVE RANGE** southeastern United States

# Chokecherry

*Prunus virginiana*

This deciduous, thicket-forming shrub or small tree has showy, fragrant flowers and edible berries and is a widely used larval host.

**BLOOM TIME** spring

**FLOWER COLOR** white

**MAXIMUM HEIGHT** 25 feet

**SOIL MOISTURE** average

**NECTAR VALUE** yes

**LARVAL HOST TO** black-waved flannel moth (*Lagoa crispata*), blinded sphinx (*Paonias excaecata*), cecropia moth (*Hyalophora cecropia*), coral hairstreak (*Satyrium titus*), cynthia moth (*Samia cynthia*), elm sphinx (*Ceratomia amyntor*), Glover's silkmoth (*Hyalophora columbia gloveri*), hummingbird

clearwing moth (*Hemaris thysbe*), imperial moth (*Eacles imperialis*), Io moth (*Automeris io*), polyphemus moth (*Antheraea polyphemus*), promethea moth (*Callosamia promethea*), red-spotted purple (*Limenitis arthemis astyanax*), small-eyed sphinx (*Paonias myops*), spring azure (*Celastrina ladon*), striped hairstreak (*Satyrium liparops*), tiger swallowtail (*Papilio glaucus*), twin-spotted sphinx (*Smerinthus jamaicensis*), Weidemeyer's admiral (*Limenitis weidemeyerii*)

**NATIVE RANGE** United States and Canada, except the southeastern states; northern Mexico

# Coastal plain willow

*Salix caroliniana*

In addition to being a larval host for many species, this deciduous small to medium tree or large shrub has male flowers that provide a source of spring pollen for bees. Requires consistently moist to wet soils.

**BLOOM TIME** spring

**FLOWER COLOR** yellow

**MAXIMUM HEIGHT** 30 feet

**SOIL MOISTURE** wet

**NECTAR VALUE** limited

**LARVAL HOST TO** black-waved flannel moth (*Lagoa crispata*), blinded sphinx (*Paonias excaecata*), cecropia moth (*Hyalophora cecropia*), elm sphinx (*Ceratomia amyntor*), imperial moth (*Eacles imperialis*), Io moth (*Automeris io*), modest sphinx (*Pachysphinx modesta*), mourning cloak (*Nymphalis antiopa*), polyphemus moth (*Antheraea polyphemus*), promethea moth (*Callosamia promethea*), red-spotted purple (*Limenitis arthemis astyanax*), viceroy (*Limenitis archippus*)

**NATIVE RANGE** southeastern United States and the Mid-Atlantic region

# False indigo bush

*Amorpha fruticosa*

This deciduous, thicket-forming shrub should not be planted outside its native range; it is considered weedy or invasive in the northeastern United States and the state of Washington. May need supplemental water during dry periods.

**BLOOM TIME** summer

**FLOWER COLOR** purple

**MAXIMUM HEIGHT** 15 feet

**SOIL MOISTURE** wet

**NECTAR VALUE** yes

**LARVAL HOST TO** clouded sulphur (*Colias philodice*), gray hairstreak (*Strymon melinus*), hoary edge (*Achalarus lyciades*), Io moth (*Automeris io*), marine blue (*Leptotes marina*), silver-spotted skipper (*Epargyreus clarus*), southern dogface (*Zerene cesonia*)

**NATIVE RANGE** central, southwestern, and southeastern United States; eastern Canada; northern Mexico

# Hollyleaf cherry

*Prunus ilicifolia*

This evergreen shrub or tree has abundant white flower spikes and shiny leaves. Requires well-drained soils.

**BLOOM TIME** spring

**FLOWER COLOR** white

**MAXIMUM HEIGHT** 15 feet

**SOIL MOISTURE** average to dry

**NECTAR VALUE** yes

**LARVAL HOST TO** California hairstreak (*Satyrium californica*), Lorquin's admiral (*Limenitis lorquini*), Nevada buckmoth (*Hemileuca nevadensis*), pale tiger swallowtail (*Papilio eurymedon*), tiger swallowtail (*Papilio glaucus*)

**NATIVE RANGE** California and Baja California

# Narrowleaf willow

*Salix exigua*

The male flowers of this deciduous shrub or tree provide pollen for bees in the spring. Requires moist soils and does not tolerate shade.

**BLOOM TIME** spring

**FLOWER COLOR** yellow

**MAXIMUM HEIGHT** 15 feet

**SOIL MOISTURE** wet

**NECTAR VALUE** limited

**LARVAL HOST TO** California hairstreak (*Satyrium californica*), Lorquin's admiral (*Limenitis lorquini*), mourning cloak (*Nymphalis antiopa*), sylvan hairstreak (*Satyrium sylvinus*), tiger swallowtail (*Papilio glaucus*)

**NATIVE RANGE** western United States and Canada; northern Mexico

# New Jersey tea

*Ceanothus americanus*

This deciduous, drought-tolerant shrub is a magnet for butterflies, bees, and many other insects. Somewhat slow growing and prone to deer browsing.

**BLOOM TIME** summer

**FLOWER COLOR** white

**MAXIMUM HEIGHT** 4 feet

**SOIL MOISTURE** average

**NECTAR VALUE** yes

**LARVAL HOST TO** mottled duskywing (*Erynnis martialis*), spring azure (*Celastrina ladon*), summer azure (*Celastrina neglecta*)

**NATIVE RANGE** eastern United States and Canada

# Oak

*Quercus* species

Oaks vary significantly in growth rate, size at maturity, and ornamental value but all provide valuable habitat for multiple life stages of numerous beneficial insects, especially if a layer of oak leaf litter is left on the ground. White oaks may be more resistant to disease and insects than other species.

MAXIMUM HEIGHT from 6 to more than 100 feet

SOIL MOISTURE variable, with some species adapted to arid environments and others to wetland habitats

NECTAR VALUE no

LARVAL HOST TO banded hairstreak (*Satyrium calanus*), black-waved flannel moth (*Lagoa crispata*), blinded sphinx (*Paonias excaecata*), California hairstreak (*Satyrium californica*), California sister (*Adelpha californica*), Edward's hairstreak (*Satyrium edwardsii*), golden hairstreak (*Habrodais grunus*), gold-hunter's hairstreak (*Satyrium auretorum*), Horace's duskywing (*Erynnis horatius*), imperial moth (*Eacles imperialis*), Io moth (*Automeris io*), Juvenal's duskywing (*Erynnis juvenalis*), mournful duskywing (*Erynnis tristis*), oak hairstreak (*Satyrium favonius*), polyphemus moth (*Antheraea polyphemus*), Propertius duskywing (*Erynnis propertius*), red-banded hairstreak (*Calycopis cecrops*), rosy maple moth (*Dryocampa rubicunda*), sleepy duskywing (*Erynnis brizo*), stinging rose caterpillar moth (*Parasa indetermina*), striped hairstreak (*Satyrium liparops*), waved sphinx (*Ceratomia undulosa*), white M hairstreak (*Parrhasius m-album*)

NATIVE RANGE broad distribution across southern Canada, the United States, and Mexico, with the exception of the inland Northwest and the northern Rockies

# Oceanspray

*Holodiscus discolor*

This deciduous, multi-stemmed shrub bears numerous sprays of fragrant tiny white flowers. Prefers partial shade.

**BLOOM TIME** summer

**FLOWER COLOR** white

**MAXIMUM HEIGHT** 12 feet

**SOIL MOISTURE** average

**NECTAR VALUE** yes

**LARVAL HOST TO** Lorquin's admiral (*Limenitis lorquini*), pale tiger swallowtail (*Papilio eurymedon*), spring azure (*Celastrina ladon*)

**NATIVE RANGE** western United States and Canada

# Oregon cherry

*Prunus emarginata*

This deciduous, thicket-forming shrub or small tree has berries that attract birds. Prefers moist soils and good drainage.

**BLOOM TIME** spring

**FLOWER COLOR** white

**MAXIMUM HEIGHT** 80 feet

**SOIL MOISTURE** average to wet

**NECTAR VALUE** yes

**LARVAL HOST TO** blinded sphinx (*Paonias excaecata*), elegant sphinx (*Sphinx perelegans*), Lorquin's admiral (*Limenitis lorquini*), pale tiger swallowtail (*Papilio eurymedon*), small-eyed sphinx (*Paonias myops*), spring azure (*Celastrina ladon*), twin-spotted sphinx (*Smerinthus jamaicensis*), western tiger swallowtail (*Papilio rutulus*)

**NATIVE RANGE** western United States, British Columbia, and northern Mexico

# Purple sage

*Salvia dorrii*

This evergreen shrub has striking blooms and silver foliage. Thrives under dry conditions and requires excellent drainage.

**BLOOM TIME** late spring and early summer

**FLOWER COLOR** purple

**MAXIMUM HEIGHT** 3 feet

**SOIL MOISTURE** dry

**NECTAR VALUE** yes

**LARVAL HOST TO** elegant sphinx (*Sphinx perelegans*)

**NATIVE RANGE** western United States

# Pussy willow

*Salix discolor*

This deciduous shrub or small tree is broadly used as a larval host. Male plants provide a source of spring pollen for bees.

**BLOOM TIME** early spring

**FLOWER COLOR** yellow-green

**MAXIMUM HEIGHT** 20 feet

**SOIL MOISTURE** wet

**NECTAR VALUE** limited

**LARVAL HOST TO** Acadian hairstreak (*Satyrium acadica*), black-waved flannel moth (*Lagoa crispata*), cecropia moth (*Hyalophora cecropia*), Compton's tortoiseshell (*Nymphalis l-album*), cynthia moth (*Samia cynthia*), dreamy duskywing (*Erynnis icelus*), eastern tiger swallowtail (*Papilio glaucus*), elm sphinx (*Ceratomia amyntor*), imperial moth (*Eacles imperialis*), Io moth (*Automeris io*), modest sphinx (*Pachysphinx modesta*), mourning cloak (*Nymphalis antiopa*), polyphemus moth (*Antheraea polyphemus*), promethea moth (*Callosamia promethea*), red-spotted purple (*Limenitis arthemis astyanax*), small-eyed sphinx (*Paonias myops*), twin-spotted sphinx (*Smerinthus jamaicensis*), viceroy (*Limenitis archippus*)

**NATIVE RANGE** northern tier United States into Canada

# Rose mallow

*Hibiscus moscheutos*

This deciduous shrub offers spectacularly showy flowers and heart-shaped leaves. Individual flowers are short lived but the species' bloom period is lengthy.

**BLOOM TIME** summer

**FLOWER COLOR** white or pink

**MAXIMUM HEIGHT** 8 feet

**SOIL MOISTURE** wet

**NECTAR VALUE** no

**LARVAL HOST TO** common checkered skipper (*Pyrgus communis*), gray hairstreak (*Strymon melinus*), Io moth (*Automeris io*), pearly wood nymph (*Eudryas unio*)

**NATIVE RANGE** eastern United States

# Rose spirea

*Spiraea douglasii*

Fuzzy terminal clusters of bright pink blossoms adorn this deciduous, thicket-forming shrub. Prefers moist soils and can spread through rhizomes.

**BLOOM TIME** summer

**FLOWER COLOR** pink

**MAXIMUM HEIGHT** 6 feet

**SOIL MOISTURE** average to wet

**NECTAR VALUE** yes

**LARVAL HOST TO** unknown

**NATIVE RANGE** northwestern United States and British Columbia

# Saskatoon serviceberry

*Amelanchier alnifolia*

This deciduous shrub has fragrant flowers, edible berries, and nice fall color. Does well in full sun or part shade.

**BLOOM TIME** spring

**FLOWER COLOR** white

**MAXIMUM HEIGHT** 12 feet

**SOIL MOISTURE** average to wet

**NECTAR VALUE** yes

**LARVAL HOST TO** pale tiger swallowtail (*Papilio eurymedon*), two-tailed swallowtail (*Papilio multicaudata*), western tiger swallowtail (*Papilio rutulus*)

**NATIVE RANGE** western United States and Canada

# Scouler's willow

*Salix scouleriana*

Male instances of this tall, deciduous shrub or tree provide bees with a source of pollen in the spring. Requires moist soil and is hardy and fast growing.

**BLOOM TIME** spring

**FLOWER COLOR** yellow

**MAXIMUM HEIGHT** 30 feet

**SOIL MOISTURE** wet

**NECTAR VALUE** limited

**LARVAL HOST TO** blinded sphinx (*Paonias excaecata*), Lorquin's admiral (*Limenitis lorquini*), modest sphinx (*Pachysphinx modesta*), mourning cloak (*Nymphalis antiopa*), twin-spotted sphinx (*Smerinthus jamaicensis*), white admiral (*Limenitis arthemis arthemis*)

**NATIVE RANGE** western United States and Canada; northern Mexico

# Spicebush

*Lindera benzoin*

This deciduous shrub provides fragrant fruits and foliage and nice fall color. Plants bear either male or female flowers; in late summer, the berries on female plants attract birds. Does well in part shade.

**BLOOM TIME** spring

**FLOWER COLOR** yellow

**MAXIMUM HEIGHT** 12 feet

**SOIL MOISTURE** average to wet

**NECTAR VALUE** no

**LARVAL HOST TO** cynthia moth (*Samia cynthia*), eastern tiger swallowtail (*Papilio glaucus*), imperial moth (*Eacles imperialis*), promethea moth (*Callosamia promethea*), spicebush swallowtail (*Papilio troilus*), tulip tree beauty (*Epimecis hortaria*)

**NATIVE RANGE** eastern United States and Ontario

# Yellow rabbitbrush

*Chrysothamnus viscidiflorus*

This important late-season nectar source has wind-dispersed seed and brilliant yellow flower clusters that are often sticky at their bases. Tolerates drought.

**BLOOM TIME** late summer and fall

**FLOWER COLOR** yellow

**MAXIMUM HEIGHT** 4 feet

**SOIL MOISTURE** dry

**NECTAR VALUE** yes

**LARVAL HOST TO** sagebrush checkerspot (*Chlosyne acastus*)

**NATIVE RANGE** western United States and British Columbia

Great butterfly gardens blur the line between garden and wilderness.

# Plant selection, installation, and maintenance

**T**HE PROCESS OF INSTALLING a butterfly garden has less in common with ornamental gardening and more in common with prairie restoration, reforestation, and other types of natural habitat reclamation. While the actual installation process may call upon many of the same skills and strategies as any gardening project, the end goal is to create something truly wild.

Remarkably few native plant communities remain in North America. Whether we look at a typical suburban yard or the vast grasslands of the West, we find that most places are now dominated by plants that originally came from somewhere else. This transformation happened slowly in many cases and was preceded or aided by the plow, herbicides, nonnative grazing animals, and well-intentioned gardeners, farmers, ranchers, and botanists. Creating these novel plant communities took time and effort. Deconstructing them and returning the landscape to something closer to native, even on a small scale, also requires time and effort.

## SOURCING NATIVE PLANTS

The struggle to define *native* has become increasingly complex among plant ecologists in recent years. In particular, many scientists and conservationists now recognize that even though a plant may be native to a wide geographic area, subpopulations within that plant's range may require different habitat conditions in order to thrive. For example, while showy milkweed (*Asclepias speciosa*) is native to much of the central and western United States, individual plants growing

Native wildflowers can fit into any size garden and can be integrated with garden art to create spaces every bit as interesting as gardens dominated by exotic ornamentals.

in Iowa may have different precipitation requirements than plants found in California. Similarly, those respective showy milkweed plants may have different temperature and day-length requirements to trigger flowering, and they may have different tolerances to local plant diseases.

With these differences in mind, the conservation community is increasingly concerned that long-distance movement of plants may reduce the success of habitat restoration efforts and that moving plants across long distances may alter the genetics of a local plant community (through cross-pollination of distinctly different members of the same plant species).

Western tiger swallowtail (*Papilio rutulus*) feeds on the nectar of showy milkweed (*Asclepias speciosa*).

Plant selection, installation, and maintenance

In response to these concerns, like most conservation organizations today, we recommend using local ecotype native plants and seeds wherever possible. An *ecotype* is a locally adapted genetic population within a species, and *local ecotype* refers to seeds and plants either harvested from a local source or grown using locally sourced parent material. Local ecotype plant materials are adapted to the soils and climate conditions in your area and are likely to establish and grow well. Another very important factor when purchasing plants, described in more detail later in this chapter, is that you must ensure that they have not been treated with pesticides that will harm insects that feed on them.

## EVALUATING THE PLANT SELECTION AT YOUR LOCAL NURSERY

Many garden centers have a limited selection of natives. To find local ecotype plants, seek out nurseries that specialize in native plants or at least have a dedicated native plant section.

Similarly, to find local ecotype seeds, we recommend companies that specialize in native wildflower seed for a particular region. In most cases, wildflower seed available from large retail chains and garden centers will not have been locally grown and many of the species offered will not be native to your region. If you

Many garden centers, like this one, have a limited selection of native plants. Specialty native plant nurseries offer better options.

# Conserving wild plants

**PLEASE DO NOT DIG** wild plants from parks, roadsides, natural areas, and other public or private lands to transplant them on your property. In addition to being illegal in most instances, doing this prevents wildlife from using the plants, deprives other people of the chance to enjoy them, and may impact the plant population's ability to reproduce. Also, the chance of plant survival may be low due to transplant shock and some plants' need for particular growing conditions. An exception to this rule is salvaging plants from areas slated for development or road construction (be sure to secure any necessary permits or permission).

shop for seed online, keep in mind that many vendors carry seed that is sourced from all over the country, and sometimes outside of the country, rather than from within the area where their company is headquartered. We encourage you to ask prospective seed vendors for information about the origin of their seed and try to use seed that is as locally sourced as possible.

The availability of native plants and seeds, and particularly of local ecotype materials, is widely variable across regions. If you do not already have a favorite native plant nursery in your area, refer to the Xerces Society's Pollinator Conservation Resource Center web page or other online native plant resources listed in "Additional Resources" in the back of the book to find options close to home. Additionally, native plant societies, botanical gardens, and soil and water conservation districts often hold annual plant sales. By contacting these organizations and signing up for their newsletters or mailing lists, you can stay informed about seasonal events such as plant swaps or local sales.

Before buying plants, ask nursery and garden center staff whether any persistent insecticides were used during propagation.

## ENSURING INSECTICIDE-FREE NURSERY PLANTS

An emerging trend in the nursery industry poses significant risk to invertebrate wildlife that feed on plants. Driven by demand for blemish-free stock, nurseries have increasingly adopted a group of insecticides with systemic action for many ornamental plant applications. Unlike older classes of insecticides that were formulated to kill pests on contact, systemic insecticides are absorbed by plants upon application and then distributed throughout plant tissues, sometimes including pollen and nectar. This mode of action provides long-lasting protection against pests such as aphids, but these chemicals also make plants potentially toxic to bees, butterflies, and other beneficial insects that eat pollen, sip nectar, or feed on plant tissues. A 2013 pilot study by Friends of the Earth revealed that more than 50 percent of common nursery plants sampled contained systemic insecticide residues. The plants were purchased from retail garden centers across the United States.

To ensure that you don't bring a toxic plant into your butterfly garden, we strongly recommend asking nursery or garden center staff whether their plants have been treated with systemic insecticides. If they are unable to provide an answer, you may want to exercise caution in making a purchase. In some cases, staff may offer to investigate your question and provide the information at a later date. Retail outlets that are not directly involved with plant propagation may not have information about insecticide use readily available; nurseries that grow their own stock, especially smaller local native plant nurseries, will be in a better position to provide such details.

## SEEDS OR TRANSPLANTS?

While establishing native plant gardens from seed may seem daunting to casual gardeners, good justifications exist for working with seed. Similarly, transplants provide several benefits that may justify their use. Pragmatically, however, you may need to seek out and use a combination of both seeds and transplants since many native plant species will only be commercially available in one form or the other. In assessing which planting approach to use, consider factors such as the plant's life cycle, your budget, how quickly you want the plants to mature, and the size of the planting area.

Planting from seed can be a low-cost approach to establishing wildflowers, particularly if you intend to plant a relatively large area (250 square feet or more). Seeding is often an economical way to introduce a broad diversity of species to your garden. For uncommon species that are not typically available from nurseries, seed may be the only available source of material to work with. Moreover, it is usually more cost effective to plant annual wildflowers from seed, and it may prove easier to obtain seed of annual species than transplants. Biennials and perennials can also be effectively established through seeding, depending on the availability of plant materials. Many of these plants, especially some annuals and biennials, will self-seed, while others may need to be replanted in consecutive years. While somewhat less effective at reseeding themselves, perennials may spread locally through lateral root growth. For trees and shrubs, there is typically no question: due to their slower growth rate, it is almost always more effective to establish them from transplants rather than from seed.

In contrast, while transplants are more expensive than seed, they typically establish and begin producing flowers more quickly, thus providing habitat sooner than plants grown from seed. Some perennial wildflowers take two or more years to bloom when started from seed, but transplants often flower the

**TOP:** Uncommon wildflowers and grasses may be available only as seeds from specialty nurseries. If they are properly planted and well tended, they can offer excellent value for the cost.
**BOTTOM:** Transplants offer the advantage of faster establishment but are relatively expensive compared to seed.

first year. Another advantage of transplants is that when provided with adequate water, they will be more competitive against weeds in their first year. In comparison, plants started from seed will be more susceptible to drought stress and competition from weeds.

## PREPARING FOR PLANTING

Whether you establish your garden from transplants or sow wildflower seed, controlling weed growth before planting is critical to the success of your efforts. Before seeding in particular, thorough preparation of the planting area to reduce competition from weeds is essential. Once the seeded wildflowers start to germinate, weed control options are limited, and it is far more effective to eliminate the weeds first.

If weed growth is sparse in the area slated for planting, and the weeds there have not been difficult to manage in past years, you may be able to prepare the area simply by pulling the weeds by hand. If the weed cover is dense and weeds have been allowed to go to seed over multiple years, we recommend at least a full

Controlling weeds before seeding or transplanting is essential to ensure the successful establishment of your chosen garden plants.

growing season of focused weed control. Nonselective herbicides, such as those available from a hardware store, may have a limited use in some cases (such as invasive species control), but they may be largely ineffective against dormant weed seed in the soil. For garden-sized butterfly habitat, solarization and smothering are the most effective alternatives for preparing a new garden area.

If you are preparing new areas for wildflower seeding, we *strongly* recommend using solarization. When performed properly, it will consistently produce a very clean, weed-free planting area.

## SOLARIZATION

Extensive multiyear and multistate field trials conducted by the Xerces Society have found solarization to be the single most effective method for removing weeds and dormant weed seed from areas identified for habitat restoration. While the use of solarization has some limitations (for example, it is difficult to conduct over a large area, and it may not be suitable for areas prone to erosion), overall the method has proven to be more effective than herbicides and is now our habitat restoration method of choice.

To solarize a weedy area that receives full sun throughout the day, place a sheet of clear, UV-stabilized plastic film (such as used for high tunnel greenhouses) over the area at the beginning of summer. By trapping heat from the sun over several months during the hottest time of the year, the plastic will raise the temperature of the upper soil layers enough to kill most weed seed. Before laying the plastic, remove existing weed growth by mowing or tilling the site to eliminate stiff stems or debris that might puncture the plastic. When laying the plastic, bury the edges with soil to prevent airflow between the plastic and the ground. If the area is large or experiences windy conditions, use a few large rocks or boards to weigh down the center of the plastic to prevent wind from

Solarization, which is done by placing clear plastic film over the soil surface and using heat from the sun to kill weeds and weed seed, is a very effective, herbicide-free approach to controlling weed growth in preparation for planting.

lifting it. Greenhouse repair tape can be used to mend tears in the plastic, as needed. After you remove the plastic in late summer or early fall (before the temperatures cool down), you can plant or seed the area immediately with little to no weed competition.

The major drawback of solarization is the waste plastic generated in the process. To reduce the amount of plastic headed to the landfill, we try to treat the sheet carefully and prevent any rips or holes from forming. By carefully rolling it up after using it, we can store it and reuse it on additional areas, gradually controlling invasive weeds and creating new areas for planting native wildflowers year after year with the same sheet of plastic. If you must dispose of the plastic, take it to a local plastic bag recycling facility.

## SMOTHERING

If you intend to plant a new garden only with transplants rather than broadcasting seed, you can also prepare new garden areas by smothering weeds with layers of newspaper or cardboard, and mulch. Most plants cannot survive without access to sunlight. This approach is most effective if started in the spring. Before laying down any materials, you will need to mow, hand weed, or rake the area to reduce the amount of vegetative cover. Black-and-white newsprint

Before you transplant, you can control weeds by covering them with layers of newspaper, cardboard, or other materials that block the plants' access to sunlight, effectively smothering them. Ideally, this gardener would have applied several overlapping layers of cardboard and held them down with mulch to ensure success.

or sturdy pieces of plain brown cardboard are the best materials to use, rather than those with a glossy coating. Five to ten layers of newspaper can be effective where weed pressure is minimal (such as areas of lawn grass); make sure to overlap the sheets significantly so that there are no gaps between them where light can enter. Wetting the sheets down as you go will help keep them in place. Alternatively, you can apply a layer of overlapping pieces of cardboard. After laying the newspaper or cardboard, cover it with up to a 6-inch layer of mulch. A variety of materials—including shredded

bark, wood chips, whole leaves, shredded leaves, or lawn clippings—can be used. Once this is done, leave the area undisturbed until the end of summer. If you intend to do some fall transplanting, you can create individual planting holes in the mulch layer rather than removing all of the materials.

## TRANSPLANTING

Before installing transplants, consider the approximate dimensions of each plant at maturity to ensure that you leave enough space for them to fill in over time. One simple trick that can help you visualize how the garden will mature is to stage the transplants in their pots over the planting area before installing them in the ground. Once you have the plants positioned, walk around the planting area and observe it from different angles, looking for gaps that might provide a space for weeds, and looking for plants that may ultimately grow much larger and shade out their companions.

When you are installing a new garden, first position the plants in their pots around the planting area to help you visualize how they will fill out the area as they grow.

Transplanting can be done any time the ground can be worked but should be timed to avoid prolonged periods of hot, dry, or windy weather. In desert areas of the southwestern United States, seasonal rainfall

Watering transplants immediately after they are installed and on a regular basis for the remainder of at least the first growing season is essential to ensure establishment.

transplanting, be sure to install the plants at least a few weeks before the first potential hard freeze. Similarly, spring transplanting should only be done after the threat of frost has passed.

Regardless of when you plant, you should water transplants thoroughly immediately after installing them. The need for continued watering will depend on local climate conditions, but transplants are likely to need at least an inch of water per week during their first year, except during natural rain events. Providing adequate water during the first summer is critical for establishment. Long, deep watering is best to encourage deep root system development; avoid shallow watering. Watering at the base of individual plants rather than overhead conserves water, decreases weed growth, and minimizes the growth of plant diseases.

Mulch around transplants to reduce weed competition and retain moisture while the plants become established. Suitable materials include wood chips, bark dust, weed-free straw, nut shells, or other regionally appropriate, weed-free mulch materials.

## SEEDING

Fall is usually the best time for planting wildflower seed. Exposure to cold temperatures and moist conditions during winter will typically stimulate

patterns dictate the best time for planting. In general, fall planting is best, particularly for spring-flowering species. This allows the plants to develop their root systems and may make them more resilient to dry summer conditions, thus reducing the need for watering during the following growing season. With fall

# Caution with tillage

**IN GENERAL,** rototilling is not an effective method in and of itself for weed control. While tilling breaks up existing weed cover and can provide a temporarily weed-free area, soil disturbance also brings dormant weed seeds to the soil surface. Those seeds, which may previously have been buried too deep to germinate, often receive the necessary water and warmth after rototilling to start growing and may ultimately contribute to more weed cover than previously existed. In addition, frequent tillage can degrade soil structure and decrease soil fertility, and it may harm beneficial soil-dwelling organisms.

germination in the spring, and winter precipitation can help work seed into the soil. Planting in early spring, when temperatures are still low and soil moisture is still high, may also be successful. Seeding in late spring or summer will usually result in somewhat lower germination and establishment during the remainder of the growing season, although some of the seed may germinate the following spring. If you plant late in the season, mixing the seed with moistened sand, vermiculite, or perlite (known as stratifying the seed) and then storing it in a household refrigerator for a few weeks beforehand may help enhance germination. After you have sown stratified seed, keep the soil in the planted area moist until the seeds germinate.

Once established, most native wildflowers grown from seed thrive with little or no supplemental water; unless you are experiencing drought conditions, it is usually not necessary to water your seedbed. However, if rainfall is scarce after the seeds germinate, you may need to do supplemental watering to ensure seedling survival. In general, keep watering to a minimum to

Wildflower and native grass seed is usually planted simply by scattering it onto the soil surface. You typically do not want to bury the seed.

help wildflowers outcompete nonnative weedy species that may require more soil moisture.

To establish wildflowers from seed, simply scatter the seed onto the soil surface by hand. Except for very large seed, you typically do not need to bury the seed (making wildflower establishment from seed different from planting a vegetable garden from seed). If your garden design features single-species blocks of color, those species can be planted separately in designated areas according to the seed package instructions. Alternatively, if you want mixed wildflowers, you can either purchase a preblended mix or assemble your own.

When you are sowing a blend of multiple seed types, it can be helpful to first mix the seed with an equal or greater volume of slightly dampened materials such as coarse-textured sand, fine-grained vermiculite, or sawdust. Including these materials ensures that species are evenly distributed within the mixture and helps you see where seed has landed on the soil surface. Wildflower seeds are highly variable in shape and size. If you have seed of multiple species that are packaged individually and are planning to blend them together, consider separating the species by seed size. For example, you may want to group the small seeds together, blend them with inert material and broadcast them, and then do the same for the large-seeded species.

You do not need to cover the seed with soil after planting, but it is important to achieve good seed-to-soil contact. For small areas (less than 100 square feet), simply walk over the seeded area to press the seeds into the soil with the soles of your shoes. For areas of several hundred square feet that are not in raised beds, a standard lawn roller (available for rent at many hardware stores) can be used to compact the seed into the ground. Once you have finished seeding, you can use floating row cover fabric as needed to protect seeds and small seedlings from predation by snails, birds, and small mammals.

## BUTTERFLY GARDEN MAINTENANCE

Because native plants are the foundation of most butterfly gardens, and because the best butterfly gardens have a slightly messy or unkempt appearance (to provide habitat for butterflies to develop through their egg, caterpillar, and pupal stages), maintenance demands are typically much less than for formal ornamental gardens of similar size. Still, on occasion, you may find that your butterfly garden is encroached upon

# Eco-lawns

**WHILE THERE IS** no substitute for native plant restoration, butterfly habitat can be enhanced across your landscape in ways other than through butterfly gardens alone. Lawns offer one such opportunity. From relatively simple changes such as letting nectar-producing weeds like dandelions grow, to more complex solutions like replacing nonnative turfgrass with low-growing native equivalents, multiple approaches are possible for enhancing the biodiversity of lawns.

When we are asked about eco-lawns, the Xerces Society typically recommends two approaches for consideration.

The first is to overseed turfgrass with low-growing Dutch white clover (*Trifolium repens*). The clover provides a source of nectar for butterflies and other insects, and is a host plant for several common butterflies such as the gray hairstreak (*Strymon melinus*), the eastern tailed blue (*Cupido comyntas*), the common sulphur (*Colias philodice*), and the orange sulphur (*Colias eurytheme*). The clover also fixes nitrogen to sustain the companion grass, eliminating the need for chemical fertilizers.

The second is to replace nonnative turfgrass with low-growing native equivalents that tolerate foot traffic and mowing. Depending on your region, native

Simple Dutch white clover (*Trifolium repens*) can add at least a little diversity to lawns, and a few species of butterflies will actually use it as a host plant. As an added benefit, clover fixes nitrogen in the soil, eliminating the need for lawn fertilizers.

grass species such as buffalo grass (*Bouteloua dactyloides*), prairie junegrass (*Koeleria macrantha*), and blue grama grass (*Bouteloua gracilis*) can all function as lawn species. These grasses have additional benefits over nonnative turfgrass in that they are host plants for many skipper butterflies, and they have deeper, more drought-resistant root systems. From this native-grass base, the turf can again be overseeded with Dutch white clover or further enhanced with lower-growing wildflowers such as blue-eyed grass (*Sisyrinchium* species) or wildflowers such as yarrow (*Achillea millefolium*) that can withstand occasional mowing.

The best butterfly gardens look semiwild and slightly overgrown, all of which makes maintenance relatively easy in comparison to more ornamental, manicured landscapes.

by some invasive weed, or one of the wildflowers that you intentionally planted is now crowding out other desirable species, or your best butterfly plants are under assault by aphids. If you live in an arid environment, you may feel compelled to reduce fire risks by tidying things up. These can all be reasons to take a closer look at the garden and make some management decisions. In most cases, some simple nudging, rather than a complete overhaul of the garden, will get things back on track.

## WEED CONTROL

Prevention is the most effective strategy for managing weeds in the butterfly garden. A layer of several

Plant selection, installation, and maintenance

While simple weeding may occasionally be necessary, it is best to leave some untidy areas even after the flowers have finished blooming.

For small spaces, hand pulling or precision hoeing is usually the most efficient and targeted method of weed control.

If you must use herbicides, such as for weed control in large meadows that are too big to hand weed, small hand sprayers or backpack sprayers allow for more targeted applications.

inches of mulch on the ground under plants may go a long way toward suppressing weeds. Even in the best of cases, however, some weeding will probably be necessary after your garden is installed. On a small scale (areas less than a few hundred square feet), hand pulling or precision hoeing is usually the most efficient and targeted approach.

For hoeing, a high-quality diamond hoe is an extremely useful tool. Unlike traditional garden hoes, which have a broad, blunt blade, diamond hoes have a blade that is narrow, thin, lightweight, and sharp (much like a kitchen paring knife). To use a diamond hoe, you pull the blade gently through the soil, severing weeds from their roots belowground. If some weeds continue to resprout from the roots, regular hoeing will eventually suppress most of the offenders. Another advantage of some diamond hoes is the longer handle length, which allows you to reach into meadow plantings for weeding without trampling desirable plants in the process.

For very large garden or meadow areas (more than a few hundred square feet), spot treatments with an herbicide might be the preferred approach to weed control. When you use any herbicide, always exercise caution to avoid harming desirable plants and to minimize risks to your health. Always read and follow all herbicide label instructions.

The same garden in fall and winter. Leaving some of the dead vegetation standing provides hibernation spots and overwintering habitat for butterflies and other wildlife.

Small hand sprayers and backpack sprayers are generally fine for most herbicide treatments. When you use a sprayer, be sure the nozzle is precise enough to not accidently spray anything other than the weed you are targeting. An even more accurate method is to wipe or brush the herbicide directly on foliage. Beyond sprayers, another very precise way to control specific plants (especially those with deep and extensive root systems) is to hand apply herbicides to the entire stem and foliage.

For hand application, first put on a tight-fitting gauntlet-type rubber glove (such as a dishwashing glove), then put a wrist-length cotton glove on top of the rubber glove. Next, spray a small amount of herbicide into the palm of the cotton glove, until it is damp. Finally, using your gloved hand, grasp low on the stem and pull the foliage through your hand, allowing the herbicide to contact as much of the plant as possible. Grip prickly plants, such as invasive thistles, carefully to avoid injury.

## ANNUAL CLEANUP

When fall arrives in temperate climates and plants begin to go dormant, the conventional management approach in ornamental gardens is to remove all the standing dead vegetation and accumulated leaf litter. However, these landscape components provide important overwintering habitat for butterflies.

Depending on the species and climate, various butterflies may spend the winter as eggs, caterpillars, adults, or pupae. Those that overwinter in the egg or caterpillar stage often do so on or near their host plants. This allows caterpillars to quickly begin feeding when new plant growth emerges in the spring. Thus, leaving larval host plants intact at the end of the season, rather than clearing away the dead aboveground growth, is very important to their survival. Similarly, butterflies that overwinter in the pupal stage usually attach their chrysalises to branches, twigs, or dead

Clean edging can help define the boundaries of the butterfly garden and make it look contained, intentional, and where necessary, in conformance with community vegetation rules.

plant stems. Avoid unnecessary winter pruning of shrubs or mowing of meadows to protect these pupation sites. Finally, leave an intact layer of leaf litter or stem thatch on the ground to provide refuge for multiple insect life stages by protecting them from extreme cold and desiccation.

If you need to selectively prune shrubs or clear away large dead stems (such as for aesthetic reasons), you can reduce your impact by stacking those branches and stems in a brush pile tucked away in the back of your garden. Winter is the time for such pruning since it will have less impact on the insect community than pruning during the growing season. With luck, insects pupating inside of those stems will still have a chance to emerge the following year, and the brush pile itself will become a nesting and overwintering feature for other insects.

## REDUCING FIRE HAZARDS

Butterfly gardens in arid climates and forested regions can require special management if the area is at risk

for wildfire. In such cases, leaving dead stems or brush piles in the garden should be avoided. Instead, maintain vegetation-free firebreaks created with pavers, rock mulch, stone walls, patios, and stone paths. Encouraging low-growing species and species that do not produce potentially flammable resins can also make a difference.

## COMMUNITY ASSOCIATION STANDARDS AND LOCAL LAWS

In some areas, butterfly garden maintenance requirements are driven by local housing association rules or municipal weed laws that restrict tall vegetation in residential landscapes. Such community rules should ideally be taken into account during the planning phase, before a new garden is established. In cases where such rules are already in place, it may be easier to conform to community standards by focusing on the removal of dried-out flower heads (deadheading) and regularly mowing immediately around the butterfly garden to maintain a clean border between the garden and the surrounding landscape. Artful picket fences, stone edging, or other ways of delineating the edges of the garden may also help contain the flowering chaos and ensure that the butterfly garden looks intentional.

A number of native plant societies offer model ordinance language for citizens seeking to change community weed and tall vegetation laws. Such model language typically requires actual native plant establishment (as opposed to simply letting existing turfgrass become overgrown), and sometimes includes setback requirements to reduce the potential for conflicts with neighbors. In some areas, additional language calling for annual mowing of any meadow-type habitat and control of specific noxious weeds is sometimes included. The various native plant organizations

This beneficial wheel bug (*Arilus cristatus*) is resting on Joe Pye weed, awaiting prey.

A Florida predatory stink bug (*Euthyrhynchus floridanus*) feeds on a brown stink bug. The same plants that attract butterflies will attract these and other beneficial insects, reducing the need for insecticides.

Extensive research now demonstrates that large wildflower plantings (such as butterfly gardens) can actually help reduce pest problems in adjacent fruit and vegetable crops by attracting beneficial insects. Similarly, the gentle wild bees that are attracted to such gardens can also be important crop pollinators.

offering support for the reform of local vegetation ordinances can often also offer resources highlighting the multiple benefits of native plants for discussions with policy makers and housing association board members.

## INSECTICIDE-FREE GARDENING

In general, no compelling reason exists to use insecticides in a butterfly garden. The appearance of various plant-feeding insects (other than butterfly caterpillars)

Plant selection, installation, and maintenance

is a positive sign of healthy biodiversity and represents a complex food web that supports other garden visitors such as songbirds and tree frogs.

In a few cases, though, introduced pest insects can wreak havoc on important butterfly plants. The most significant example of this is the invasive oleander aphid (*Aphis nerii*), a Eurasian pest that found its way to North America where it has become a damaging pest of milkweeds. In addition to feeding on the same plants that monarch butterflies depend upon (often weakening the plants in the process), oleander aphids likely transfer diseases between milkweed plants. In extreme cases those diseases may kill the plants completely. If significant numbers of these yellow-orange aphids are feeding on milkweed in your garden, the safest method of control is simply to crush any large and obvious aphid colonies or to carefully knock them off the plant stems with the spray of a garden hose.

Even some organic-approved insecticides like pyrethrins and rotenone can be harmful to pollinators. For the health and well-being of your butterflies, avoiding insecticides altogether is the best option.

## NATURAL PEST CONTROL

Rather than requiring insecticides to suppress pest populations, a well-designed butterfly garden usually hosts an abundance of beneficial predators that attack pests. Typically, beneficial insects such as syrphid flies, tiny parasitoid wasps, lacewings, fireflies, soldier beetles, and others depend upon diverse sources of food—including in many cases wildflower pollen or nectar. The same native plants you use to attract butterflies will also sustain these other insects—helping to effectively control garden pests such as spider mites, aphids, and stinkbugs.

Extensive research now demonstrates that large wildflower plantings (such as butterfly gardens) can actually help reduce pest problems in adjacent fruit and vegetable crops. Thus a butterfly garden not only is a source of beauty and a refuge for beautiful insects but can also help protect nearby food plants. Similarly, butterfly gardens attract and support vast numbers of gentle native bees that are highly effective farm and garden pollinators. Researchers at Michigan State University found that large wildflower plantings on blueberry farms significantly increased the yield of berries by several hundred pounds per acre (worth several hundred dollars in additional annual income). Those yield increases were the direct result of higher numbers of wild bees on the farms where the wildflowers were planted, resulting in more pollination of the blueberry flowers.

While the wild insects sustained by butterfly gardens offer tremendous benefits to their surrounding landscapes, the intentional release of garden predators (such as lady beetles) is questionable. The available research suggests that such releases pose several risks to wild insect populations such as the spread of insect diseases, hybridization between locally native and locally nonnative subspecies, possible competition between wild insects and the insects being released, and more. Moreover, intentionally released beneficial insects are often not even adapted to local conditions and often are not effective for pest control. For these reasons, we recommend fostering locally native wild beneficial insect populations through habitat restoration using a diverse selection of native grasses, wildflowers, and other plants. While in a few cases the results can be surprising—such as when a "beneficial" insect attacks a butterfly caterpillar on one of your plants—the overall result is a healthy, resilient, and life-filled landscape.

## DIVIDING PLANTS TO REVITALIZE AND PREVENT OVERCROWDING

After several years, butterfly gardens can become overcrowded. Perennials may start to outgrow their planted areas, show signs of declining health (such as smaller

Digging up and dividing plants that have outgrown their space can help revitalize them and can help you expand your butterfly garden or share with others.

flowers), or develop a bald center or dead spot in the middle of the plant. Simply digging up and dividing plants (cutting the crown and root mass into multiple pieces) can solve these common problems. Dividing can help revitalize plants and encourage new growth, often resulting in more vigorous, abundant blooms and sometimes extending their life span. Dividing is also a great project if you want to increase the number of plants in your garden, expand your garden size, or share plants with a friend.

Spring is usually the best time to divide plants, when soil moisture is adequate, temperatures are cool, and the plants have just begun to put on new growth.

Dividing plants during the summer comes with a greater risk of drought stress and transplant shock. It is best not to divide plants when they are flowering since they are expending energy at that time and it will be more difficult for them to recover from disturbance. Fall division is possible but must be done at least four weeks before the first potential hard freeze to allow the roots enough time to establish.

To divide a perennial plant, first water the soil around the plant a day or so in advance to make digging easier. Next, dig up the entire plant by inserting a shovel around it as deeply as necessary to keep the root mass intact. The roots of some species can be

Plant selection, installation, and maintenance

pulled apart with bare hands while others will need to be cut apart with a knife or other sharp tool. If plants have older, dead roots at their centers, removing those will stimulate the production of new roots. When you break apart the original plant, ensure that each division has a good portion of healthy roots and at least a few shoots. Keep the divisions moist and protected from direct sun until you can get them into the ground. Plant them as soon as possible at the same depth as the original plant and water them deeply. Supplemental watering will likely be needed in the following weeks to keep the soil moist.

Individual plants vary in how often they benefit from division, but as a general rule, when plants have reached their maximum potential size or have outgrown their space, they are ready. Groups of plants that typically divide well are asters (*Symphyotrichum* species), beebalm (*Monarda* species), blanketflowers (*Gaillardia* species), blazing stars (*Liatris* species), coneflowers (*Rudbeckia* and *Echinacea* species), penstemon (*Penstemon* species), and tickseed (*Coreopsis* species). In contrast, plants that do not lend themselves to division include wild indigo (*Baptisia* species), lupines (*Lupinus* species), and milkweeds (*Asclepias* species).

## COLLECTING YOUR OWN WILDFLOWER AND GRASS SEED

Along with dividing perennials, another great project for making more plants from your existing butterfly garden is seed collection. Seed collection allows you to propagate annuals as well as perennials and is a very low-cost way of either expanding your own garden or sharing part of your garden with others. While some wildflowers readily self-sow, collecting and planting your own seed gives you greater influence over garden design and the success of plant establishment, and allows you to spread the seeds far beyond where they may naturally fall.

A first step is simply to familiarize yourself with the life cycle of your native wildflowers and grasses by watching the seed heads form after the flowers fade. In some cases this is easier said than done since the seeds of some plants such as mountain mint (*Pycnanthemum* species) and black-eyed Susan (*Rudbeckia* species) can be extremely tiny and difficult to distinguish from the structural parts of the seed heads. While there are no comprehensive seed identification resources, a few plant conservation organizations, such as the Rancho Santa Ana Botanic Garden, offer website photo collections of many common native plants and their seed. Often a simple web search for images will reveal various photos for reference.

Along with being able to identify the seeds of a plant, it's also essential to know when they are actually ready for harvest. In general, seeds of native grasses, as well as annual and perennial wildflowers, are ready for collection two to five weeks after peak bloom. If you are harvesting shrub and tree seeds, those can sometimes take two months or longer to mature. Mature seeds are dry and firm and are typically brown, tan, black, or gray. Seeds that are moist or pliable and that are green, yellow, or white are likely to be immature and not ready for collection.

When seeds are ready for collection, it may be easiest to collect them by hand or use garden shears to clip seed heads from their stems for later separation. In the case of native grasses, it is sometimes more efficient to use a fine-toothed metal hair comb to rake seeds from their stems than it is to strip them off by hand. For plants such as milkweed that have light, wind-borne seeds that burst from their pods, or plants such as lupines with pods that explode and scatter their seed, a convenient option is to bag the unripe seedpods with a small, fine-meshed gauze bag. The bags can simply be left in place and then retrieved after the seed has matured and the pods begin to break open.

Clipping and collecting flower heads as they dry out can provide a source of seed to share or to use in expanding your garden.

When you hand collect seed, it is sometimes easy to separate the actual seed from chaff (fine plant material such as seed coverings) as you go. In other cases, you may need to work at separating the seed from chaff, flower parts, and stems. If the seed heads are tough and the seeds deeply embedded in the seed head (such as with *Echinacea*), you will need to carefully pull the dry seed heads apart with gloved hands. Alternatively, tough seed heads can be broken apart using an old kitchen food processor (pulsing the seed head a couple of times to chop it up). The resulting mix of seeds, chaff, and stems can be further separated with hardware cloth, window screens, and kitchen sieves of various mesh sizes.

As a final step, heavier seed can be separated from lightweight chaff by winnowing the seed in front of a small fan. To winnow seed, pour it from a bowl held several feet in the air into another bowl positioned in front of a low-speed fan (it is best to do this outside!). The heavier seed will fall into the lower bowl despite

Plant selection, installation, and maintenance

To remove chaff, leaves, and debris from wildflower seed that you harvest, you can sift it through screens of various sizes.

the airflow, while lightweight dust and chaff will be blown beyond the bowl. Note that it is perfectly okay if some debris or inert material remains among the seed.

Even when seeds are ripe and hard to the touch, they often still benefit from additional drying before you store them, to prevent mold from developing and to increase their longevity. The best approach to drying seeds is to leave them in an open bin or bag where they receive good air circulation. Heated locations or areas that receive direct sunlight are not good for drying and can kill otherwise viable seed. Often just a few weeks of additional drying at ambient temperatures are sufficient. After this the seeds should be kept in a cool, dark location with low humidity away from direct sunlight, in a sealed container such as a jar, paper bag, or envelope to protect them from rodents or seed-feeding insects. Seed should never be stored in the freezer because the formation of ice crystals can damage it.

Finally, don't forget to label your seed packages. Basic information such as the species, location of the parent plant, and date of collection will help you keep track of your seed. Such information also provides a legacy for friends and family members who you might share the seed with, and a sense of connection with other butterfly gardens that you help to make possible.

The nighttime garden is shared with a host of species such as the luna moth (*Actias luna*).

# Gardening for moths

**F**EW PEOPLE TAKE NOTICE of moths, despite their close relationship with butterflies. Even fewer people intentionally create gardens for them. The muted colors of many species, along with the reputation of a tiny fraction of them as crop or wardrobe pests, has done little to endear moths to the average gardener. But the truth is that moths are a beautiful and interesting wildlife group that anyone can attract into a garden.

Our relationship with moths and moth gardening is ancient. The domestication of the Asian mulberry silkmoth (*Bombyx mori*) likely began around 2600 BC. According to legend, one day a wild silkworm cocoon fell from an overhead mulberry tree into the cup of tea held by the Chinese empress Leizu. Retrieving the warm, soaked cocoon, the empress realized that she could carefully unwind the wet silk of the cocoon around her finger. Leizu recognized that a caterpillar

While often eclipsed in the public imagination by butterflies and songbirds, moths are a beautiful and interesting wildlife group that anyone can attract into a garden. These painted schinia moths (*Schinia volupia*), for example, might visit if you grow their host plant, Indian blanket (*Gaillardia pulchella*).

was the source of this amazing material and went on to establish a grove of mulberry trees (and hence the world's first moth garden) for silkworm cultivation. Today more than 700,000 tons of silk are produced annually by silkworms, all of them still relying on the same kind of leaves first identified by empress Leizu.

Your moth gardening aspirations might be more modest. But with more than 11,000 moth species in North America (placing them among the most diverse and abundant insect groups), you are assured of infinite opportunities for fascinating observation. Perhaps equally valuable to many gardeners is the fact that moths are an important source of food for countless other animals such as bats, tree frogs, flying squirrels, songbirds, and even small owls.

## COMMON MOTH FAMILIES

Vastly more moths than butterflies are found across the world, including more than 140,000 identified species and many others that still await discovery. This is in sharp contrast to the roughly 20,000 butterfly species identified globally. North America's moth diversity is represented by more than three dozen families. While many of these families may be present in your garden, a few families are more common and obvious than others.

## SPHINX AND HAWK MOTHS (FAMILY SPHINGIDAE)

Often mistaken for hummingbirds, sphinx and hawk moths are a particularly striking group that you might commonly see in the garden visiting plants such as beebalm and morning glory. The large size of these moths (a few are actually larger than hummingbirds), along with the fact that many are active during the day, places them among the most obvious and accessible moth groups.

Sphinx and hawk moths are also some of the fastest flying insects known, with a few species capable of flying more than 30 miles per hour. Like hummingbirds, these moths use rapidly beating wings to hover above flowers. From this hovering position, they can extend

# Tactics to evade bat predators

**EVERYONE KNOWS** that bats are supreme nighttime hunters of moths. Fewer people know that some moths display clever defenses against being eaten. Researchers in North Carolina have concluded that Grote's tiger moth (*Bertholdia trigona*) emits a series of ultrasonic clicks in midflight when it senses the high-pitched sounds of echo-locating bats—and it increases the frequency of the clicks as a bat approaches. The clicking sounds seem to jam the sonar of potential bat predators by returning noises that are difficult to separate from one another, making exact location of the moth by this method difficult. In another example of moths confusing bats, recent research has shown that the fluttering tails of luna moths (*Arctias luna*) cause bats to miss more often than capture these moths.

In other moths, researchers have identified earlike organs that can recognize the sound of echo-locating bats and can even gauge the relative distance of those bats. Detecting a far-off bat sound will cause the moth to simply change direction and to fly away from the source of the sound. Detecting a close-up bat sound may result in a zigzag or looping flight, or may even cause the moth to simply stop flying and free-fall below the bat's hunting range.

The snowberry clearwing moth (*Hemaris diffinis*, above) and the white-lined sphinx (*Hyles lineata*, below) are two incredibly fast, hovering fliers that are sometimes mistaken for hummingbirds at first glance.

their extremely long proboscis deep into the blossoms without ever landing. The beating wings of sphinx and hawk moths also allow them to fly sideways, in addition to simply hovering or flying forward. This provides a handy advantage when they are trying to access hard-to-reach flowers or to evade predators.

In the tropics these moths often have a close relationship with some of the larger orchids they pollinate. The classic example of this is the relationship between Madagascar's famed Christmas star orchid (*Angraecum sesquipedale*), which has nectar tubes up to a foot long, and *Xanthopan morganii* subsp. *praedicta*, a hawk moth with a very long proboscis. North American sphinx and hawk moths are a bit smaller by comparison but still often large, showy, and fascinating. Roughly a hundred species are known across the continent.

## WILD SILKMOTHS, ROYAL MOTHS, AND IMPERIAL MOTHS (FAMILY SATURNIIDAE)

The title for the largest North American moths probably goes to the family Saturniidae, often referred to as wild silkmoths. Numerically the family is small in the United States and Canada, with perhaps forty-some species north of Mexico. Many, however, are intensely patterned, colorful, and huge (some roughly equal in size to an average adult human's hand).

Because wild silkmoths do not feed as adults and

# Darwin's prediction

**IN 1862,** Charles Darwin received a package of orchids from Robert Bateman, a British orchid grower. Darwin had been studying the pollination of orchids for many years, so it was no great surprise that people would send him specimens. What *was* surprising, however, was that one of the orchids sported nectaries, tubular spurs from the flowers containing nectar at the bottom, nearly a foot long. In disbelief, Darwin wrote to his good friend, botanist Joseph Hooker, "Good Heavens! What insect can suck it?"

The orchid was *Angraecum sesquipedale*, a beautiful species from Madagascar with large, six-pointed white flowers, now often called comet orchid or Darwin's orchid. After examining the orchid and experimenting with pushing tubes down into its nectaries, Darwin reached the conclusion that the only insect capable of reaching the nectar would be a moth with a tongue that was extraordinarily long—far longer than that of any moth known at the time. Later that year, Darwin published *The Various Contrivances by Which Orchids Are Fertilised by Insects*, in which he made his now-famous prediction that there "must be moths with proboscides capable of extension to a length of between ten and eleven inches!"

His prediction was widely dismissed by his contemporaries, the most notable of which was the Duke of Argyle. Other scientists supported Darwin, including Alfred Russel Wallace, who added his not-inconsiderable scientific weight to the prediction. Darwin and Wallace were eventually proven correct, although it was more than forty years before anyone found such a moth on Madagascar, a subspecies of the African hawk moth *Xanthopan morganii* with a 12-inch-long tongue. It was given the subspecies name *praedicta*, meaning "the predicted one," in recognition of Darwin's statement.

have no digestive system, they don't visit flowers. Instead their short adult lives consist of simply living off the energy reserves they stored as caterpillars while they seek out mates. Even though you cannot attract them with typical flowering garden plants, you can nurture their populations by protecting and planting the trees they typically feed upon as caterpillars, such as wild cherries, oaks, hickories, walnuts, and other hardwoods. In eastern North America, some well-known members of this family include the luna (*Actias luna*), cecropia (*Hyalophora cecropia*), Io (*Automeris io*), rosy maple (*Dryocampa rubicunda*), royal walnut (*Citheronia regalis*), imperial (*Eacles imperialis*), and polyphemus (*Antheraea polyphemus*) moths. In the West, the enormous ceanothus silkmoth (*Hyalophora euryalus*) and Glover's silkmoth (*Hyalophora columbia gloveri*) are two of the largest and most well-known family members.

For all their glory, wild silkmoths tend to be distinctly nocturnal. Thus, aside from occasionally sighting them around porch lights (to which some species are attracted), most of us don't get to see them. Nonetheless, they are a captivating group of moths and worth watching for.

## TIGER MOTHS (FAMILY ARCTIIDAE)

While some moths rely on camouflage to protect themselves from predators, many members of the tiger moth family flaunt bright colors and make no effort to disguise themselves. Among these brightly colored tiger moths are some species that produce chemical defenses, making them toxic to predators. As in the case of the monarch butterfly, the bright colors of these moths are a warning to potential predators. Another common visual characteristic of this group is the "woolly bear" appearance of many tiger moth caterpillars.

One of the better-known tiger moths found in gardens, roadsides, and meadows of eastern Canada and the United States is the Arge moth (*Grammia arge*), a

The Io moth (*Automeris io*) is equally stunning in appearance as a caterpillar and an adult.

species that stands out for its white, orange, or sometimes bright pink 2-inch wingspan that is crisscrossed with black stripes and angular dots. While the Arge moth visits flowers such as blazing star (*Liatris* species), its caterpillar is less discriminating and readily feeds on sunflowers and weeds such as lamb's quarters.

Other colorful and relatively common tiger moth visitors include the harnessed tiger moth (*Apantesis*

The striking-looking caterpillar of the milkweed tussock moth (*Euchaetes egle*) has a habit of dropping to the ground and curling into a ball when disturbed.

*phalerata*), the great leopard moth (*Hypercompe scribonia*), and the milkweed tussock moth (*Euchaetes egle*). Like the monarch butterfly, the latter moths feed on milkweeds to acquire poisonous cardiac glycosides to protect themselves from predators. The very hairy caterpillar stage of the milkweed tussock moth also has the curious habit of dropping to the ground and curling into a ball when disturbed.

Wasplike coloration and slender wasplike appearance contribute to another visual defense employed by some tiger moths. Ctenucha moths (*Ctenucha* species) represent this strategy with metallic blue-green bodies and wings that are sometimes complemented with red or yellow color patterns around the head. While adult ctenucha moths may be found visiting flowers, their caterpillars tend to feed on grasses.

Gardening for moths

A red-shouldered ctenucha moth (*Ctenucha rubroscapus*) mimics a wasp as it feeds on flower nectar.

Another common wasplike member of this family is the cinnabar moth (*Tyria jacobaeae*). The striking orange-and-black-striped caterpillars are perhaps even more striking as adults with bright red warning stripes imposed on sleek bluish-black forewings. The cinnabar moth is not native to North America but rather was introduced to control its larval host plant, tansy ragwort (*Senecio jacobaea*), an invasive, nonnative weed.

## OWLET MOTHS (FAMILY NOCTUIDAE)

Owlet moths are a very common and large group of flower visitors. In a typical garden, this group is often represented by various cutworm and plusiine moths; both groups are small, heavy-bodied moths that usually hover while feeding. The cutworm moths are typically drab colored, while the plusiines are distinguished

Owlet moths such as this *Plagiomimicus dimidiata* tend to have stout, feathery bodies, hence their common name, which means "baby owl."

Among the owlets, flower moths such as this arcigera flower moth (*Schinia arcigera*) are rare but strikingly colorful flower visitors.

by silvery marks on their forewings. One plusiine, the green-patched looper (*Diachrysia balluca*), is notable for its striking brassy metallic green forewings.

Less common among owlets are the flower moths (*Schinia* species). This group, which includes many rare species, represents perhaps the most strikingly colorful moths in North America. Members of this group also tend to have very specific plant associations, sometimes nectaring on the same plant they fed on as caterpillars. The painted schinia moth (*Schinia volupia*) and the gaillardia flower moth (*Schinia masoni*) both have orange markings that almost exactly match the flower petals of their host plant, blanketflower (*Gaillardia* species). Rivaling the gaillardia flower moths for color intensity is the bright pink bleeding flower moth (*Schinia sanguinea*), a species that almost perfectly blends in with the flower buds of its host plants, the blazing stars (*Liatris* species). The cotton-candy-pink primrose moth (*Schinia florida*) is perhaps the most abundant and well-known example

of owlet flower moths. Many gardeners are amazed by their first glimpse of this otherworldly looking moth when they spot it perched among the bright yellow flowers of its host plant, evening primrose (*Oenothera biennis*), in the eastern United States and Canada.

The largest owlet in North America is steeped in folklore. With a wingspan reaching more than 6 inches, an attraction to night lights, and a unique striped and dotted pattern on a brown background, the black witch (*Ascalapha odorata*) makes an immediate impression on those who see it. The black witch is most common in the southern United States, where it feeds on leguminous trees and bushes such as Kentucky coffeetree (*Gymnocladus dioicus*) and mesquite (*Prosopis* species). In Mexico and Jamaica, the moth is associated with ghosts or a pending death in the family, while in other places such as the Bahamas its sudden appearance is associated with good fortune and future wealth. In Hawaii (where the moth is introduced), it is believed to be a deceased loved one coming back to say goodbye.

Gardening for moths

The muted color of underwing moths such as the penitent underwing (*Catocala piatrix*) shown here offers them camouflage from predators, but when the underwings are exposed, they may be every bit as colorful as the similarly sized painted lady butterfly.

## UNDERWING MOTHS (FAMILY EREBIDAE)

The muted gray-and-brown but intricately patterned forewings of underwing moths offer them excellent camouflage and protection from predators. When they are startled, however, these moths may suddenly expose the striking red, orange, or yellow color bands on their underwings. One species common in the western United States, the Aholibah underwing (*Catocala aholibah*), which feeds on oaks as a caterpillar, has such colorful orange underwing patterns that at first glance in midflight it might be mistaken for the similarly sized painted lady butterfly.

The diversity of underwings provides a succession of different species throughout the summer in many areas, although their nocturnal nature makes them difficult to readily observe. Aside from just waiting and watching for underwings in the garden at night with a flashlight, you can sometimes actively attract them to overripe bananas or other fermenting fruit. Underwing caterpillars usually feed on the leaves of trees such as willows, aspens, oaks, hickories, and hawthorns, underscoring the value of native trees for landscaping and gardening.

The humble inchworm caterpillars familiar to most gardeners grow to become subtle, butterfly-like adults—like this large maple spanworm moth (*Prochoerodes lineola*)—that visit garden flowers at night.

## GEOMETER MOTHS (FAMILY GEOMETRIDAE)

Resembling small, drab butterflies, geometer (or geometrid) moths are common nighttime flower visitors. Their common and scientific names come from the Latin and Greek words for "earth-measurer," a reference to the distinct movement of their "inchworm" caterpillars.

Some of the more colorful and thus noticeable geometers include the white slant-line moth (*Tetracis cachexiata*) and the infant moth (*Archiearis infans*),

both of which feed on forest trees and are found across most of temperate North America. One of the larger members of the group is the large maple spanworm moth (*Prochoerodes lineola*), which prefers maples and oaks, and whose caterpillar resembles a brown twig while the adult stage roughly resembles a brown leaf. The wavy-lined emerald moth (*Synchlora aerata*) uses similar camouflage, resembling a pale green leaf as an adult and as a caterpillar attaching bits of flowers or leaves to its body to blend in with its host plant. You can attract the wavy-lined emerald with its preferred

The currant borer moth (*Synanthedon tipuliformis*), like other clearwings, has a distinctly wasplike appearance.

host plants: various asters (*Symphyotrichum* species), blazing stars (*Liatris* species), black-eyed Susans (*Rudbeckia* species), goldenrods (*Solidago* species), and other members of the sunflower family.

## CLEARWING MOTHS (FAMILY SESIIDAE)

The clearwing moths are notable for looking almost nothing like other moths. Lacking the heavy bodies, muted colors, and fuzzy appearance of many other moth families, the clearwings tend to be distinctly wasplike in appearance, complete with transparent wings and metallic or striped yellow-and-black color patterns that discourage birds and other predators from attacking them. This appearance works in their favor since most clearwings are active in the daytime and frequently visit flowers to feed on nectar. In contrast, the larvae of clearwings tend to hide away within the stems, bark, or roots of host plants where their boring and tunneling feeding habits sometimes cause damage. A butterfly garden rich in native wildflower diversity might attract the eupatorium borer

The hag moth (*Pheobetron pithecium*) caterpillar has a flattened, hairy, branched appearance and is sometimes mistaken for the shed exoskeleton of a spider.

(*Carmenta bassiformis*), which feeds within the stems of ironweed and Joe Pye weed as a caterpillar, and Riley's clearwing (*Synanthedon rileyana*), a striped yellow-and-black moth that at first glance looks deceptively like a yellowjacket wasp.

## SLUG MOTHS (FAMILY LIMACODIDAE)

The slug moths are so called because many of the caterpillars in this family have a uniquely sluglike appearance. While slug moth adults tend to be chunky and brown, a few stand out with bright green color patterns on their forewings.

One slug moth you might encounter is the hag moth (*Pheobetron pithecium*), a squat moth that closely resembles a bee as an adult but has a hairy, branched appearance like the shed exoskeleton of a spider while a caterpillar. Its relative the stinging rose caterpillar moth (*Parasa indetermina*) looks like a green and brown folded leaf; the caterpillars are bright yellow and orange and are covered with stinging, fleshy projections. A third species, the spiny oak slug (*Euclea delphinii*), is a bright green caterpillar protected by stinging orange projections. As an adult this dark brown moth with two bright green wing patches feeds on various trees across the eastern United States.

## OTHER NOTABLE MOTHS

Countless other interesting moths can make an appearance in gardens that offer an abundance of diverse native plant habitat, structure for egg laying and overwintering, and protection from pesticides. Among these are the flannel moths (family Megalopygidae) and in particular the southern flannel moth (*Megalopyge opercularis*), which has been described as the Persian cat of moths. As both a caterpillar and an adult, this species is covered in lush, downy orange-brown hair that looks tempting enough to pet. Be warned, however—the southern flannel moth's hairs

While moths are sometimes thought of as brown and drab, as a group they are actually much more diverse in appearance than butterflies, as this Texas wasp moth (*Horama panthalon*) illustrates.

contain venomous spines that can cause extreme reactions in unwitting humans, from headaches and nausea to abdominal cramps, chest pains, difficulty breathing, and skin rashes. The southern flannel moth is found in the southern United States, where it feeds on various trees.

The goldenrod gall moths (family Gelechiidae, genus *Gnorimoschema*) are species that frequent meadows, roadsides, and abandoned pastures in the eastern United States. The gray-brown adult females lay their eggs in the fall in leaf litter near goldenrod plants (*Solidago* species), where they overwinter. In the spring, newly hatched larvae seek out their nearby host plant, burrowing into the stem and feeding on the plant from the inside out. Responding to this feeding, goldenrods

# After-dark moth-watching tricks

**WHILE SOME MOTHS** commonly appear in the garden during the day, many are much more likely to be active after dark, making observation difficult. Fortunately, a few time-tested after-dark moth-watching methods exist. Here are two:

**1** Drape a white sheet over an overhead tree branch or something similar and use strings tied to each corner of the sheet to create a semi-taut flat surface (like the sail of a ship). Then steadily shine a stationary bright light (such as a powerful flashlight) to illuminate the entire sheet. Moths as well as many other types of insects are attracted to such lights and within several minutes will begin fluttering against the sheet. After an hour or so of this type of moth watching, shut off the light and allow the moths to get on with their nighttime business.

**2** Place a red lens over a flashlight and use it to investigate insect activity on various garden plants. This is an especially good way to explore larger meadows, where the red light can reveal not just moths but many other interesting nocturnal insects at all levels—from those flying across the landscape to those living out their lives along the stems and leaves of the meadow plants and those moving in the thatch below.

The best nights for such moth watching are the relatively warm nights between late spring and early autumn in most temperate areas.

This deceptive sallow moth (*Feralia deceptiva*), an owlet, was spotted early one morning by our communication director, Matthew Shepherd, on the siding of his house.

form a tumorlike gall over the larvae, protecting them from predators and providing a proliferation of new plant cells as food for the caterpillar. Goldenrod moth larvae pupate in summer and emerge in the fall to mate and lay eggs.

Yucca moths (family Prodoxidae) are a group of several genera that live out their entire lives in and around their namesake host plants. Famous as an example of specific pollinator dependence, female yucca moths collect pollen from the anthers of yucca flowers and directly deposit it into the stigmata (female organs). After pollinating a flower, the female yucca moth then turns around and immediately lays her eggs in the flower's ovaries. As the yucca seeds develop, they provide a food source for the moth larvae, but fortunately the yucca plant is able to produce enough extra seeds that some inevitably survive to become new plants. In this symbiotic relationship, each species is of critical importance to the other, since yuccas are only pollinated by yucca moths, and yucca moths only lay their eggs on yuccas. When yuccas are planted from seed outside of their native range, they typically fail to produce seed without their moth companions.

## THE MOTH LIFE CYCLE

In general, the life cycles of moths and butterflies are very similar. Both begin life as eggs and then hatch into caterpillars, feed for a time, pupate, undergo metamorphosis, and emerge as adults. Some differences exist, however—one of the most notable being that moth caterpillars feed on a somewhat more diverse range of foods than butterflies. Like butterflies, the vast majority of moths feed on a host plant during their caterpillar stage. But rather than limiting themselves to leaves as most butterflies do, some moths also eat seeds or roots, or, by boring into woody stems or branches, eat the plant from the inside. Fewer than 1 percent of moth species (only in the family Tineidae) eat fabrics such as wool.

Plants that you might already be growing for butterflies, such as butterfly milkweed (*Asclepias tuberosa*), are a good foundation for attracting common flower-visiting moths, such as this corn earworm moth (*Helicoverpa zea*).

This wide range of larval food sources is reflected in the broad range of ways moths lay their eggs. Those with specific host plant requirements, such as most tiger moths, seek out and lay their eggs on those specific plants. In a few extreme cases, such as that of the yucca moths, individuals may live out their entire life cycle on that host plant alone. In other cases, such as that of the swift moths, females may scatter their eggs far and wide as they fly above grassy meadows, as though they are scattering seeds.

Another difference in life cycles between butterflies and moths is the pupal stage, which for butterflies consists of a chrysalis (a hardened outer casing that forms when the caterpillar sheds its skin) but for moths typically consists of a cocoon of tough silk fiber they spin around themselves before undergoing metamorphosis. Depending on the species, the silk fibers may harden into a tough casing or remain soft and pliable. Similarly, the fibers may be completely opaque or translucent. A number of moths add defenses to their cocoons such as shed larval hairs that contain painful skin irritants. Still other moths hide their cocoons in bark crevices or leaf litter, or even spin bits of twig and plant debris into the cocoon as camouflage.

A final notable distinction between butterflies and moths in North America is the fact that some moths do not have functional mouths or digestive tracts as adults. These moths, which include the wild silkmoths, do all of their feeding as caterpillars, then emerge later as nonfeeding adults that live for only a few days before they mate and die.

## SELECTING PLANTS FOR MOTHS

Common wisdom has it that moths visit night-blooming plants with flowers that are typically white or pale in color such as sacred datura (*Datura wrightii*), morning glory (*Convolvulus* species), and common evening primrose (*Oenothera biennis*). While there is certainly some truth in this, the relationship between moths and plants is infinitely more complex. For moths that do not feed as adults, it is critical to recognize and protect their larval host plants. All the moths that do feed as adults rely on sugar sources for food, primarily flower nectar but in some cases also tree sap or rotting fruit. Those active in daylight readily visit the same wildflowers you might already be planting for a butterfly garden. Like butterflies, nectar-feeding moths usually have long tongues, allowing them to reach nectar located deep within showy tubular flowers.

The flower preferences of nocturnal or crepuscular (active at dawn and dusk) moths are less well understood. We know that these species are often extremely important pollinators of night-blooming plants since other pollinators such as bees are generally inactive at night.

In creating a moth-friendly garden, your focus should be on selecting as a foundation many of the same native plants you would use to attract bees and butterflies. From there, you should be sure to select any additional plants known to be important for specific moth groups you want to attract, and possibly include lots of those plants to increase the chances of the moths you are interested in visiting your garden.

# BEST MOTH GARDEN PLANTS BY REGION

The options listed in this table, most of which are described in further detail in "Butterfly Garden Plants of North America," are good choices for moth gardening in various regions. When supplemented by a diversity of other native plants, they will create a landscape rich in interesting insect life.

| PACIFIC NORTHWEST AND BRITISH COLUMBIA | | | |
|---|---|---|---|
| **COMMON NAME** | **SCIENTIFIC NAME** | **ASSOCIATED MOTHS** | **NECTAR VALUE** |
| blanketflower | *Gaillardia aristata* | gaillardia flower moth | * |
| Douglas aster | *Symphyotrichum subspicatum* | | * |
| fireweed | *Chamerion angustifolium* | bedstraw moth, white-lined sphinx moth | * |
| Garry oak | *Quercus garryana* | blinded sphinx | |
| Oregon checkermallow | *Sidalcea oregana* | | * |
| Oregon cherry | *Prunus emarginata* | blinded sphinx, elegant sphinx, small-eyed sphinx, twin-spotted sphinx | * |
| Puget Sound gumweed | *Grindelia integrifolia* | | * |
| Scouler's willow | *Salix scouleriana* | blinded sphinx, modest sphinx, twin-spotted sphinx | |

| CALIFORNIA | | | |
|---|---|---|---|
| **COMMON NAME** | **SCIENTIFIC NAME** | **ASSOCIATED MOTHS** | **NECTAR VALUE** |
| buckbrush | *Ceanothus cuneatus* | ceanothus silkmoth, white-streaked saturnia | * |
| California goldenrod | *Solidago californica* | | * |
| California morning glory | *Calystegia macrostegia* | | * |
| foothill penstemon | *Penstemon heterophyllus* | | * |
| hollyleaf cherry | *Prunus ilicifolia* | Nevada buckmoth | * |
| hummingbird trumpet | *Epilobium canum* | | * |
| meadow checkermallow | *Sidalcea malviflora* | | * |
| Pacific aster | *Symphyotrichum chilense* | | * |
| purple sage | *Salvia dorrii* | elegant sphinx | * |
| sacred datura | *Datura wrightii* | | * |

## DESERT SOUTHWEST

| COMMON NAME | SCIENTIFIC NAME | ASSOCIATED MOTHS | NECTAR VALUE |
| --- | --- | --- | --- |
| chokecherry | *Prunus virginiana* | small-eyed sphinx | * |
| golden crownbeard | *Verbesina encelioides* | | * |
| Indian blanket | *Gaillardia pulchella* | Bina flower moth, painted schinia moth, and *Schinia varix* | * |
| Palmer's penstemon | *Penstemon palmeri* | | * |
| prince's plume | *Stanleya pinnata* | | * |
| Rocky Mountain bee plant | *Peritoma serrulata* | | * |
| Spanish bayonet | *Yucca baccata* | ursine giant skipper, yucca giant skipper, various yucca moths | * |
| white-tufted evening primrose | *Oenothera caespitosa* | white-lined sphinx moth | * |

## MIDWEST AND GREAT PLAINS

| COMMON NAME | SCIENTIFIC NAME | ASSOCIATED MOTHS | NECTAR VALUE |
| --- | --- | --- | --- |
| chokecherry | *Prunus virginiana* | blinded sphinx, cecropia moth, elm sphinx, hummingbird clear-wing moth, small-eyed sphinx, twin-spotted sphinx | * |
| cup plant | *Silphium perfoliatum* | | * |
| evening primrose | *Oenothera biennis* | primrose moth, white-lined sphinx | * |
| foxglove beardtongue | *Penstemon digitalis* | | * |
| oak | *Quercus* spp. | blinded sphinx, imperial moth, polyphemus moth, rosy maple moth, waved sphinx | |
| prairie blazing star | *Liatris pycnostachya* | bleeding flower moth | * |
| prairie phlox | *Phlox pilosa* | phlox moth | * |
| pussy willow | *Salix discolor* | blinded sphinx, elm sphinx, Io moth, modest sphinx, Nevada buckmoth, polyphemus moth | |
| Rocky Mountain blazing star | *Liatris ligulistylis* | bleeding flower moth | * |
| spicebush | *Lindera benzoin* | cecropia moth, large bark-patterned moth, promethea moth, tulip tree beauty | |
| wild bergamot | *Monarda fistulosa* | hermit sphinx, orange mint moth, raspberry pyrausta | * |

| NORTHEAST AND MID-ATLANTIC | | | |
|---|---|---|---|
| **COMMON NAME** | **SCIENTIFIC NAME** | **ASSOCIATED MOTHS** | **NECTAR VALUE** |
| black huckleberry | *Gaylussacia baccata* | brown elfin, Gordian sphinx, Henry's elfin, huckleberry sphinx | * |
| chokecherry | *Prunus virginiana* | black-waved flannel moth, cecropia moth, cynthia moth, elm sphinx, Glover's silkmoth, hummingbird clearwing moth, imperial moth, Io moth, polyphemus moth, promethea moth | * |
| evening primrose | *Oenothera biennis* | primrose moth, white-lined sphinx | * |
| foxglove beardtongue | *Penstemon digitalis* | | * |
| oak | *Quercus* species | black-waved flannel moth, imperial moth, rosy maple moth, stinging rose caterpillar moth, waved sphinx | |
| pussy willow | *Salix discolor* | black-waved flannel moth, cecropia moth, cynthia moth, elm sphinx, imperial moth, Io moth, modest sphinx, polyphemus moth, promethea moth, small-eyed sphinx, twin-spotted sphinx | |
| scarlet beebalm | *Monarda didyma* | hermit sphinx, orange mint moth, raspberry pyrausta | * |
| spicebush | *Lindera benzoin* | cynthia moth, imperial moth, promethea moth, tulip tree beauty | |
| spotted Joe Pye weed | *Eupatoriadelphus maculatus* | Clymene moth, Eupatorium borer moth, ruby tiger moth, three-lined flower moth | * |
| wrinkleleaf goldenrod | *Solidago rugosa* | | * |

| SOUTHEAST | | | |
|---|---|---|---|
| **COMMON NAME** | **SCIENTIFIC NAME** | **ASSOCIATED MOTHS** | **NECTAR VALUE** |
| buttonbush | *Cephalanthus occidentalis* | hydrangea sphinx, royal walnut moth | * |
| Chickasaw plum | *Prunus angustifolia* | black-waved flannel moth, blinded sphinx, cecropia moth, elm sphinx, hummingbird clearwing moth, imperial moth, lo moth, polyphemus moth, promethea moth, small-eyed sphinx | * |
| coastal plain willow | *Salix caroliniana* | black-waved flannel moth, blinded sphinx, cecropia moth, elm sphinx, imperial moth, lo moth, modest sphinx, polyphemus moth, promethea moth | |
| false indigo bush | *Amorpha fruticosa* | lo moth | * |
| hollow Joe Pye weed | *Eupatoriadelphus fistulosus* | Clymene moth, three-lined flower moth | * |
| oak | *Quercus* species | black-waved flannel moth, blinded sphinx, imperial moth, rosy maple moth, stinging rose caterpillar moth, waved sphinx | |
| rattlesnake master | *Eryngium yuccifolium* | rattlesnake-master borer moth | * |
| rose mallow | *Hibiscus moscheutos* | lo moth | * |
| spicebush | *Lindera benzoin* | promethea moth, tulip tree beauty | |
| wingstem | *Verbesina alternifolia* | | * |
| wrinkleleaf goldenrod | *Solidago rugosa* | | * |

Like many other interesting and important insects, moths need overgrown areas of stumps, snags, logs, brush piles, and leaf litter in the landscape for overwintering.

## MOTH CONSERVATION

The same conservation strategies intended to support butterflies also support moths in most landscapes. Protecting existing natural areas from degradation, restoring native plant communities, and eliminating insecticide use are all basic but important strategies.

Beyond these basics, and perhaps more significant for moths, is the need to preserve overgrown areas with decaying stumps, snags, logs, brush piles, and leaf litter. The latter can be especially important in temperate climates where many moth species use leaf litter for overwintering cover. In fact, gardeners should consider leaving piles of unraked autumn leaves where they fall rather than raking, bagging, or shredding them and in the process sentencing possibly thousands of moths and other interesting creatures to certain death.

Another conservation consideration of special relevance to moths is protection from light pollution. Artificial lights are believed to be a factor in the decline of nocturnal wildlife such as moths and fireflies, and may disrupt the migration of birds that navigate by starlight such as the indigo bunting (*Passerina cyanea*).

In the case of some moths, the reason for their attraction to artificial lights is still not well understood. One theory is that moths navigate by maintaining a constant angular relationship to a celestial light such as the moon or a bright star. Because of the vast distance between the moth and those light sources, the orientation changes very little, allowing a moth to fly in a relatively straight path. Because its orientation to a nearby light source changes quickly as a moth flies toward it, however, the moth may become disoriented and fly in circles around the light. Another theory is that moths fly high into the sky during sunrise and then scan the ground below looking for a protected location to hide during the day ahead. At night, when the ground remains dark, a moth may continue flying toward what it perceives to be the rising morning sun (in this case an artificial light), only to return to the light again and again in a state of confusion.

Calls to address light pollution are increasing in many parts of the United States. While many of the proposed solutions are a good start, the emphasis is often on strategies to improve the visibility of the night sky (such as replacing older street lights with downward-facing models). Moths need more. The best way to protect moths from light pollution is to turn off lights where possible. If you must use outdoor lighting, consider dim low-voltage landscape lighting systems, red lights (which are typically not visible to insects and are more effective than yellow "bug lights" at reducing the impact of light pollution on moths), or lights operating on a motion detector that turns them on when movement is detected and then shuts them off after a few minutes.

Finally, and amazingly, electronic bug zappers are still manufactured and readily available for purchase despite a now overwhelming body of research demonstrating that they are useless for controlling pests such as mosquitos. One study examining the effectiveness of bug zappers found that of the 13,789 moths and other insects killed during a summer season by one typical residential bug zapper, only 31 of them were actually biting insects. The research, conducted in the 1990s, estimated that 4 million bug zappers were in use across the United States, and operating for an average of forty nights per year, those bug zappers were killing roughly 71 billion harmless and beneficial insects. Additional research suggests that the mist of dead airborne insect parts created by bug zappers can actually harm your health. For all of these reasons, plus the fact that they cost money to purchase and operate, it's clear that bug zappers deserve scorn and ridicule rather than a place in your yard.

In many places, wildflowers—like this milkweed (*Asclepias* species) growing in a roadside ditch—have been pushed into the margins. New habitat can reclaim land for butterflies and connect existing patches.

# Helping butterflies beyond the garden fence

**M**ANY LANDSCAPES CAN SUPPORT butterflies. Gardens, farms, greenspaces, roadsides, and rooftops all matter if we hope to provide a secure future for these animals. The needs of butterflies are the same in every place—flowers throughout the seasons, host plants for adults to lay eggs on, and safe niches for spending the winter. Maintaining a flowering landscape in these larger areas does take some special consideration. For example, the proper mowing regimen is vital to maintain habitats along roadsides and in parks, and some large areas may also benefit from controlled burning. This chapter discusses these considerations and other aspects of how larger landscapes (as well as unique ones like rooftops) can be restored and managed for the benefit of butterflies.

## ECO-ROOFS FOR BUTTERFLIES

With careful planning and maintenance, flower-rich meadows and prairies will grow on roofs, offering an abundance of nectar and caterpillar host plants. Sod roofs have been used in parts of northern Europe for centuries because sod is cheaply available and can withstand gales and rain. In recent decades, this old concept has been adapted for the modern landscape as a way to manage stormwater in urban areas. These unique rooftops also provide other benefits, including offering habitat in areas where the potential to create traditional habitat on the ground is limited. Research has demonstrated that a diversity of invertebrates— including butterflies—colonize green roofs, even in densely populated neighborhoods and even when these sites are tens of stories above the ground.

Green roofs can be built on any structure, from a garage or shed to large skyscrapers or warehouses. Such roofs go by many names and can take many forms, from a formal flower garden to a re-creation of a riverside sandbar. A *roof garden* can have a formal layout and may feature shrubs and trees in addition to

This eco-roof brings a field of seablush (*Plectritis congesta*) into an industrial district of Portland, Oregon.

flower borders. A *green roof* is primarily designed for stormwater management and is often a uniform mat of sedum, grown off-site and installed much like laying sod to create a lawn. A green roof designed to provide diversity of both plants and structure, also called an *eco-roof*, allows for greater variation in soil depths, which leads naturally to a greater diversity of conditions supporting a greater diversity of wildlife.

An eco-roof can be designed to replicate local habitats and conserve local biodiversity. In Zurich, Switzerland, the roof of a municipal water station has a century-old wildflower meadow in which 175 plant species have been recorded, including a large population of orchids. Such a roof need not be green: *brown roofs* have been constructed that feature few plants and often mimic rocky or bare-ground habitats that existed in the area before urbanization. These have typically been designed to suit ground-nesting birds—the black redstart (*Phoenicurus ochruros*) in London, England, for example—but bare ground should be a feature of any roof for butterflies as it can offer basking sites and the possibility of puddling locations.

Helping butterflies beyond the garden fence

When planning a green roof for butterflies, the first step is to assess the structure of the building, which must be able to support the soil and plants. Natural soil is heavy, and many green roofs use a lighter-weight growing medium, usually a mixture of compost. However, local, natural soils are better suited to locally native plants, so use a mixture that is as similar to the local soils as possible, and ideally incorporate local soils into some areas of the roof.

Research done in Basel, Switzerland, showed that the depth of the soil or growing medium was the primary determinant of the wildlife diversity on green roofs. Uniformly thin soils exacerbated the already harsh growing conditions, leading to less diversity. Consider having a minimum soil depth of 6 inches and vary the depth across the roof area. Mounds of soil (up to 12 inches deep, if the roof structure allows) allow roots to go deeper and support taller vegetation, whereas areas with soils thinner than 6 inches support sparser, more open vegetation. This kind of small-scale structural diversity provides a greater range of ecological niches than does a uniform soil depth.

In choosing plants for your roof, remember that a roof is a more extreme environment than a ground-level garden. The roof is likely to be more exposed, hotter in the summer, colder in the winter, and windier. Plants adapted to rocky places may be a good choice, which is one reason sedum is widely used. An eco-roof can also include artificial components. Solar panels, for instance, can add to the variety of microclimates by introducing areas of shade or increased wetness where rain drips from the structure.

Once a green roof is established, like any garden it will need some maintenance. This should be minimal, limited to inspecting the roof membrane and removing any weeds.

Bioswales like this one with milkweed can provide habitat for a variety of butterflies while beautifying neighborhood streets.

## RAIN GARDENS AND BIOSWALES

A rain garden, bioswale, or filter strip is a vegetated area designed to manage stormwater. By slowing runoff, these areas increase absorption and reduce the speed at which rainwater reaches storm drains or creeks. The increased retention time allows a rain garden or bioswale to act as a filter to remove pollutants and gives time for sediment to settle, releasing cleaner water into local waterways. These special areas can be constructed beside houses or other buildings to catch roof runoff, in parking lots, on street corners, or at the edge of a neighborhood.

Although a rain garden manages rainwater similarly to a green roof, it has none of the concerns over soil weight or roof strength and thus has the capacity to grow larger plants and shrubs. This allows for planting trees that are preferred hosts for the caterpillars of many butterfly and moth species.

Several things should be considered when selecting a location for a bioswale or rain garden. First, because it is designed to hold water only briefly, a rain garden should be constructed where soils drain well. If your yard has a low point where standing water gathers during wet periods, you know drainage is not good enough there. Partway up a gentle slope is best. Also, to avoid the risk of disturbing foundations, the rain garden should be more than 10 feet from any building and should drain away from it. Finally, it must be large enough to cope with the amount of runoff expected from the adjacent roof or parking lot. Detailed guidelines and instructions for creating a successful rain garden or bioswale are easily found on the Internet, and many state and local governments offer information.

The most appropriate plants for a rain garden in a smaller yard are perennials and prairie plants that provide abundant nectar, along with caterpillar host plants. Since a rain garden is periodically damp as it catches runoff and then may be dry for long periods, you should choose plants that can withstand periods of wet and dry. Include shrubs or trees where space allows—larger yards, edges of parking lots. Willows (*Salix* species), for example, are hosts for tiger swallowtails (*Papilio glaucus*), mourning cloaks (*Nymphalis antiopa*), green commas (*Polygonia faunus*), and other butterflies.

Maintenance of a bioswale is limited to typical gardening activities like weeding and deadheading, although you may occasionally need to dig out accumulated silt.

## CORPORATE AND COLLEGE CAMPUSES

Manufacturing facilities, railway corridors, urban brownfields, and other industrial sites as well as corporate and college campuses typically offer large land areas that must be managed for safety, operations, and in some cases aesthetics. Even though these sites may not provide suitable habitat for most large wildlife species, butterfly conservation can in many cases be completely compatible with other management priorities. In addition, butterfly conservation may provide an opportunity for industries to meet business sustainability benchmarks.

One example of a company that has integrated butterfly-friendly habitat into an industrial operation is hair and skin care company Aveda. Aveda's headquarters in Blaine, Minnesota, are surrounded by diverse mass plantings of native wildflowers and wetland plants. Sitting in Aveda's cafeteria, for example, warehouse employees can look out at songbirds and butterflies visiting mass plantings of cup plant (*Silphium perfoliatum*) and black-eyed Susan (*Rudbeckia hirta*). These plantings extend into parking lot areas and blend seamlessly into the surrounding plant community as it transitions into mature stands of native trees. The use of native plants provides a landscape for Aveda that is not dependent on supplemental irrigation or fertilizers and helps absorb runoff from parking lots and rooftops. These benefits build upon a larger corporate sustainability mission, which includes sourcing energy from wind, using recycled materials in packaging, and raising public awareness of pollinators.

The central emphasis of Aveda's approach directly applies to any industry wanting to position itself as a butterfly conservation leader. Specifically, a design for a new landscape or a plan to revegetate a disturbed area should give priority to planting locally native species, including native butterfly nectar and host plants. For an existing area slated for redevelopment or significant disturbance, the priority should be to conduct an inventory of plants and butterfly populations to identify opportunities to protect what already may be present. Conservation groups with expertise in butterflies and natural resources agencies can often help or provide consultation on such a process.

Butterfly gardens like this one at the University of Minnesota provide multiple benefits to both human and butterfly visitors.

Maintenance of these sites needs to follow specific mowing guidelines. For example, where possible, mowing, herbicide application, brush hogging, and other vegetation management should be as targeted as possible, focusing on controlling invasive weeds or vegetation that poses a risk to safety and operations while leaving other areas as intact as possible. Similarly, where possible, practicing rotational mowing on just a third or a quarter of the landscape per year provides better odds that butterfly populations can remain stable and find refuge in the areas not currently being mowed.

## PARKS AND GREENSPACES

In Tigard, Oregon, a formal butterfly garden in Cook Park allows visitors to watch butterflies up close from a network of curving paths or view them from a distance in a raised gazebo. At Memorial Park in Wilsonville, Oregon, a wide hedgerow of flowering shrubs flanked by a broad strip of flower-rich prairie offers a haven for butterflies and bees between a creek and a community garden. In Beaverton, Oregon, a 1-acre pollinator meadow is being created beside a heavily trafficked walking and biking trail, replacing featureless mowed grass beneath powerlines. These three examples,

Taller vegetation, like this native aster flowering along a suburban creek corridor, can provide an important nectar source for butterflies.

separated by no more than a handful of miles, illustrate that there is no single best way to create habitat for butterflies in parks. The approach should be tailored both to local conditions and to community desires. Park facilities encompass everything from business offices and maintenance yards to ball fields and creek corridors. Butterfly habitat can be incorporated into any of these.

Instead of being landscaped with bedding plants, office buildings can be surrounded with native plantings so that the flutter of butterfly wings greets visitors. Flower borders can be enhanced by ensuring appropriate caterpillar host plants are growing alongside nectar plants. Reducing the frequency of mowing along park margins, beside hedgerows, or on the banks of creeks will allow taller vegetation to grow and provide undisturbed areas where caterpillars can develop or chrysalids overwinter. The flower diversity of these areas can be improved by adding more native species. Natural areas can be managed with butterflies in mind, ensuring that the habitat offers host plants, nectar sources, and overwintering sites. Many of these actions may also help park managers achieve districtwide sustainability goals.

Greenspace and park managers should not be discouraged from planning butterfly habitat because a greenspace or park facility is too developed. These creatures have a remarkable ability to survive in even the most urbanized of areas. Several species of butterflies—such as the red-banded hairstreak (*Calycopis cecrops*) and the eastern black swallowtail (*Papilio polyxenes*)—are regularly seen in community gardens in the Bronx and Harlem.

Just like for corporate and college campuses, maintenance of these sites should take butterfly needs into consideration. If the experience from a suburban park in the English town of Saltdean is anything to go by, a change as simple as not mowing can have dramatic benefits for butterflies—and park patrons won't be upset. In 2012, the mowing regimen of the Saltdean Oval changed. Most was mowed every two weeks as it had been for years, but several patches were left unmowed and allowed to grow. The following year, the unmowed patches had three times as many flowers as the mowed areas and nearly five times as many butterflies—and 97 percent of park visitors approved of the changes.

Because parks are public places, they offer an additional benefit for butterflies: education. Many park districts and local councils have natural resources departments, and many of these are tasked with environmental education and community outreach. An interpretive panel could be installed in a butterfly garden to explain what visitors see and what they can do at home. Guided walks can pass through (or beside) the habitat. Butterfly gardening workshops can be hosted. Volunteer parties can care for the habitat or garden. The gardens and the education can lead to much greater adoption of these practices in yards, which in turn will benefit more butterflies. If you live in a neighborhood near a park, you can contact the park manager and volunteer to put in or manage habitat or help with educational outreach.

## ROADSIDES AND UTILITY CORRIDORS

In an increasingly modified and fragmented landscape, important habitat for butterflies can be provided by utility corridors and the areas alongside roads and railroads. They cover more than 17 million acres of land in the United States, stretching across agricultural and urban landscapes. In urban areas, roadside vegetation serves as a wildlife corridor connecting areas of habitat, or as a significant patch of habitat in its own right. The same is true for farmland, where most ground is under the plow.

Studies show just how important these areas are for butterflies. One study in Iowa found that 42 percent of the butterfly species in the state were observed along

Land alongside highways, country roads, and urban streets can be managed to provide important host and nectar plants and overwintering sites for butterflies and their caterpillars.

roadsides, and another in Britain found that 47 per-cent of all British butterfly species were present along roadsides. Some roadsides and utility corridors are increasingly important for rare butterflies; species like the endangered Fender's blue butterfly rely on road-side habitat for their survival. Data even suggests that well-maintained roadsides with native plants help keep butterflies and other pollinators from being killed by cars. In a landscape that has a lot of resources (flowers and host plants), butterflies do not need to move as far

to get everything they need. Because of this, they are less likely to fly across the road and get hit by a car.

Roadside managers can take a more active role in enlarging the population of pollinators by increasing the abundance of pollen and nectar resources with a diverse range of plants that flower throughout the growing season and by encouraging vegetation that provides egg-laying and overwintering locations for butterflies. This habitat restoration can take the form of mass wildflower plantings, interseeding of

Helping butterflies beyond the garden fence

North Carolina farmer Van Burnette uses butterfly conservation as a means to draw customers to his farm.

low-growing pollinator-attractive plants in existing turfgrass areas, and establishing flowering shrubs and trees in living snow fences, windbreaks, or slope stabilization efforts. Wherever possible, foraging habitat should be enriched with native plants.

Managing for butterflies in these areas means taking into account several key maintenance considerations. In many places, the current maintenance regimen will probably sustain the open conditions that are beneficial for butterflies. In other situations, specific management efforts are required to maintain optimum conditions, and a biologist should be consulted. Mowing of species-rich grassland alongside

highways and railroads should be timed so that flowers can bloom and long grass can remain for butterfly egg laying; this may mean mowing only in the late fall or winter every other year. Dividing an area into plots and cutting them on a three- or four-year rotation will maintain a suitable diversity of conditions. Insecticides should not be used, and managers should realize that herbicides will kill most of the plants that pollinators depend on for egg laying and foraging.

Gardeners who live alongside roadways can help provide habitat as well. If you want to undertake a roadside planting for butterflies and caterpillars, be sure not to plant anything so large or tall it will

New habitat, such as this insectary planting on an Oregon farm, brings many benefits from the pollinators and other beneficial insects it supports.

obstruct the view of traffic, and contact the entity that manages the roadway to let them know about your project so they do not mow or spray there.

## BUTTERFLY CONSERVATION ON FARMS

Van Burnette is a North Carolina farmer who has made butterfly conservation a cornerstone of his business. Tucked in an Appalachian mountain valley, Van's Hop'n Blueberry Farm includes spreading meadows of native wildflowers, a flowering shrub hedgerow, garden strips of butterfly host plants, and an entire educational program on butterfly conservation that is integrated into farm tours and field trip visits from local schools.

While his primary farm business is growing hops for a local brewery and blueberries for the local market, Van's longtime personal interest in butterflies has provided a springboard for larger community engagement. This engagement attracts new customers for his blueberries and at the same time increases butterfly conservation awareness among everyone who visits the farm. The model has proven successful enough that Van has begun drawing an income from admission tickets for butterfly and pollinator tours at the farm, and in his own take on the corn maze concept, he has even established a winding strip of giant sunflowers, milkweed, and other tall wildflowers that function as a "pollinator maze."

Even without Van Burnette's specific passion for butterflies, farmers can find easy opportunities and an enormous need to engage in butterfly conservation. For example, one of the major drivers of the decline in monarch butterfly numbers has been the widespread adoption of herbicide-resistant corn and soybean varieties in the Upper Midwest, which has increased herbicide use on farmlands and thus resulted in farm fields and field edges that are increasingly devoid of milkweeds. While the average Corn Belt farmer may not want to give up herbicides, these farmers can make a major contribution to monarch recovery by protecting or restoring small patches of milkweed and other native plant habitat and protecting those habitat patches from pesticides. Beyond sustaining butterflies, such small patches can sustain songbirds as well as pheasants and quail, provide areas for kids and grandkids to play and explore, and add beauty to the landscape.

In fact, the creation of such farm habitat is supported through conservation programs of the USDA's Natural Resources Conservation Service. These programs routinely offer both technical advice and financial assistance (cost-sharing grants) to farmers who want to create wildlife habitat on their land. In recent years, pollinators, including butterflies, have become a larger priority for these USDA programs. To find out more about program deadlines and qualification requirements, contact your local USDA Natural Resources Conservation Service office or your local soil and water conservation district office.

## WILD AREAS AND BUTTERFLY CONSERVATION

Wild areas are often a mosaic of distinct habitats—including woodlands, scrublands, and herb-rich grasslands—in which butterflies thrive. Managing for butterflies does not generally require a major overhaul of existing wildlife management plans and goals. However, butterfly conservation in wild—or partially wild—areas, such as nature preserves, state parks, and national parks and monuments, does require a different approach from many of those previously discussed because of both the size of the sites and the diversity of management goals.

Typically, managers of natural areas focus on maintaining their site's ecological integrity, often measured by its relative biodiversity. In other instances, site goals may be directed at the conservation or restoration of

individual species or groups of species (for example, waterfowl conservation in national wildlife refuge wetlands), and butterflies may not be a focus in the management of these areas. Three of the major land-management issues affecting butterflies are grazing, fire management, and control of invasive species.

Some areas managed for wildlife are overgrazed and trampled by livestock. This can be highly damaging, leading to a loss of both nectar sources and host plants; in addition, the disturbance of fragile areas

Native and restored prairie like this area at the Kerr Center for Sustainable Agriculture in Poteau, Oklahoma, provides excellent habitat for butterflies and moths.

Controlled burning is a valuable technique for prairie management, but if butterflies are not considered in the management plan their populations can be devastated. Although adult butterflies are mobile and some may be able to avoid fire, their eggs, larvae, and pupae cannot. Under a well-designed fire-management plan that considers all of the area's species, managers burn only a small percentage of the site in any given year. At some sites, an extended rotation of ten years or more may be appropriate so that insects can recolonize unburned habitat after the fire.

Invasive species must be controlled—and indeed, such control is generally beneficial to butterflies—but land managers should be cautious and measured in their methods. Using broad-spectrum herbicides to control weeds can indirectly harm butterflies by removing either caterpillar host plants or foraging flowers that provide nectar for existing populations.

Some management practices may unnecessarily harm butterfly populations, but if managers recognize the needs of butterflies and moths these can be avoided. In the end, ensuring that butterflies are considered in management helps all pollinators and all of the animals that rely on them.

allows invasive weeds to become established. Light rotational grazing can in some cases help butterflies by keeping down tall vegetation that crowds out butterfly plants. A grazing plan that takes into account the needs of butterflies is essential for their conservation.

Sometimes butterflies make it very easy to watch them. This pearl crescent (*Phyciodes tharos*) alighted on the photographer's shoe.

# Observing and enjoying butterflies

ONCE YOU START GARDENING for butterflies you will begin noticing them—and a variety of other flower visitors like bees and hummingbirds—all around your garden. You may already be familiar with the thrill of finding an unexpected winged visitor gathering nectar from your daisy or a fantastically striped caterpillar quietly munching away on some willow leaves. To watch butterflies is to become intimately familiar with their habits and needs, which ultimately leads to a greater understanding of how your garden can provide for them. Before you know it, this familiarity will be influencing everything you do in the garden, from changing your mowing and fall cleaning regimens to planting specific host and nectar plants to entice certain butterflies to become frequent visitors or permanent residents.

As you watch your butterflies and learn more about them, you may want to start recording their appearances and noting your observations. This may take the form of photographs or sketches, which can be shared with other enthusiasts. You may even start to build a list of local species. These observations can propel you to become involved in citizen science projects where you can collect data to inform large-scale science and conservation projects. Eventually you may find that your butterfly watching even leads to becoming a local expert, organizing classes or giving talks at the local library or schools. It may take you out into the natural world at large, where you can look for butterflies in all of their varied habitats.

This chapter provides tips for finding and observing butterflies. We also briefly explain how you can rear your own adults from larvae collected in the field.

Not all butterflies occupying your garden are obvious. Fallen oak leaves provide a camouflaged perch for low-profile butterflies such as the common roadside skipper (*Amblyscirtes vialis*).

## FINDING BUTTERFLIES TO WATCH

The first step in becoming a butterfly watcher is figuring out where to look for them. The best search technique depends on the life stage you are seeking. Adult butterflies with their colorful, graceful flights through the landscape are easy to notice, particularly if they are large and showy like admirals, swallowtails, and monarchs. The smaller butterflies are more often overlooked in the garden, even though they are no less beautiful. Grass skippers keep a low profile, flitting near the ground and blending in with grasses and forbs with their tawny brown or tan bodies. Blues, coppers, and hairstreaks can be the size of your thumbnail and display iridescent blues, bright orange chevrons, chunky black spots, and delicate tails. Once you know where to look in your garden, you may be surprised how many of these small animals have been flying under your nose the whole time.

The best time to search for adult butterflies is between the hours of ten in the morning and four in

Observing and enjoying butterflies

the afternoon because this is the warmest part of the day, and they are most active when the sun is shining and temperatures are above 60 degrees F. It doesn't hurt to have a calm day, either, especially if you're hoping to take photographs. Keep in mind that in mid-summer many butterflies seek shelter in the middle of the day as temperatures peak and then become active again later in the afternoon. This is especially true in southern regions.

When approaching a butterfly to identify it, move with smooth, fluid steps so that you do not startle it into flight. Also be sure to keep your shadow from falling across the butterfly as you approach. Sometimes seemingly inconsequential things can have an effect on your observations. For example, even clothing can make a difference: a brightly colored shirt combined with a quick movement can surprise a butterfly into flight, whereas the same movement might not cause alarm when cloaked in plain colors. On the other hand, bright colors attract males of certain species, so you may get a few inquisitive darts until they determine you are not an intruder or a potential mate.

Immature stages of butterflies can be equally rewarding but trickier to find. If you are hoping to find eggs, larvae, or even pupae you will need to carefully search known host plants, turning over leaves and stems, and check nearby structures and safe places where caterpillars may have crawled to pupate. When you search for these stages, knowledge of specific host plants and what time of year you are likely to see each species is particularly important and can help you home in on the right spots to look.

Another way to find eggs is to closely watch for an ovipositing female laying eggs on host plants. When she flies away, step in and carefully look for the tiny egg, often on the undersides of leaves or along stems. Identify the plant and check to see if it is a known host plant for a specific species, and then see if you can corroborate that with your sighting of the female. The

A young Gulf fritillary caterpillar leaves clues to its location in the form of frass and chewed leaves. Use these clues to home in on caterpillars, which are often hidden on the undersides of leaves.

host plant is a good way to narrow down species iden-tification when no adult is in sight and only an egg or a larva is found. When you are searching for caterpillars, look for frass and signs of chewing.

Learning to search for and find immature stages of butterflies is an entirely different way of butterfly watching and will enable you to learn quite a bit about each species' life history and special requirements. It is also a great way to continue your observations when conditions are not ideal for adults.

## EQUIPMENT FOR BUTTERFLY WATCHING

Butterfly watching is quickly becoming a popular pastime, rivaling the popularity of bird watching. Tools for butterfly watching are simple: a good regional field guide, a notebook and a pen, a pair of binoculars, and perhaps a camera. When choosing binoculars, be sure to select a model that allows for close focusing (a minimum of 6 feet or less). A small plant press may be useful for collecting plant specimens to be identified later. Other potential equipment includes nets, jars,

Practice and simple equipment such as a net and a viewing jar allow up-close viewing of butterflies.

and maps. Look for regional butterfly checklists online and in print (see "Additional Resources" and "Suggested Reading") to get an idea of which species exist in your area and whether they are rare or common.

Some butterfly enthusiasts observe butterflies strictly with their eyes and binoculars, while others prefer to use a net to temporarily capture butterflies for closer inspection and identification. If you use a net, realize that you are handling a living thing. People have been netting butterflies for hundreds of years, and you can safely net and release butterflies without injuring them. Correct net technique involves not just catching the butterfly but also handling it properly after you catch it. You can remove the butterfly from the net by gently grasping its wings with your forefinger and thumb and removing it from the net, or by using spatulate forceps, similar to those used by stamp collectors. Forceps that are serrated or more pointed may inadvertently tear a butterfly's wings. You can also use a jar or buy a container with a magnifying glass in the top to look at the butterfly. If you use a jar, make sure it is large enough for the butterfly and always look at the butterfly in the shade. The inside of the jar can get hot quickly in the sun and the butterfly will become more active, which makes it hard to see details.

Observing and enjoying butterflies

## RECORDS AND FIELD NOTES

The vast majority of what we know about butterflies has come from extensive notes, letters, and records written by amateur butterfly enthusiasts. The importance of writing down your observations cannot be overstated. Each piece of information you keep gains significance as time goes on and may one day be used by researchers.

As you get to know the species in your garden and afield, consider keeping a small notebook of your observations. At a minimum, keep track of the species (including number of individuals observed), its behavior, associated habitat and/or host or nectar plants, time of day (preferably in military time), date (formatted day/month/year, with month spelled out), weather (temperature, cloud cover, wind speed, unusual weather events before or during your observation), and specific location. Be sure to include your name as the observer.

Behavioral notes can be especially important in studies of poorly understood species. The location is also very important, as an observation without this information means little. Many records from the past are accompanied by vague location information such as "Dallas, TX" or "the Appalachians," information that is not very helpful to someone trying to relocate a population. These days, with Internet resources, smartphones, and an abundance of maps, locations can be specified much more precisely. Perhaps the best way to record a sighting is to use latitude and longitude. Numerous smartphone apps are now available that can pinpoint your latitude and longitude. Additional locality information such as directions, place names, street names, and names of water bodies is also helpful. This could be something as simple as your address if the butterfly was sighted in your home garden.

It is best to write down your notes and observations immediately, as letting even a short period of time elapse between sighting and notes can alter your

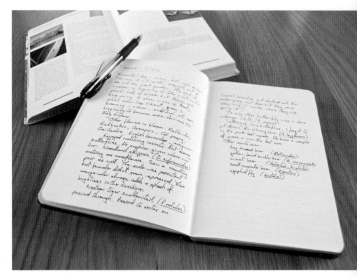

Keeping detailed notes about your observations is a great way to start learning about the various butterfly species visiting your garden.

memory and blur important details. As you keep these records and observations, think about starting your own "life list" or county list, a practice adopted from birders that many butterfly watchers enjoy using.

## COLLECTING BUTTERFLIES RESPONSIBLY

Collecting has been vital to our understanding of butterflies and has led to great steps forward in knowledge of species' life history and distributions—as well as to some of our most ardent butterfly conservationists. It has helped scientists, naturalists, and land managers understand these animals, identify species, and document biodiversity. Collecting can also be an extremely helpful source of information for setting conservation priorities, monitoring climate change, and educating others. Much important research rests firmly on responsibly gathered, well-curated collections made by amateurs and professionals alike.

If you are going to collect, you need the proper equipment and the know-how to ensure that you do it responsibly. Collecting of butterflies should always be

# Sample field record

```
3 May 2013
Oregon: Polk County
Cedar Wind Ridge
Observers: C. Fallon and M. Conner
Survey time: 1140 to 1218
Air temperature: 75° F (24° C)
Precipitation: Dry
Light index: Full sun
Wind: Calm
Aspect: NE
Elevation: 2200 ft.
```

**SITE DESCRIPTION** Surveyed several very steep, small pockets of meadows spread along a dry, rocky, forested ridge. Meadows characterized by abundant grasses, rock mosses, and assorted forbs and ferns. Flowering plants included strawberry, paintbrush, parsley, balsamroot, wild cucumber, oceanspray, and Saskatoon. Various buckwheats were growing all along the rocky parts of the ridge, not yet in bloom. Surrounding forest patches composed of Douglas-fir, bigleaf maple, Oregon white oak, and Pacific madrone.

**BUTTERFLY OBSERVATIONS** Dominant butterflies at this site were echo blues (*Celastrina echo*) and Sara's orangetips (*Anthocharis sara*), which could be seen flitting throughout the meadows. Three green hairstreaks (*Callophrys* species) were also observed; one was netted for closer observation. The netted individual had been flying low to the ground, occasionally perching on various forbs. No other butterfly species observed. The site is very dry even this early in the season, and nectar plants look stressed.

done with consideration of its possible consequences. Collecting will not impair most butterfly populations, but intensive collecting can potentially harm very rare and ecologically vulnerable species. Instances of this are uncommon but can happen, especially through aggressive and heedless commercial collecting.

Xerces recommends the following practices for collectors, whether scientists, amateur enthusiasts, or children making a study collection:

- Have specific objectives for your activity rather than just killing insects randomly.

- Collect no more individuals than are needed, particularly of females, even in cases where a series of specimens must be secured for studies in variation and evolutionary biology.

- Always follow the law. Do not collect from areas such as national parks or state parks where collecting is prohibited without a permit. Never collect specimens of a species protected by federal or state laws, local ordinance, or any relevant international treaty. Use common sense.

- Do not collect specimens of a single species in large numbers year after year from the same locality in the same season. If regular sampling is necessary, be conservative and take more males than females, whose removal makes much more difference to the population.

- Honor each specimen collected by recording the precise location and date of collecting along with the name of the collector on the envelope or pin label. If these facts are not noted, nothing can be learned and a potentially valuable scientific specimen becomes a mere curio—just a dead insect on a pin.

- Do as little damage as possible to the habitat in collecting (and watching) locales.

Taking photographs is an effective alternative to collecting for many purposes. With high-quality digital cameras and smartphones, you can often get diagnostic photos for identification. Binoculars can be a great help in observing species that are otherwise difficult to reach or when you want to see intimate details of a butterfly's life. You might also consider making a collection from road-killed butterflies. The son of one of the authors has a nice educational collection assembled from already-dead specimens, and one Xerces member collected every species of butterfly known in New Jersey in this manner.

## PHOTOGRAPHING BUTTERFLIES

Photography is an excellent way to observe butterflies in your garden and capture them in their natural settings. While they can be difficult to photograph because they startle easily and are often busily moving from flower to flower in search of nectar, and while it takes some patience, photographing butterflies can be a great pleasure. Photography will allow you to closely observe their behaviors and to document and identify species without handling them. Photographs are also an excellent aid to identification once you have left the field or garden. Just be sure to capture multiple perspectives of each butterfly you see, as minute details are not always easily visible in photos, and diagnostic features may be on both the undersides and upper sides of the wings.

Numerous online communities exist to help with identification or let you track all of your sightings. For example, both e-Butterfly.org and the Butterflies and Moths of North America website allow users to upload photographs of species, which are then pinned to a map of nationwide observations. Each upload is vetted by a regional expert, adding to a large and quickly growing collection of citizen-gathered data. A similar resource, the Butterflies I've Seen portal through the North American Butterfly Association website, allows users to upload photos and observations, categorized by field trips, to a greater database, in addition to creating their own life lists of butterflies.

An easy way to photograph butterflies is to set up your camera near flowers that attract adults. Tripods or

Photographing butterflies takes a bit of patience but can be a very rewarding way to document the species in your garden and local area.

monopods are especially useful for this method, as they allow for clear shots without camera shake. If using a tripod, consider leaving the head partially untightened so you can easily swivel the camera around to keep your target in focus. If you want to follow a subject around, be slow and quiet, and do not let your shadow fall across the butterfly as you approach. You may want to gradually move forward on your knees, focusing and snapping a few shots along the way in case the butterfly spooks and flies away. Butterflies need to heat up in order to fly, so early morning hours when butterflies are still cool and potentially even damp with dew are the best time to search for and photograph them.

A digital single lens reflex (DSLR) camera with interchangeable lenses is ideal for photographing butterflies, although digital compact cameras have increasingly sophisticated zoom lenses and produce good quality images. Many other cameras, including simple point-and-shoot and smartphone cameras, will also work for the beginner. The standard for butterfly photography is a macro zoom lens, which will allow you to take fairly close photographs without needing to get so near your subject that you startle it away. Many photographers prefer lenses with a range of 70 to 180 mm. Handheld flashes and diffusers may be helpful in achieving crisp shots with good lighting, but natural light (especially in the golden morning and evening hours) can also work very well. A flash can help fill in details on the wings and will also eliminate some movement (blurring), but if you do use a flash, try to place it in the same position as the sun in order to make shadows look more natural.

There are many other aspects of photography to consider, including the size of the aperture, the depth of field, and the shutter speed (using a faster shutter may help you get a clear shot if your butterfly is on the move). Most cameras these days feature a range of automatic settings from high-speed sports to portrait, with a close-up setting (typically marked with a flower icon) for shooting at shorter distances. As you become more comfortable with photography, you may want to move on from these automatic settings. In the meantime, program mode is a good place to start, letting the camera select shutter speed and aperture while you concentrate on the butterflies.

Regardless of your camera type, the best way to improve your butterfly photography is to practice. Get to know your particular camera and its settings and practice with not just butterflies but other animals and stationary subjects as well. Numerous books are dedicated to butterfly, insect, and nature photography, all of which offer great tips on techniques and the latest equipment.

## RAISING AND RELEASING BUTTERFLIES

Raising butterflies can be a way to observe all of the life stages and to help kids understand metamorphosis. Children and adults alike can be filled with wonder at the sight of a tiny caterpillar growing, pupating, and then emerging as an adult. This takes planning, equipment, and time, but many resources are available to help those who are interested.

Not all butterflies are good candidates for rearing. Some have specific life cycle strategies such as association with ants and do not do well in captivity. It is best to pick a well-known species such as monarch (*Danaus plexippus*), painted lady (*Vanessa cardui*), or cabbage white (*Pieris rapae*). Eggs can be harder to find than caterpillars and harder to rear.

To rear a caterpillar, you first need to find one in your garden. Follow the tips earlier in the chapter on finding and observing butterflies to locate a suitable caterpillar. Try to find a feeding caterpillar so that you know which host plant it is eating; if you find a caterpillar away from its host plant, it is best to leave it alone. Monarchs are a good choice as they eat only milkweed. Cabbage whites are another good choice as you can often find them on the cabbage or broccoli growing in your yard. The host plant should be easy to access and harvest; you will need fresh leaves every day. Caterpillars eat many times their weight in plant materials, so you will need an ample supply of the host plant to raise a caterpillar.

Be sure to collect some of the host plant when you collect the caterpillar. Place your cuttings in a moist bag and your caterpillar in a dry collection container

Eggs can be hidden on the undersides of leaves or along stems. This tiny egg has already been vacated by its Fender's blue inhabitant; note the tiny exit hole that gives the egg a donutlike shape.

with some of its host plant. When you get inside, put your plant cuttings stems down in their own jar or vase with a small amount of water in the bottom to keep them fresh, and then place your caterpillar on the leaves of the plant. You may want to cover the mouth of the jar or vase to keep your caterpillar from accidentally falling into the water. Then place the plant and the caterpillar in an enclosure so the caterpillar cannot escape.

Caterpillars can be kept in an aquarium, a large jar, a bug cage, or another container. You will need to clean it every day, so the container should be easy to open. It should have a screen covering or holes for air flow and should allow you to see the caterpillar inside. Make sure the air exchange is ample by either using a mesh cover or poking holes in the container lid. Unless you plan to move the chrysalis, the cage should be large enough for the adult to expand its wings when it emerges.

Caterpillars are voracious eaters and can quickly decimate your host plant supply. Be sure to give them plenty of fresh food and the space they need to complete their life cycles.

Keep the caterpillar's new home out of direct sun and be sure to replace any wilted leaves with fresh ones from the appropriate host plant. It is critical you provide the correct host plant, as many caterpillars will eat from only one plant or plant family. Be sure to clean out the container frequently—your caterpillar is an eating machine and will produce a lot of droppings. Add some twigs and small branches to the container so the caterpillar has something other than the container lid to attach to when it pupates.

The life cycles of butterflies vary, but caterpillars will usually eat for seven days to more than two weeks before they pupate. The chrysalis may last for a similar period of time before the butterfly emerges. Always release the butterfly where you found it. This helps ensure it will have the necessary resources to complete its life cycle, and it means you are not releasing a butterfly into an area where that species may not have been found before.

## CITIZEN SCIENCE OPPORTUNITIES

Recently, citizen science programs around the world have harnessed the enthusiasm of volunteers to collect and contribute scientific data. Citizen science is a way for the public to engage in important scientific discovery and allows for outdoor classrooms that can inspire young and old alike. The first naturalists

Observing and enjoying butterflies

and scientists were almost all self-taught, not being trained at universities, but as science shifted from our backyards to university labs it became harder for people to engage in scientific activities. Now with the advent of technology like smartphones and because of advances in identifying species, everyone can help scientists better understand the natural world so we can better conserve it.

This tagged monarch is ready for its migration to Mexico. Tag recoveries at overwintering sites give scientists a better understanding of migration pathways throughout North America.

Smartphones are enabling a new generation of citizen scientists to collect and submit photographs and other observations in real time.

The power of citizen science is the ability to collect huge data sets across large geographic areas, which is often impossible for the single researcher or research team. People from all walks of life now participate in projects that run the gamut from analyzing the extent of sea star wasting diseases to understanding rangewide shifts, migrations, and population declines of dragonflies. Local bioblitzes (rapid inventories of all plants or animals that generally take place over a twenty-four-hour period) are often hosted by parks and schools in an attempt to identify all species in a given area. These blitzes rely on volunteers to help find, photograph, and collect specimens that are identified or verified by regional experts, and they are

a great way to become familiar with your local species and get to know other enthusiasts in your area.

Numerous citizen science programs focus on butterflies. Great Britain has the longest-running butterfly citizen science programs, and the United States boasts a growing number of projects and participants, particularly relating to monarch butterflies. Many of these projects depend on volunteers to count monarchs at overwintering sites, monitor larval populations and monarch health, track migrations, tally species at annual events, and upload photos and location information to get a sense of global distributions over time.

# Butterfly citizen science projects in North America

## Butterflies and Moths of North America (BAMONA)

**butterfliesandmoths.org**

BAMONA strives to bring verified lepidopteran occurrence data and natural history information together in a single publicly accessible database. Citizen scientists can contribute observations and photographs to be included in the database, and knowledgeable individuals can apply to become regional monitors.

## eButterfly

**e-butterfly.org**

eButterfly is an international citizen science project dedicated to butterfly biodiversity, conservation, and education. Researchers associated with the website use citizen-contributed observations to study how global climate change is affecting our natural environments and how we can make decisions to help mitigate the effects on butterfly biodiversity and abundance.

## Journey North

**learner.org/jnorth/monarch/**

Journey North is a global study of wildlife migration, including monarch butterflies. This organization provides information on tagging and monitoring monarch butterflies as they migrate in the eastern United States.

## Monarch Larva Monitoring Program (MLMP)

**mlmp.org**

The MLMP is a project of the University of Minnesota's Monarch Lab. Volunteers in the United States and Canada collect long-term data on larval monarch populations and milkweed habitat in order to better understand how and why monarch populations vary in time and space.

## Monarch Monitoring Project

**monarchmonitoringproject.com/index.html**

The Monarch Monitoring Project conducted by New Jersey Audubon's Cape May Bird Observatory seeks to better understand the fall migration of monarchs along the Atlantic coast. Volunteers assist by tagging thousands of monarchs every year, some of which are rediscovered at the Mexican overwintering grounds later in the year.

## Monarch Watch

**monarchwatch.org/index.html**

Based at the University of Kansas, Monarch Watch is a nonprofit education, conservation, and research program that focuses on the monarch butterfly, its habitat, and its spectacular fall migration. Monarch Watch has a broad network of volunteers who tag migrating monarchs and report tag sightings.

## National Moth Week

**nationalmothweek.org**

National Moth Week is held during the last full week of July to celebrate the beauty, life cycles, and habitats of moths. "Moth-ers" of all ages and abilities are encouraged to learn about, observe, and document moths in their backyards, parks, and neighborhoods. Moth information gathered at NMW events can be submitted via the website.

## North American Butterfly Association (NABA) butterfly counts

**naba.org/butter_counts.html**

Regional NABA chapters host butterfly counts each year, most often around the Fourth of July but also in the spring and fall. New members are welcome to join counts as well as other field trips to monitor butterfly populations and report sightings.

## Project MonarchHealth

**monarchparasites.org**

Project MonarchHealth seeks to understand host-parasite interactions by tracking the spread of a protozoan parasite (*Ophryocystis elektroscirrha*) in wild monarch populations across North America. Citizen scientists collect parasite spores from captured-and-released monarchs and send them in to the MonarchHealth lab for testing.

## Red Admiral and Painted Lady Research Site

**vanessa.ent.iastate.edu**

Citizens help researchers at Iowa State University to monitor red admirals and painted ladies by providing observations of territorial behavior, migration, life history, number of broods, and seasonal variations. Includes the Vanessa Migration Project.

## Southwest Monarch Study (SWMS)

**swmonarchs.org**

The Southwest Monarch Study studies the migration patterns of monarch butterflies in Arizona. Their activities include tagging monarchs, monitoring milkweed populations, and searching for habitats that attract and support monarchs. People of all ages are welcome to participate. The Southwest Monarch Study also provides educational programs to raise monarch awareness.

## Xerces Society's Western Monarch Count

**westernmonarchcount.org**

The Western Monarch Count is an annual effort of volunteer monitors to collect data on the status of monarch populations overwintering along the California coast. Thanks to the extraordinary efforts of a cadre of volunteers, more than a decade of data demonstrates that monarchs have undergone a dramatic decline in the western United States.

## METRIC CONVERSIONS

| INCHES | CM |
|--------|-----|
| 1/10 | 0.3 |
| 1/6 | 0.4 |
| 1/4 | 0.6 |
| 1/3 | 0.8 |
| 1/2 | 1.3 |
| 3/4 | 1.9 |
| 1 | 2.5 |
| 2 | 5.1 |
| 3 | 7.6 |
| 4 | 10 |
| 5 | 13 |
| 6 | 15 |
| 7 | 18 |
| 8 | 20 |
| 9 | 23 |
| 10 | 25 |

| FEET | M |
|-------|-----|
| 1 | 0.3 |
| 2 | 0.6 |
| 3 | 0.9 |
| 4 | 1.2 |
| 5 | 1.5 |
| 6 | 1.8 |
| 7 | 2.1 |
| 8 | 2.4 |
| 9 | 2.7 |
| 10 | 3 |
| 100 | 30 |
| 1,000 | 300 |

## Temperatures

$$°C = (5/9 \times °F) - 32$$

$$°F = (9/5 \times °C) + 32$$

## ADDITIONAL RESOURCES

### Biota of North America Program

**bonap.org**

Provides county-level distribution maps, images, and other plant data for all North American species.

### Butterflies of America

**butterfliesofamerica.com**

Gives information on taxonomy, identification, distribution, habitat, and life history for more than 8,300 species of butterflies in America. Includes color images of live adults, specimens, caterpillars, food plants, and habitats.

### Calflora

**calflora.org**

Offers a searchable database of more than eight thousand California native plants that provides images and information on range, bloom time, and other species characteristics.

### Colorado Plant Database

**jeffco.us/coopext/intro.jsp**

Lets users search for plants by name, specific characteristics, or bloom season. Hosted by the Colorado State University Extension and sponsored by the Colorado Native Plant Master Program.

### Flora of Delaware Online Database

**wra.udel.edu/de-flora/Introduction**

Provides information on the status, habitat, and distribution of Delaware natives and offers special search categories for gardeners. Hosted by the University of Delaware.

### Floridata

**floridata.com**

Native plant database with detailed profiles including photos, habitat preferences, and cultural information.

### Florida Wildflower Foundation

**flawildflowers.org**

Source of propagation guidelines, native plant news, and educational materials.

### Grow Native!

**grownative.org**

A program of the Missouri Prairie Foundation, offers a native plant database, native plant lists, and gardening guidelines.

### Illinois Wildflowers

**illinoiswildflowers.info**

Provides detailed profiles, including photos and insect associations, of Illinois native trees, shrubs, vines, grasses, sedges, and rushes.

### Kansas Wildflowers and Grasses

**kswildflower.org**

Database of Kansas native forbs, grasses, sedges, rushes, and woody plants with image galleries and the option of searching by flower color and bloom time.

## Lady Bird Johnson Wildflower Center

**wildflower.org**

Based in Texas, features native plant gardens, meadows, nature trails, and an arboretum, seed bank, and herbarium. The Center offers events including garden tours, nature nights, seminars, and indoor and outdoor art exhibits. The website hosts the Native Plant Information Network, a database with images and profiles of more than eight thousand native plant species, and provides how-to articles on native plant gardening. Via the Special Collections webpage, users can create customized plant lists based on species range, wildlife value, and other characteristics. Main source of information for plants native to the Southern Plains.

## Minnesota Native Wildflowers

**minnesotawildflowers.info**

Provides detailed profiles, with photos, of Minnesota native trees, shrubs, vines, grasses, sedges, and rushes.

## Monarch Joint Venture

**monarchjointventure.org**

Offers a variety of ways to get involved with conserving monarch butterflies, from creating monarch habitat to studying the butterflies. More than two dozen conservation, education, and research partners from across the United States are behind this venture.

## National Gardening Association

**garden.org**

Through its KidsGardening.org project, provides grants and free materials for educators and families that promote garden-based learning.

## National Wildlife Federation's Garden for Wildlife Program

**nwf.org/how-to-help/garden-for-wildlife.aspx**

Provides guidance on creating gardens that attract and support wildlife in commercial and residential areas. Your garden may qualify to become an official Certified Wildlife Habitat®.

## Native Plant Network

**nativeplantnetwork.org**

Provides technical and practical information on growing and planting North American native plants. Features a searchable propagation protocol database with the option of uploading and sharing your own protocols.

## New England Wild Flower Society

**newenglandwild.org**

Headquartered in Massachusetts, offers educational programs and volunteer opportunities throughout New England. Its native plant botanic garden, called Garden in the Woods, is open to the public. Its online Go Botany database (gobotany.newenglandwild.org/) provides extensive native plant information for New England.

## NorthWest Plants Database System

**pnwplants.wsu.edu**

Provides images, detailed species descriptions, and cultivation information. Hosted by the Washington State University Clark County Extension.

## Pennsylvania Department of Conservation and Natural Resources

**dcnr.state.pa.us/forestry/plants/nativeplants/**

Provides native plant publications, a plant database, and garden design templates.

## Plant Iowa Native

**plantiowanative.com**

This initiative of the Tallgrass Prairie Center at the University of Northern Iowa connects people with native plant resources for horticultural, conservation, and habitat improvement purposes.

## Southwest Environmental Information Network

**swbiodiversity.org/portal/index.php**

Lets users search for plant images, species descriptions, and occurrence information from multiple herbaria in the southwestern United States. Plant games, including flash card quizzes, are also offered.

## USDA Natural Resources Conservation Service PLANTS database

**plants.usda.gov/**

Provides county-level distribution maps, an image gallery, fact sheets, and plant guides, and offers the option of conducting advanced database searches for detailed plant data.

## Wild Ones

**wildones.org**

Provides information on landscaping with native plants and promotes the preservation, restoration, and establishment of native plant communities.

## Xerces Society's Pollinator Conservation Resource Center

**xerces.org/pollinator-resource-center/**

By region, provides lists of recommended native plants for pollinators, lists of native plant nurseries, habitat conservation guides, and guidance on establishing pollinator habitat.

## SUGGESTED READING

Allen, Thomas J. *The Butterflies of West Virginia and Their Caterpillars.* Pittsburgh, PA: University of Pittsburgh Press, 1997.

Allen, Thomas J., James P. Brock, and Jeffrey Glassberg. *Caterpillars in the Field and Garden: A Field Guide to the Butterfly Caterpillars of North America.* New York: Oxford University Press, 2005.

Beadle, David. *Peterson Field Guide to Moths of Northeastern North America.* New York: Houghton Mifflin, 2012.

Bebbington, John. *Insect Photography: Art and Techniques.* Ramsbury, England: Crowood Press, 2012.

Belth, Jeffrey E. *Butterflies of Indiana: A Field Guide.* Bloomington, IN: Indiana University Press, 2012.

Brock, Jim P., and Kenn Kaufman. *Kaufman Field Guide to Butterflies of North America.* New York: Houghton Mifflin, 2006.

Burris, Judy, and Wayne Richards. *The Life Cycles of Butterflies: From Egg to Maturity, a Visual Guide to 23 Common Garden Butterflies.* North Adams, MA: Storey, 2006.

Carson, Rachel. *Silent Spring.* New York: Houghton Mifflin, 1962.

Chu, Janet R., and Stephen R. Jones. *Butterflies of the Colorado Front Range: A Photographic Guide to 80 Species.* Boulder, CO: Boulder County Nature Association, 2011.

Clevenger, Ralph A. *Photographing Nature: A Photo Workshop from Brooks Institute's Top Nature Photography Instructor.* San Francisco, CA: New Riders, 2010.

Covell, Charles V. Jr. *A Field Guide to Moths of Eastern North America.* Martinsville, VA: Virginia Museum of Natural History, 2005.

Cullina, William. *The New England Wild Flower Society Guide to Growing and Propagating Wildflowers of the United States and Canada.* New York: Houghton Mifflin, 2000.

Dole, John M., Walter B. Gerard, and John M. Nelson. *Butterflies of Oklahoma, Kansas, and North Texas.* Norman, OK: University of Oklahoma Press, 2004.

Douglas, Matthew M., and Jonathan M. Douglas. *Butterflies of the Great Lakes Region.* Ann Arbor, MI: University of Michigan Press, 2005.

Folsom, William B. *Butterfly Photographer's Handbook: A Comprehensive Reference for Nature Photographers.* Buffalo, NY: Amherst Media, 2009.

Glassberg, Jeffrey. *Butterflies of North America.* New York: Sterling, 2011.

———. *Butterflies Through Binoculars: A Field Guide to Butterflies in the Boston-New York-Washington Region.* New York: Oxford University Press, 1993.

———. *Butterflies Through Binoculars: The East, A Field Guide to the Butterflies of Eastern North America.* New York: Oxford University Press, 1999.

———. *Butterflies Through Binoculars: The West, A Field Guide to the Butterflies of Western North America.* New York: Oxford University Press, 2001.

Guppy, Crispin S., and Jon H. Shepard. *Butterflies of British Columbia.* Seattle, WA: University of Washington Press, 2001.

James, David, and David Nunnallee. *Life Histories of Cascadia Butterflies.* Corvallis, OR: Oregon State University Press, 2011.

Leslie, Claire Walker, and Charles E. Roth. *Keeping a Nature Journal: Discover a Whole New Way of Seeing the World Around You*, 2nd ed. North Adams, MA: Storey, 2003.

Link, Russell. *Landscaping for Wildlife in the Pacific Northwest.* Seattle, WA: University of Washington Press, 1999.

Mikula, Rick. *The Family Butterfly Book: Projects, Activities, and a Field Guide to 40 Favorite North American Species.* North Adams, MA: Storey, 2000.

Neill, William, and Doug Hepburn. *Butterflies of the Pacific Northwest.* Missoula, MT: Mountain Press, 2007.

Ogard, Paulette Haywood, and Sara Bright. *Butterflies of Alabama: Glimpses into Their Lives.* Tuscaloosa, AL: University of Alabama Press, 2010.

Opler, Paul A. *A Field Guide to Western Butterflies.* New York: Houghton Mifflin, 1999.

———. *Peterson First Guide to Butterflies and Moths of North America.* New York: Houghton Mifflin, 1998.

Opler, Paul A., Roger Tory Peterson, and Vichai Malikul. *A Field Guide to Eastern Butterflies.* New York: Houghton Mifflin, 1998.

Pyle, Robert Michael. *National Audubon Society Field Guide to North American Butterflies.* New York: Knopf, 1981.

———. *Handbook for Butterfly Watchers.* New York: Houghton Mifflin, 1992.

———. *Chasing Monarchs: A Migration with the Butterflies of Passage.* New Haven, CT: Yale University Press, 1999.

———. *The Butterflies of Cascadia.* Seattle, WA: Seattle Audubon Society, 2007.

———. *Mariposa Road. The First Butterfly Big Year.* New Haven, CT: Yale University Press, 2010.

Russell, Sharman Apt. *An Obsession with Butterflies: Our Long Love Affair with a Singular Insect.* New York: Basic Books, 2004.

Schappert, Phil. *A World for Butterflies: Their Lives, Behavior, and Future.* Ontario, Canada: Firefly Books, 2000.

Scott, James A. *Butterflies of North America: A Natural History and Field Guide.* Redwood City, CA: Stanford University Press, 1992.

Smith, Miranda. *The Plant Propagator's Bible.* Emmaus, PA: Rodale Books, 2007.

Stewart, Bob. *Common Butterflies of California.* Arcata, CA: West Coast Lady Press, 1998.

Summers, Carolyn. *Designing Gardens with Flora of the American East.* New Brunswick, NJ: Rutgers University Press, 2010.

Sutton, Patricia Taylor, and Clay Sutton. *How to Spot Butterflies.* New York: Mariner Books, 1999.

Tallamy, Douglas W. *Bringing Nature Home: How You Can Sustain Wildlife with Native Plants.* Portland, OR: Timber Press, 2007.

Wagner, David. *Caterpillars of Eastern North America: A Guide to Identification and Natural History.* Princeton, NJ: Princeton University Press, 2005.

Wright, Amy Bartlett. *Peterson First Guide to Caterpillars of North America.* New York: Houghton Mifflin, 1993.

Xerces Society. *Attracting Native Pollinators: Protecting North America's Bees and Butterflies.* North Adams, MA: Storey, 2011.

## ACKNOWLEDGMENTS

The authors would like to thank our families and friends for providing countless words of encouragement and endless patience throughout long hours of writing and revision. The best parts of this book are a reflection of their support. Thanks to Bob Pyle for his feedback on this book and his unwavering support of butterfly conservation. A special thanks to Sara Morris and Emily Krafft for assistance with plant profiles and to the Lady Bird Johnson Wildflower Center for the excellent resources on butterfly host plants and nectar sources. Thanks to Paul Opler for information on moths, Van Burnette for allowing us to profile Hop'n Blueberry Farm, and to both Debbie Roos and Native American Seed for practical plant and gardening advice. We would also like to thank members of the International Union for Conservation of Nature (IUCN) Butterfly Specialist Group for fielding questions about butterflies that came up in writing this book. Our thanks also go to the scores of people whose lovely photos grace the pages of this book. And finally, thank you to the fantastic staff and members of the Xerces Society.

# PHOTO CREDITS

©Benjamin Vogt, Monarch Gardens, pages 68 bottom, 206 top and bottom, 264
©Bill Bouton, pages 42 top, 43 top, 111, 119 right
©Bonnie L. Harper, Lady Bird Johnson Wildflower Center, page 163
©Brianna Borders, The Xerces Society, page 243
©Bruce Newhouse, page 165 left
©Bryan E. Reynolds, pages 1, 9, 10, 12, 14, 15 top and bottom, 16, 22, 24, 25 top, 36, 38 top and bottom, 39, 40, 41 top and bottom left, 42 bottom, 43 bottom, 44, 46 top and bottom, 48 top and bottom, 49 top and bottom, 51 middle and bottom, 55, 56, 58, 61, 65, 66, 71, 72, 73 right, 104, 112 left, 154 left, 158 left, 164, 216, 219 top and bottom, 221 top and bottom, 224 left and right, 225, 226, 232, 229, 254, 256, 261
©Candace Fallon, The Xerces Society, pages 142, 152, 258, 263
©Carly Voight, The Xerces Society, pages 26, 67
©City of Portland, courtesy Casey Cunningham, Bureau of Environmental Services, page 242
©Claudia Street, Yuba–Sutter Farm Bureau, page 194 bottom
©Debbie Roos, pages 47, 62, 88, 90, 115, 150 left, 156 right, 194 top, 205 top left, 209 top and bottom, 210
Dennis Krusac, USDA Forest Service, pages 91, 110 left, 126, 140 right, 168, 265 right
Eric Eldrege, NRCS Great Basin Plant Materials Center, page 143
©Eric Lee-Mäder, The Xerces Society, pages 154 right, 161 right, 197 top, 214
©Heritage Seedlings, Inc., page 128 left
©Hilary Cox, pages 57, 74, 89, 121 left, 192, 204
©iStock.com/49pauly, page 60
©iStock.com/Bertl123, page 28
©iStock.com/BorislavFilev, page 41 bottom right
©iStock.com/bruceman, page 205 right
©iStock.com/dlewis33, page 248
©iStock.com/JeffGoulden, page 30
©iStock.com/jpll2002, page 195
©iStock.com/janniswerner, page 34
©iStock.com/LailaRberg, page 119 left
©iStock.com/LordRunar, page 23
©iStock.com/plinney, page 20
©iStock.com/VvoeVale, page 205 bottom left
©iStock.com/WoodenDinosaur, page 32
©Jason Sharp, page 178
©Jennifer Hopwood, The Xerces Society, pages 68 top, 138 left, 241, 252–253
©Kenneth Setzer, pages 21, 45, 53 left
©Mace Vaughan, The Xerces Society, page 202
©Mari Lee-Mäder, page 215
©Mary K. "Mare" Hanson, page 52
©Matthew Shepherd, The Xerces Society, pages 25 bottom, 29, 76, 103, 106 left, 128 right, 133 right, 155, 184 left, 188, 189, 196, 197 bottom, 198, 200 left and right, 201, 203, 212, 223, 238, 230–231, 246, 250, 259
©Minnesota Native Landscapes, page 139
©MJ Hatfield, page 134
©Nancy Lee Adamson, The Xerces Society, pages 146, 156 right, 199, 249
©Native American Seed, page 217
©Penny Stowe, pages 11, 53 right, 54 all, 64, 70, 207, 265 left
©Peter Veilleux, East Bay Wildlands, pages 112 left, 125 right, 130, 149 right
©Richard Trelease, page 169 right
©Robert Sivinski, page 138 right
©Robert Wager, pages 51 top, 257
©Rod Gilbert, pages 50 all, 106 right, 116 right, 177, 187 right
©Steve Woodhall, page 19
©Sue Carnahan, page 167
©Thomas Palmer, page 124
USDA-PLANTS Database, page 191
©Wendy Caldwell, page 245

## Bugwood
**USED UNDER A CREATIVE COMMONS ATTRIBUTION 3.0 GENERIC LICENSE**
Charles T. Bryson, USDA Agricultural Research Service, page 157
Dave Powell, USDA Forest Service, page 172 right
David Cappaert, Michigan State University, pages 122, 208, 222
Howard F. Schwartz, Colorado State University, page 162
Jerry A. Payne, USDA Agricultural Research Service, page 228
John D. Byrd, Mississippi State University, page 174 right
Rob Routledge, Sault College, pages 150 left, 173
Whitney Cranshaw, Colorado State University, page 227

## Flickr
**USED UNDER A CREATIVE COMMONS ATTRIBUTION–SHAREALIKE 2.0 GENERIC LICENSE**
Fritz Flohr Reynolds, pages 120, 171
Jami Dwyer, pages 182–183
Joe Decruyenaere, page 179 right
Joshua Mayer, pages 131 right, 137 right, 153 left
Kid Cowboy, page 176
M. Dolly, page 114
Marvin Smith, page 127 right
Matt Lavin, pages 73 left, 149 left, 161 left, 165 right
Pfly, page 117
Tom Page, page 186

**USED UNDER A CREATIVE COMMONS ATTRIBUTION–NODERIVS 2.0 GENERIC LICENSE**
Debbie Ballentine, page 129
John Flannery, page 170
Will Pollard, pages 160, 179 left

**USED UNDER A CREATIVE COMMONS ATTRIBUTION 2.0 GENERIC LICENSE**
Forest and Kim Starr, page 59
Frank Mayfield, pages 133 left, 166 right
Miguel Vieira, page 174 left
NatureShutterbug, page 163 right
Oliveoligarchy, pages 131 left, 159
plerd, page 144
Scott Zona, page 190
The Marmot, page 121 right
Tim Walker, page 75

## Wikimedia
**USED UNDER A CREATIVE COMMONS ATTRIBUTION–SHAREALIKE 2.0 GENERIC LICENSE**
Udo Schmidt, page 113
Walter Siegmund, pages 109, 137 left, 184 right
**USED UNDER A CREATIVE COMMONS ATTRIBUTION–SHARE ALIKE 2.5 LICENSE**
Curtis Clark, pages 123 left and right, 169 left
**USED UNDER A GFDL AND CREATIVE COMMONS ATTRIBUTION–SHARE ALIKE 3.0 UNPORTED LICENSE**
ArtMechanic, page 17
Christian Ferrer, pages 117, 166 left
Cody Hough, page 108
D. Gordon E. Robertson, page 147
Hedwig Storch, page 125 left
H. Zell, pages 140 left, 181, 187 left
Jerry Friedman, page 141
Kenpei, pages 127 left, 158 right
Petr Vilgus, page 172 left
Stan Shebs, pages 116 left, 132, 135 right, 136, 143 right, 145 left and right, 153 right, 175, 180, 185
**RELEASED INTO THE PUBLIC DOMAIN**
Hardyplants, page 151
Masebrock, pages 135 left, 148
Stickpen, 110 right

Butterflies, dragonflies, beetles, worms, starfish, mussels, and crabs are but a few of the millions of invertebrates at the heart of a healthy environment. Invertebrates build the stunning coral reefs of our oceans; they are essential to the reproduction of most flowering plants, including many fruits, vegetables, and nuts; and they are food for birds, fish, and other animals. Yet invertebrate populations are often imperiled by human activities and rarely accounted for in mainstream conservation.

Established in 1971 and named after the extinct Xerces blue butterfly (*Glaucopsyche xerces*), the Xerces Society is at the forefront of invertebrate protection, harnessing the knowledge of scientists and the enthusiasm of local citizens to implement conservation and education programs. For more than four decades, we have protected endangered species and their habitats, produced groundbreaking publications on insect conservation, trained thousands of farmers and land managers to protect and manage habitat, and raised awareness about the invertebrates of forests, prairies, deserts, and oceans.

## The Work We Do

Of the more than 1 million species of animals in the world, 94 percent are invertebrates. The services they perform—pollination, seed dispersal, food for wildlife, nutrient recycling—are critical to life on our planet. Indeed, without them whole ecosystems would collapse. But when decisions are made about environmental policy and land management, these vital and diverse creatures are often overlooked. The Xerces Society works to address this situation in a variety of ways.

## Education

We educate farmers, land managers, and the public about the importance of invertebrates by demonstrating that habitat protection and management are keys to their conservation. Xerces Society staff train farmers, agency officials, gardeners, park managers, and others to protect, restore, and enhance areas for pollinators and other beneficial insects; protect at-risk species such as bumble bees, tiger beetles, and butterflies; and help managers understand how to monitor the health of streams, rivers, and wetlands.

## Advocacy

Xerces advocates on behalf of threatened, endangered, and at-risk invertebrates and their habitats. From the world's rarest butterflies, to caddisflies that live solely in one stream, to declining bumble bees, Xerces is dedicated to protecting invertebrates and the ecosystems that depend on them.

## Policy

We work with federal agencies to incorporate the needs of pollinators and other invertebrates into national conservation programs. We work with lawmakers to pass legislation to improve habitat for invertebrates. We also promote invertebrate protection using the Endangered Species Act and other federal and state laws.

## Publications

Via our biannual color magazine for members (*Wings: Essays on Invertebrate Conservation*) and through our books and website, we disseminate scientific information, updates on advocacy efforts, and practical suggestions for helping invertebrates. Wings features articles by leading conservationists and scientists as well as extraordinary color images from renowned wildlife photographers. Xerces also publishes guidelines, fact sheets, and identification guides that help citizens take action to protect pollinators and other beneficial insects. Many of these publications are free on our website, xerces.org.

## Scientific Research

We work on a variety of applied research projects that help us to protect habitat, ranging from studying how to effectively restore pollinator habitat on farms to understanding the life history of endangered species. Through the Joan Mosenthal DeWind Award, the Xerces Society offers grants to students conducting research on Lepidoptera conservation. Our staff members regularly write scientific papers and magazine articles, coordinate field work, and take leading roles in national and international scientific coalitions.

## Join Us

As a Xerces Society member, you will receive *Wings: Essays on Invertebrate Conservation* twice a year as well as timely bulletins on invertebrate conservation efforts. Most important, your support helps fund innovative conservation programs, effective education and advocacy, and scientific and popular publications, helping to spread the word about the vital role invertebrates play in our lives. Please join us today!

**LEFT TO RIGHT:** Candace Fallon, Eric Lee-Mäder, Scott Hoffman Black, Brianna Borders, Matthew Shepherd

**Scott Hoffman Black**, the Xerces Society's executive director, holds a master's degree in ecology and a bachelor's degree in horticulture, both through the College of Agricultural Sciences at Colorado State University. He has authored more than two hundred scientific and popular publications, co-authored three books, and contributed chapters to several others, and his work has been featured in newspapers, magazines, and books, and on radio and television. He also serves as chair of the International Union for Conservation of Nature (IUCN) Butterfly Specialist Group, chair of the Migratory Dragonfly Partnership, co-chair of the Monarch Joint Venture, and deputy chair of the IUCN Invertebrate Conservation Subcommittee. Scott has received the 2011 Colorado State University College of Agricultural Sciences Honor Alumnus Award and the U.S. Forest Service Wings Across the Americas 2012 Butterfly Conservation Award, among other awards.

**Brianna Borders** was the Xerces Society's plant ecologist from 2010 to 2015 and helped launch Project Milkweed, a nationwide initiative to promote milkweed conservation and increase milkweed seed availability for use in monarch butterfly and pollinator habitat restoration projects. Brianna has a master's degree in biological sciences from California State University, Chico, where her research focused on the restoration of riparian forests on the Sacramento River. She has also managed a native plant seed production program in California's San Joaquin Valley, taught biology at Bunker Hill Community College and Clark College, and assisted with plant-based ecological research on Nantucket Island and at Mount St. Helens.

**Candace Fallon,** conservation biologist for the Endangered Species Program at the Xerces Society, has worked for more than a decade in field ecology, botany, and land management throughout the western United States. She manages several aspects of Xerces' Western Monarch Conservation Campaign, including the Western Monarch Thanksgiving Count, a citizen science program based in California. She has extensive experience in habitat restoration and species inventories and monitoring.

**Eric Lee-Mäder**, M.S., is co-director of the Pollinator Conservation Program at the Xerces Society. In this role Eric works across the world with farmers and agencies like the U.S. Department of Agriculture and the United Nations Food and Agriculture Organization to enhance functional biodiversity in working agricultural lands. This includes consulting support for a USDA private lands conservation program targeting the federally endangered Karner blue butterfly. He previously worked as an extension farm educator, a commercial beekeeper, and a crop consultant for the native seed industry. Eric is the co-author of several books including the best-selling *Attracting Native Pollinators*, and *Farming with Beneficial Insects: Strategies for Ecological Pest Management*.

**Matthew Shepherd** has been with the Xerces Society since 1999, currently serving as the communications director and previously working on the Pollinator Conservation Program. Matthew has authored or co-authored numerous articles and other publications, including the Xerces Society's *Pollinator Conservation Handbook* and *Attracting Native Pollinators*. Before joining Xerces, Matthew worked in both England and Kenya on community-based conservation programs and with partners in business and the local community to manage Samphire Hoe, an award-winning nature park in Kent. Matthew started gardening at his mother's side and has created and maintained gardens that provide for insects and other wildlife everywhere he has lived.

**Robert Michael Pyle** (foreword) founded the Xerces Society in 1971 while studying butterfly conservation as a Fulbright Scholar in England. He holds a PhD in butterfly eco-geography from Yale University. His eighteen books include *The Audubon Society Field Guide to North American Butterflies, The Butterfly Watcher's Handbook, The Butterflies of Cascadia, Chasing Monarchs,* and *Mariposa Road*.